GW01395995

SCOTTISH HISTORY SOCIETY

SIXTH SERIES

VOLUME 19

Florentius Volusenus: Christian Humanist

1   Facsimile of the title page of the *Commentatio quaedam theologica*, 1539 (NLS RB.s.296). Reproduced under a Creative Commons Attribution 4.0 International (CC-BY) licence with the permission of the National Library of Scotland. https:// creativecommons.org/licenses/by/4.0/.

Florentius Volusenus: Christian Humanist
The *Commentatio quaedam theologica* (1539)

Edited by
Alasdair A. MacDonald, Betty I. Knott and J. Craig McDonald

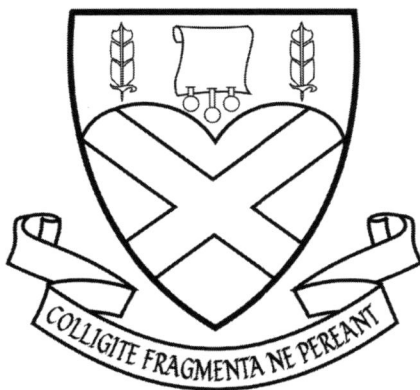

COLLIGITE FRAGMENTA NE PEREANT

SCOTTISH HISTORY SOCIETY
2024
THE BOYDELL PRESS

First published 2024
ISBN 978-0-906245-49-1

A Scottish History Society publication in association with The Boydell Press.
The Boydell Press is an imprint of Boydell & Brewer Ltd
PO Box 9, Woodbridge, Suffolk IP12 3DF, UK
and of Boydell & Brewer Inc.
668 Mt Hope Avenue, Rochester, NY 14620-2731, USA
website: www.boydellandbrewer.com

A CIP catalogue record of this publication is available
from the British Library

The publisher has no responsibility for the continued existence or accuracy of URLs for
external or third-party internet websites referred to in this book, and does not guarantee
that any content on such websites is, or will remain, accurate or appropriate

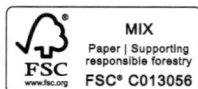

MIX
Paper | Supporting
responsible forestry
FSC
www.fsc.org   FSC® C013056

Printed and bound in Great Britain by
TJ Books Limited, Padstow, Cornwall

CONTENTS

PREFACE

The *Commentatio quaedam theologica* of the Scottish humanist Florentius Volusenus (born c.1504 near Elgin; died c.1557 near Lyon) is a most interesting work of early modern religious literature. It merits particular attention on account of both its unusual literary nature as a series of aphorisms and its somewhat challenging neo-Latin prose style; this latter aspect makes an English translation highly desirable. The text articulates the faith of an evangelical humanist of the Renaissance, and this Aberdeen-educated student found a niche in, and made a contribution to, the intellectual life of the Continent. Before the mid-twentieth century, the *Commentatio* was believed totally lost from sight. Only four copies of the first edition (Lyon, 1539) are known to have survived, and a mere two of the reissue (Basel, 1544). The text has been little studied, and has never been edited or translated.

The reputation of Volusenus has hitherto rested on only one of his published writings – the philosophical dialogue *De animi tranquillitate* (1543). That is doubtless because the latter topic, associated with Seneca and Plutarch and with many Christian writers of the Middle Ages and later, has been found especially relevant at periods of heightened political, social and cultural anxiety – such as were those of the Reformation, of the mid-seventeenth-century civil wars, and (in Scotland) of the union of parliaments and the Jacobite rebellions. The final British reprint (Edinburgh, 1751) was explicitly designed during the age of the Scottish Enlightenment for students and schoolboys who, via this work, would receive a solid training in Latin prose and poetry and also an education in moral philosophy.

The career of Volusenus was spent almost entirely outside his native country. At Aberdeen he was a pupil of Hector Boece, while in England he was a client of Thomas Cromwell; at the University of Paris he was a friend of George Buchanan; in the Comtat Venaissin, within the papal enclave centred on Avignon, he was an associate and *protégé* of the scholarly and reform-minded bishop of Carpentras, Jacopo Sadoleto; at Lyon he was one of the evangelical humanist intellectuals at the Collège de la Trinité, and who were attached to the circle of the printer-publisher Sebastian Gryphius. He was in touch with reform-minded humanists in England, Scotland, France, Italy and Switzerland.

The research of John Durkan and Dominic Baker-Smith has illuminated the significance of Volusenus within the contemporary European intellectual and cultural context. The *Commentatio* is the work of an eirenic and philologically minded Catholic scholar at the crucial point just before the religious fissure became irreversible. It is in no sense a work of religious partisanship, but rather gives a unique insight into the existential problems of an age of rapid and violent cultural change. It anticipates and expresses in a condensed way many of the issues touched on in the better-known *De animi tranquillitate*. Buchanan's tribute to his Scottish friend is both classically laconic and moving:

Hic musis, Volusene, jaces carissime, ripam
    Ad Rhodani, terra quam procul a patria.
Hoc meruit virtus tua, tellus quae foret altrix
    Virtutum, ut cineres conderet illa tuos.

[Most dear to the Muses, Volusenus, here you lie by the bank of the Rhône, how very far from your fatherland! This your talent has deserved, that the country which was to be the nourisher of your talents should lay your ashes to rest.]

The *Commentatio* is unlike any contemporary religious literature in the vernacular, and its generic and formal affinities are rather with such a famous text as the *Oratio de hominis dignitate* of the brilliant Pico della Mirandola. As a witness to the impact of Renaissance humanism upon Scotland, Volusenus is worthy to be set beside his contemporaries Gavin Douglas, translator of the *Aeneid*, and George Buchanan, poet, dramatist and Protestant historian. The *Commentatio*, written at a moment of general religious and spiritual crisis, may be found to have a relevance for readers at the present time.

The present volume begins by placing Volusenus within the historical and cultural context, before providing an edition of the original text with translation. This is followed by accounts of the literary aspects of the *Commentatio* and the character of the Latin in which it was composed, and by an analysis of the literary and religious source-texts on which Volusenus drew. The three editors have co-operated closely at all stages, but, on the Contents page, initials of names indicate who is principally responsible for any particular section.

ILLUSTRATIONS

The editors and publisher are grateful to all the institutions and persons listed for permission to reproduce the materials in which they hold copyright. Every effort has been made to trace the copyright holders; apologies are offered for any omission, and the publisher will be pleased to add any necessary acknowledgement in subsequent editions.

ACKNOWLEDGEMENTS

In the preparation of this collaborative study of the *Commentatio quaedam theologica* of the Scottish humanist scholar Florentius Volusenus, the editors have benefited from the philosophical, theological and historical expertise of Professors Alexander Broadie and Ian Hazlett, both of the University of Glasgow. At particular places, help was received from the following: the Rev. Dr Brian Alderman (King University, TN); Mr I.C. Cunningham (Edinburgh); Dr Theo van Heijnsbergen (Glasgow); Dr Kristine Johnson (Calvin University, MI); Prof. Michael Lynch (Edinburgh); Prof. David Parkinson (Saskatchewan); Prof. Steven Reid (Glasgow).

We are grateful for the courteous and efficient support given by the staffs of the following libraries: Bristol, TN, King University Library; Cambridge, University Library, Rare Books; Edinburgh, National Library of Scotland; Edinburgh, University Library; Glasgow, University Library; Knoxville, TN, University of Tennessee Library; San Francisco, The Internet Archive. The illustrations in the book were kindly supplied by the National Library of Scotland and Edinburgh University Library.

We thank the Council of the Scottish History Society for accepting this volume for publication in their scholarly series. In recognition of the groundbreaking research of Dr John Durkan (Glasgow) in all aspects of the Renaissance in Scotland, the present volume is respectfully dedicated to his memory.

Alasdair A. MacDonald
Betty I. Knott
J. Craig McDonald

ABBREVIATIONS

Aen	Virgil, *Aeneid*
annot.	annotated by
c.	chapter or *circa*, depending on context
cc.	chapters
DAT	Volusenus, *De animi tranquillitate* (Lyon, 1543)
DCD	Augustine, *De civitate Dei*
DCP	Boethius, *De consolatione philosophiae*
DDN	pseudo-Dionysius, *De Divinis Nominibus*
ed.	edited by
Epist	*Epistolae*
IR	*Innes Review*
l(l).	line(s)
Met	Aristotle, *Metaphysics*
ODNB	*Oxford Dictionary of National Biography*
OHD	Pico della Mirandola, *Oratio de hominis dignitate*
p(p).	page(s)
PG	J-P Migne, *Patrologia Graeca*
PL	J-P Migne, *Patrologia Latina*
Pr	Prose
Ps L	Volusenus, *In Psalmum 50 enarratio*
Ps XV	Volusenus, *Psalmi quintidecimi enarratio*
PSAS	*Proceedings of the Society of Antiquaries of Scotland*
qtd.	quoted
Scholia	Volusenus, *Scholia seu commentariorum epitome in Scipionis somnium*
SHR	*Scottish Historical Review*
SHS	Scottish History Society
trans.	translated by
v(v).	verse(s)

Books of the Bible are abbreviated according to common usage.
Abbreviations for citations by Aquinas are illustrated as follows:

ST I.Q1.A1   *Summa Theologiae* Part 1, Question 1, Article 1

SCG 1.C1   *Summa Contra Gentiles*, Part 1, Chapter 1

DDN 1.L1   Lectures on pseudo-Dionysius's *De Divinis Nominibus*, Part 1,
                Lesson 1

I.D1.Q1.A1   Commentary on the *Sententiae* of Peter Lombard, Book 1,
                Distinction 1, Question 1, Article 1

INTRODUCTION

VOLUSENUS: LIFE AND WRITINGS

The multifaceted phenomenon that is humanism began to manifest itself in Scotland towards the end of the fifteenth century, its impact being felt in the spheres of education, law, religion, philosophy, literature, art, architecture and science. This important development has been well discussed in many publications by Durkan (see the Bibliography) and by other scholars (cf. MacQueen 1990; Royan 2024). In a quick introduction to the present chapter, therefore, only a few of the most prominent Scottish figures of literary humanism need be mentioned.

Perhaps the first Scot to write Latin in a classical style was Archibald Whitelaw (1415/6–1498) – ecclesiastic, university teacher at Cologne and St Andrews, book collector, diplomat and royal secretary to James III. In 1513 the St Andrews graduate bishop Gavin Douglas (c.1476–1522) completed his epic masterwork, the *Eneados*, only the second vernacular translation of the entire *Aeneid*. In the decades that followed, Latin verse in Classical metres was composed by two otherwise very different Scottish contemporaries: the Edinburgh-based James Foulis (d.1549?), student at Paris and Orléans, and subsequently lawyer and lord of session; and the Highlander Roderick MacLean (d.1553), who is believed to have studied at Aberdeen during the principalship of the historian Hector Boece (c.1465–1536), himself a graduate of Paris and associate of Erasmus. The hundred years during which humanism reached Scotland were also distinguished by the presence of a vigorous literary culture in the vernacular, in which many late-medieval habits of thought and expression lingered on and were developed – one example being Gavin Douglas's *Palice of Honour* (1501), a poem that employs the conventions of dream-vision allegory in the manner of Chaucer. The period was thus one of overlap between the traditional and the novel, and various points of contact, and varying degrees of accommodation, between the two patterns of culture are encountered.

The Scottish humanist Florentius Volusenus is another important, if less familiar, figure in this context of cultural change. Although he was the author of several printed works, he has almost exclusively been remembered for his philosophical dialogue *De animi tranquillitate* (Lyon, 1543). This is presumably

2   'Elgin Cathedral in 1538', by John Grant. In Adam White, *Symbolae Scoticae* volume 7: Aberdeen, Angus, Elgin, Banff, Inverness, Argyle (circa 1850), f. 61. Coll-10/7, University of Edinburgh Heritage Collections. Reproduction courtesy of the Edinburgh University Library.

the work listed under 'Tranquillitie of the mynd' in the 1579 *post mortem* inventory of the stock of the Edinburgh bookseller, printer and publisher Thomas Bassandyne (Dickson and Edmond 1890: 298); however, despite this title, no early vernacular translation of the work is known. Reprints of the Latin text issued during the seventeenth and eighteenth centuries show that the dialogue long maintained its interest. The Edinburgh 1751 edition was expressly designed for the benefit of student readers, and Volusenus and his book were evidently considered familiar enough to merit a patriotic mention in *The Reprisal: or, The Tars of Old England* (1757), a comedy by the novelist and dramatist Tobias Smollett (MacDonald 2009a: 133).

By contrast, another production by Volusenus – his *Commentatio quaedam theologica* (Lyon, 1539) – has achieved no such fame. The aim of the present volume is therefore to rescue this neglected, but very interesting, work from the penumbra, by presenting an edition and translation, together with an accompanying study. This involves discussion of the book in relation to the career of the author, to the historical background, to the intellectual and theological sources used by him, and to the cultural context of early modern humanism; later chapters examine his work as a literary creation, and discuss his Latinity. At the time of the first extended study of Volusenus (Taylor 1861), only the title of the *Commentatio* was known, and no actual specimen was available for consultation. Today, copies are found in four libraries: Edinburgh, National Library of Scotland; Manchester, University Library; Paris, Bibliothèque Nationale; Vienna, Österreichische Nationalbibliothek. In his Cambridge thesis (1969), Baker-Smith was able to survey the complete output of the Scottish author, and the information reported in the following pages of this chapter should be understood as being grounded upon his account, which he developed in a series of subsequent articles. That account, however, is now supplemented from the publications of other scholars.

SCOTLAND

On one page of the *De animi tranquillitate* Volusenus writes that he and his friend John Ogilvie went walking by the banks of the river Lossie while discussing the poetry of Horace (*DAT*: 140–1). The Lossie, in the northeast of Scotland, flows by Elgin, in the county of Moray, and this rare biographical detail has given rise to the statement that Volusenus was born at that town (Biot 1996: 86; Baker-Smith 2006: 88). Such precision, however, is unsafe, since, while the story as narrated implies that Volusenus was acquainted with the area, it says nothing whatsoever about his place of birth. Rather, Ogilvie's observation that his companion has spent four years in the study of philosophy indicates a friendship between two adult friends, both enthusiastically devoted to the Classics, and men who are either university students or, more likely, graduates. A plausible date for their conversation – assuming that it did in reality occur – would be 1525, before the departure of Volusenus to England, and before Ogilvie in the following year became rector of Cruden, north of Aberdeen (Durkan 1980a: 269).

Nonetheless, there is no reason to impugn the long-standing common opinion that would refer the author's origins to somewhere at least in the vicinity of Elgin. In that part of Scotland there were several institutions capable of contributing to the formation of the future humanist. Elgin contained the splendid cathedral (now a sorry ruin) of the diocese of Moray, and the chanter was responsible for teaching song and elementary reading, while the chancellor in 1489 was tasked with the teaching of grammar in a general school (Taylor 1861: 3; Macintosh 1914: 38–61; Durkan 2006: 27). The bishop had his imposing residence at the nearby Spynie Palace, overlooking the seaward course of the Lossie, north of the town. Dominican and (Observant) Franciscan houses were present, and the friars would doubtless have provided some instruction in theology. A few miles to the southwest was the Valliscaulian monastery (after 1454 a Benedictine priory) of Pluscarden, and only a few miles further west lay the wealthy Cistercian abbey of Kinloss (Cowan and Easson 1976: 61, 84; 76). Of all these, Kinloss in the early sixteenth century has probably the best claim to be considered an intellectual and cultural powerhouse, especially under abbots Thomas Crystall and Robert Reid.

These two men had studied at the Collège de Montaigu in the University of Paris, where they had been exposed to the late-medieval reformist movement known as the *devotio moderna*. This movement, from its late fourteenth-century beginnings at Deventer in the northern Low Countries with the pious but secular Brethren of the Common Life, gave rise to the internationally extended Congregation of Windesheim, organised into houses of Augustinian canons (Ross 1962: 190–4, 214–7; Post 1968; Durkan 1980a: 261). One of the most important of these houses was Montaigu, which was noted for its rigorous, spiritual, moral, educational and ascetic ethos, especially during the Mastership of Jan Standonck (d.1504). The Collège was widely recognised as a locus of reformism (Tracy 1972: 57–8) and, among those who studied there, were Erasmus, Calvin and Ignatius of Loyola, as well as the Scotsmen John Mair, Hector Boece and John Knox. Via Paris the influence of the *devotio moderna* was transmitted to Scotland, where it proved to be a catalyst in the growth of humanistic studies (Durkan 1962b: 295). This is seen at several places in Scotland and in relation to several prominent churchmen – for example at King's College Aberdeen, where Hector Boece was the first principal, and where John Vaus, a former student under Boece and himself a distinguished grammarian, taught Latin (Durkan 1980a; Macfarlane 1985: 290–402; Durkan 1990; Mapstone 2010: 39–44). In this connection a significant figure is the Piedmontese scholar Giovanni Ferrerio, who in 1528 was invited by Robert Reid to teach at Kinloss and to assist with preparing commentaries on certain important religious works. Ferrerio, who in all remained more than 15 years at Kinloss, and who wrote *vitae* of abbots Crystall and Reid (Stuart 1872: 17–63; Durkan 1981; Holmes 2008), was sufficiently impressed by his experience in Scotland to publish his own continuation (Paris, 1574) of Boece's *Scotorum Historiae* (Paris, 1527), a work noted *inter alia* for the humanistic style of its Latin (Stevenson and Davidson 2009: §§13–17, 27, 34–6).

Although nothing is known of the family background of Volusenus, it has regularly been said that he was born c.1504 at or near Elgin, that the vernacular form of his surname may have been Wilson, and that he received his earliest instruction at the cathedral school. It seems likely that he would have been given a vernacular baptismal name, but, if so, none is recorded. For its part, the uncommon and learned-sounding 'Florentius' might have been a cognomen acquired at some later date, not improbably in an ecclesiastical connection, once the lad's aptitude for learning had become apparent. This name could be a Latinisation of the Flemish 'Florens', though it would be unsafe to conjecture a Low Countries element in his ancestry simply on that basis. On the other hand, a religious figure of great importance in the fifteenth century was Florens Radewijns (d.1400), the associate of Geert Groote, the founder of the Brethren of the Common Life. If the name Florentius was chosen as a tribute to Radewijns, thereby indicating influence from the *devotio moderna*, some particular connection between the young Volusenus and Kinloss might be posited. A parallel is perhaps to be seen with the case of Erasmus (Gerrit Gerritszoon) who, at the age of nine was sent for his schooling to the chapter of St Lebuin's church at Deventer, in the very heartland of the *devotio moderna* (Tracy 1972: 21). The fact that in 1555 a later Florentius is recorded as a canon of Elgin cathedral (Taylor 1861: 1) may be a sign that Volusenus was remembered with honour in his home region.

At around the age of 15, as was then the custom, the youth would have proceeded to King's College Aberdeen, situated some 65 miles southeast of Elgin. The university, the third in Scotland, had been founded in 1495 by bishop William Elphinstone (1431–1514), the most important ecclesiastical adviser of James IV. Hector Boece, the principal, was a friend and admirer of Erasmus, and for Volusenus King's College would have been a congenial place at which to prosecute his education (Durkan 1980a; Macfarlane 1985). As a student at Aberdeen, he would have coincided with the Gaelic-speaking Roderick MacLean (c.1504–53), the later commendator of Iona, bishop of the Isles, and accomplished neo-Latin poet (Macquarrie and Green 2022). Volusenus is likely to have graduated as master sometime between 1522 and 1525. It is uncertain what he did immediately after graduation (apart from strolling with John Ogilvie). If he went on to Paris, a step that would have been natural for a student from Scotland, he might have benefited from a legacy from James Hepburn (d.1524), bishop of Moray; the intention behind such a bursary was to facilitate the training in Greek of young men from the diocese. However, a visit by Volusenus to France at that time is undocumented and, if it did occur, could have been of only short duration.

LONDON AND PARIS

Between 1526 and 1535 Volusenus becomes a much better attested figure, and he can be traced in a variety of roles – as tutor to the son of Cardinal-Archbishop Thomas Wolsey, as humanist and friend of humanists in both England and France, as associate of several prominent figures in and around the court of Henry VIII, as rector of Speldhurst (in Kent), as client of Thomas Cromwell, and as emerging author. During this period, he made several journeys back and forth across the Channel, although he apparently revisited Scotland only once, in 1535.

Volusenus is mentioned in a letter of 1526 to Cromwell from Sir George Lawson, Builder of the English King's Works, in which Lawson asks that his 'gossip' in London, one Antonio Bonvisi, should contact Volusenus to see to it that George junior be kept continually at school. It would therefore seem that Volusenus was at that date already acting as a tutor. Cromwell was a member of Wolsey's household and, through Cromwell, the tutor – like several other Scots – would have been admitted to the periphery of the powerful (Durkan 1982: 128–31). Later that year, Volusenus was incorporated at Cardinal College Oxford, founded by Wolsey, where he supervised not only the young Lawson but also Thomas Winter, the founder's natural son. The tutoring was continued at Paris, where in 1529 Volusenus may have been charged with an attempt to recruit John Mair as reader in theology for Cardinal College (the later Christ Church). Although in this initiative Volusenus was ultimately unsuccessful (cf. Broadie 1983: 15–16), it was perhaps for his efforts in that direction that he received the benefice of Speldhurst, which he held until 1532. The latter grant might be taken to imply that Volusenus had been ordained, but such a conclusion is unnecessary, since from the benefice a curate could have been appointed. While at a few places in the *Commentatio* (§§3, 347) the speaking persona does apply the term 'priest' to his own role, it seems likely that this is intended metaphorically. Nonetheless, the Speldhurst link may have been responsible for a meeting with the diocesan bishop, the saintly John Fisher, about whom Volusenus would speak with deep respect (*DAT*: 345).

Volusenus's social contacts in this period lay very clearly within the circles of humanists. He is known in London to have met the following: John Bekinshaw, who taught Greek at New College Oxford; Richard Pate, a pupil of Juan Luis Vives; Thomas Lupset, a Cambridge friend of Erasmus, appointed by Wolsey to Corpus Christi College Oxford, and friend of Sir Thomas More; and Antonio Bonvisi, a merchant banker originally from Lucca and an intimate of More (Baker-Smith 2006). It was at Bonvisi's house that Volusenus would later (1535) reveal the news of Fisher's elevation to cardinal. Other like-minded spirits either certainly or possibly encountered by Volusenus include More himself, Reginald Pole and Thomas Starkey.

He is likely to have encountered several of these figures also in Paris, where his other associates were humanists at the Faculty of Arts and the Collège Royal (founded by François I in 1530). The latter institution quickly became embroiled in disputes with the Faculty of Theology, concerning the extent to which expertise in the *linguae sacrae* was necessary or permissible in the matter of the correct interpretation of Scripture. A significant event was the commotion arising from the 1531 Lenten sermons of Gerard Roussel, preacher to the king's sister, Marguerite de Navarre. In October 1533, during this tense cultural and religious atmosphere, the queen's poem, *'Le miroir de l'âme pécheresse'* [*The mirror of the sinful soul*] (in 1544 translated by Elizabeth Tudor) was denounced by the Sorbonne (Salminen 1979: 21–30), and the humanist Roussel was attacked as a 'Lutheran' by the Faculty of Theology. Information on such happenings, which were not without potential implications for the marital situation of Henry VIII, was relayed by Volusenus to Cromwell in London, to whom he sent books purchased in Paris. The Scot also met Sir Francis Bryan, friend and emissary of the English king and nephew of John Bourchier, Lord Berners, the translator of Marcus Aurelius (completed in 1532); though himself not truly one of the humanist scholars, Bryan was keenly interested in the education of the young. Further contacts included the following: Guillaume du Bellay, the learned and skilful diplomat of François I; his no less learned diplomat brother Jean, bishop of Paris from 1532, poet, and patron of Rabelais; and Jean de Guise, cardinal of Lorraine. An associate less socially exalted was his fellow-countryman George Buchanan, a regent (teacher) at the Collège Sainte-Barbe, and from 1529 the procurator of the German Nation (to which Scottish students belonged). Buchanan had followed Mair to Paris in 1526 (McFarlane 1981: 24–47), and one of the things he and Volusenus had in common was an interest in Hebrew. It was therefore fitting that, before Buchanan left France for Scotland in 1534, Volusenus should have presented him with his copy (now in Edinburgh University Library) of Sebastian Munster's *Dictionarium Hebraicum* (Basel, 1523). This volume had been published with a dedication to John Fisher, and the gift could only have gained in significance after the bishop's martyrdom on Tower Hill, London (22 June 1535).

It was therefore against a background of religious, intellectual and political tension that the first works by Volusenus appeared. His choice of subject-matter – the Hebrew language and interpretation of the Psalms – immediately ranged him on the side of the humanists engaged in elucidating and correcting the text of the Vulgate. The first of these works, the *Enarratio psalmi quintidecimi* (Paris, 1531), was dedicated to the cardinal of Lorraine, to whom Volusenus had been introduced by Guillaume du Bellay and Sir Francis Bryan. This was followed by the *Enarratio in psalmum 50* (Paris, 1532), dedicated to Stephen Gardiner, secretary to Henry VIII and, since 1531, bishop of Winchester (in which function he had succeeded Wolsey). In the dedication to the latter volume (sig. Aii), Volusenus records his great debt to England and expresses his praise of France, Paris, and the stimulating intellectual environment in and around the university: *Multis de causis, illustris Antistes, mihi Gallia placet* [France pleases me, distinguished bishop, for many reasons]. These early publications stem directly from the author's professional experience as a tutor, and they testify to his ability as an expositor of texts.

The same talents are no less in evidence in his *Scholia seu commentariorum Epitome in Scipionis Somnium ad egregium adolescentem Gregorium Crumwellum* (London, [1535]). The *Scholia* was addressed to Volusenus's outstanding pupil, who, most importantly, was the son of his teacher's most powerful patron, Thomas Cromwell. The text of the *Somnium Scipionis* – the only part of Cicero's *De re publica* to survive, and from the time of Macrobius (early fifth century) onwards a work studied as an educational textbook (cf. Stahl 1952) – is presented here in parallel with a commentary by Volusenus.

It is possible that these were not the only productions of this Paris period. In the early seventeenth century, a four-book synopsis of Aristotelian philosophy was attributed to Volusenus by the antiquarian Thomas Dempster (Irving 1829: II.669–70). Unfortunately, the latter is not always the most trustworthy of writers (Morét 2000; Durkan 2003), and one cannot be confident that the alleged work was actually written, let alone printed. The two volumes *De Consolatione* with which Dempster also credits Volusenus constitute another puzzle, unless this entry should represent a coupling of the *Commentatio* and the *De animi tranquillitate*, both of which might not altogether inappropriately be brought under such a label.

CARPENTRAS

The religious tensions in Paris came to a head with the 1533 All Saints Day address in the Church of the Mathurins given by Nicholas Cop, the rector of the university. He spoke in a tone of moderation, referring to both Luther and Erasmus, but the reaction was extreme, and several of those in the evangelical humanist party – including Cop himself, and the young Jean Calvin – felt obliged to flee to places of safety. Volusenus too evidently wished to leave the city, and in 1535 he revisited his homeland. There he reconnected with John Ogilvie and borrowed a horse from him. This detail is recorded on a flyleaf of a copy (location no longer known) of the *Apophthegmata* of Erasmus (Paris, 1533) sent to Ogilvie by Volusenus, who writes of his delight in that work and passes on his greetings to the aged Hector Boece (d.1536). An allusion in Volusenus's *Scholia* to lumberjacks riding logs down the river Tay (sig.

Di^v–Dii) may conceivably have been elicited by this return of a native (Linnard 1981). However, one cannot be sure: the passage in question was triggered by a mention in the original of the cataracts on the Nile that impede the flow of the water, and the allusion to the Scottish river – which does not flow in Volusenus's home province of Moray – seems fetched from some memory of indeterminable date (*si memini*). From Scotland Volusenus proceeded to London, where, in the early summer and in the garden of Antonio Bonvisi, he again met Thomas Starkey, from whom he received a positive account of a visit which Reginald Pole and Starkey had in 1532 paid to Jacopo Sadoleto, at the latter's episcopal seat of Carpentras, in the papal enclave of Avignon. A few months later, these words would have important consequences.

Having returned to Paris, Volusenus set out for Rome in the train of Jean du Bellay, who was commissioned by the French king to procure a last-minute assent from the pope to the divorce plans of Henry VIII (the attempt was unsuccessful). For his part, the Scot had intended to seek employment at an Italian university, but things turned out otherwise, and at Avignon illness prevented him from continuing with the travelling party. Instead, recalling Starkey's commendations of Sadoleto, which when recently passing through Lyon he had heard echoed by Bonvisi, he betook himself to Carpentras. His meeting there with Sadoleto is recounted with vivid detail in a letter of 7 November 1535 from the bishop to his nephew Paolo. The unknown stranger had presented himself late one evening, and his host had quizzed him as to his educational and professional experience, observing his skill in Latin. The next day, Volusenus gave an equally good account of himself to the local magistrates and was forthwith appointed master of the municipal grammar school (Douglas 1959: 65–6). At the end of the month he wrote to Starkey, declaring his intention to remain at Carpentras for several years: far from the madding crowd (*procul turbis, procul ambitu, procul denique curis omnibus*), he intended to devote himself to philosophy (Laing 1827: 336). In his positive opinion of Carpentras he evidently concurred with Sadoleto who, in his *Interpretatio* of Psalm 93/94 (1530: sig. a2), had praised the town as an excellent place in which to attain peace and tranquillity of mind (*pacis et tranquillitatis in animo retinendae*). However, despite his initial resolution, Volusenus apparently moved on to Lyon by late 1537 or early 1538. Though his period of residence at Carpentras was therefore not long, it was of great significance, since it proved to be the turning-point in his development from being primarily an explicator of existing and familiar texts to becoming a more truly original writer.

Sadoleto (1477–1547) was not merely a bishop and, as such, desirable as a patron (on 22 December 1536 he was raised to the cardinalate), but was a humanist scholar sharing the outlook of men such as Lorenzo Valla, John Colet, Erasmus and Matteo Giberti. On every count he was suited to be a mentor to Volusenus. Like the Scot, he had written neo-Latin verse and composed works of exegesis on the Psalms. His concern for education – as witness, his frequently printed treatise *De liberis recte instituendis* [*On the proper instruction of the young*], written in 1530 – would have struck a chord with the man who himself had tutored the sons of men of authority. His *De laudibus philosophiae* and *Hortensius* (1523) belong to the Renaissance literature on the dignity of man, a theme indelibly associated with Pico della Mirandola. Most importantly, Sadoleto, who had been a member of the Oratory of Divine Love, favoured the path of conciliation in the matter of ecclesiastical reform (*renovatio ecclesiae*), and his instinctive and institutional affinities lay with such important figures as Gasparo Contarini and Reginald Pole (McNair 1967: 130–8). He was much involved with the reform initiatives under Paul III, which led to the 1537 *Consilium de emendanda ecclesia* [*Proposal on amending the Church*]. In 1539, with such an experience behind him, Sadoleto sent an *Epistola ad Senatum Populumque Geneuensem* to the authorities and people of Geneva, who had succumbed to reformist ideas, to urge them to return to the traditional path of orthodoxy. This missive, couched in a tone of paternalistic pastoral reproof, and which warned the Genevans of their danger (*'hoc illud est biuium, quod diuersa duo in itinera scinditur'*: p. 22) [this is that fork in the road, which divides in two separate directions], quickly drew a vigorous rejoinder from Calvin, with articulations of his standpoints on a number of key issues of theology (e.g., the Eucharist, auricular confession, intercessory prayers to saints), together with his views on scholastic philosophy in general, which he denounced as 'a species of secret magic' (Beveridge 1844: 15, 40; Douglas 1959: 143–8; Olin 1966).

At Carpentras, there was clearly a meeting of minds and a sympathy of humours between Volusenus and Sadoleto. The bishop wrote about him to the cardinal of Lorraine *'mihique in quotidiana consuetudine admodum jucundus et gratus est'* [I find him most pleasant and agreeable in the daily routine] (Baker-Smith 1969: 45), and in another letter to the Cardinal he described the Scot as *'elegantia morum et literis Latinissimus'* [the most thorough Latinist, in the elegance of his life and in his writings] (Irving 1829: II.670). In turn, Volusenus could not have failed to be aware of the religious controversies in which his patron was engaged, and of the doctrinal positions that he represented. It was presumably in this period that the *Commentatio* would have been conceived, drafted and circulated among the friends mentioned in the prefatory letter to the 1539 publication. It is unknown whether Volusenus discussed with Sadoleto the work in progress, but that would seem highly likely, and the fact that, in its completed state, the *Commentatio* appeared in the same year as the *Epistola* to the Genevans is a piquant coincidence. Though different in form and purpose, these works belong within the larger European context in which scholastic traditionalism was under challenge from both humanists and reformers (Nauert 1973; Cameron 1991). At the same time, those of a conservative inclination were quite liable to fall back on proffering

vetust formulations concerning the authority of the Church – such as those
famously crystallised in the fifth-century *Commonitorium* of Vincent of Lérins,
and deployed (though not explicitly named) by Sadoleto in his *Epistola* – as
a hopefully adequate and authoritative counterweight to the reasonings of
the reformers.

Despite Volusenus's close association with Sadoleto and the affinity of
outlook between the two men, he did not follow the bishop into the arena of
religious polemic: on the contrary, in the *Commentatio* he prefers to skirt round
potentially dangerous material (e.g., the Eucharist, Purgatory, the Papacy). The
avoidance of controversy is typical of the position of an evangelical humanist
whose main purpose is not to advance an argument but to stir an affective
response (Baker-Smith 1969: 275). While fervent praise of God permeates
the text, comment about either the institutional Church, with its hierarchy
and organised devotion, or about the social and sacramental dimensions of
religious life at parish level, is absent. There were good reasons for Volusenus
to exercise caution: in July 1538 Charles V and François I met at Aigues-
Mortes and agreed to combat Lutheranism, a step that betokened the end of
the dream of a 'French middle way' in religion (El Kenz 1997: 41–2). In such
a situation, Volusenus opted to arrange his collected aphorisms so that they
would lead in the safer direction of fideism, by expressing enthusiastic approval
of those who manage to avoid worldly temptations through cultivation of
an intense love for the crucified Jesus (§§242–3) – whether that might be by
living an eremitical or cenoebitic existence, and whether without or within
towns (§§272–80). This particular emphasis may owe something either to
the lifestyle of the Observant mendicant orders, or to that of the pious laity
of the Brethren of the Common Life: the latter case might suggest some
residual influence from the ideals of the *devotio moderna*, possibly remounting
ultimately to either Kinloss or Montaigu. In any event, it cannot be doubted
that it was during the time spent at Carpentras, and as a consequence of his
encounter with Sadoleto, that Volusenus developed into an author capable
of responding creatively, and indeed movingly, to the troubles of the times.

LYON

Although the composition of the *Commentatio* owed much to the author's
residence at Carpentras, the work was perfected at Lyon, where it was published
by Sebastian Gryphius in 1539. In the prefatory letter, Volusenus records that
he had originally compiled his aphorisms at the request of an unspecified
amicus, and it is hard not to suspect that this perhaps discreetly anonymous
'friend' may be none other than Sadoleto. Yet however that may be, the text
was now presented for general publication at the suggestion of two other
friends, openly acknowledged: Sir John Borthwick, captain in the Scots

Guard in France, and Panagius Hocedius (Toussaint d'Hocédy), secretary to the cardinal of Lorraine. Volusenus further declares that he is the less reluctant to accede to their request, in that the work had already pleased both the bishop of Winchester (Stephen Gardiner) and the latter's secretary (Germain Gardiner). This preamble allows the Scot to insinuate that he has both royal and ecclesiastical support for his writing, and from both France and England. His group of contacts is of particular interest when viewed in a longer historical perspective. Borthwick (d.1569), a keen supporter of Thomas Cromwell, was back in Scotland by 1539, where in his absence he was tried for heresy by Cardinal David Beaton; Germain Gardiner was a Catholic layman, who in 1544 would be executed under Henry VIII; Hocedius, once an evangelical and associate of Erasmus at Louvain, died (1565) as bishop of Toul; Stephen Gardiner (d.1555) would defend royal supremacy and the execution of John Fisher, and survived to become lord chancellor under Mary Tudor. In 1539, however, the members of this coterie could pass as moderate and sufficiently orthodox in religion, for all that they might have flirted with certain heretical or schismatic ideas; at that early time, and whatever the eventual convictions of their later years, all of them were keenly interested in the views of the early reformers. To such men, open to considering a range of religious opinion, the *Commentatio* would have been well suited.

From this background story presented by Volusenus it is evident that a great deal of care went into the preparation of the book, and the Latin style employed therein may have been adopted with those very associates (named or unnamed) in mind. However, the author of the *Commentatio* may also have had an eye to an impending career move relocation from Carpentras to the Collège de la Trinité in Lyon, a place where the highest standards of Latinity were cultivated; in this connection one recalls Sadoleto's praise of Volusenus as *Latinissimus*. Given the prospect of attachment to such a prestigious institution, Volusenus may have wished to provide the critical humanists who were to be his future colleagues with a demonstration of his talents. The attraction of this hypothesis is that it offers an explanation – over and above the intrinsic and abiding interest of the philosophical and religious content – for the fact that Volusenus should have embarked upon and published this concise but ambitious work, of a sort unparalleled in his oeuvre.

After the quiet of his residence in the small town of Carpentras, Volusenus must have experienced the prosperous and bustling city of Lyon – then the chief financial centre in France, and with four trade fairs per year – as a great, and perhaps not unwelcome, change. Moreover, it was different from what he had known in Paris, since the southern city had the advantage of having neither a difficult *parlement* nor an aggressive faculty of theology. Indeed, Volusenus must have appreciated the fact that, between 1536 and 1539, the local archbishop was none other than his Paris patron, the cardinal of Lorraine. The geographical situation of Lyon, at the confluence of two great rivers, meant that there were easy and continual contacts – personal, commercial, intellectual and religious – with both northern Europe and the Mediterranean, Switzerland and Italy, the Empire and the Papacy. Before the outbreak of the French wars of religion in 1562, more than 40 printer-publishers were at work there, many of whom sympathised with the reformers. From Lyon, books were disseminated throughout western Europe (Johnson 1922), and the writings of Sadoleto and Volusenus were among those published by the Swabian-born Gryphius, who brought out a stream of works by leading writers – such as Erasmus, More, Poliziano, Rabelais, Maurice Scève, Clément Marot and Santes Pagnini – in addition to numerous editions of the Classics (Christie 1907; Margolin 1974; Davis 1983). Appropriately, Volusenus was called upon to act as a corrector for the printer. This was in fact an honour, seeing that among the other humanists who performed that role were the prominent figures of Alciato, Sadoleto, Rabelais, Claude Baduel and Gilbert Ducher (Biot 1996: 85, 88). It seems likely that the entry of Volusenus to this charmed circle would have been facilitated by commendations from Sadoleto; at the same time, he may also have benefited from his long-standing friendship with Bonvisi, whose financial network linked his bases at London, Lyon and Lucca.

Volusenus's chief occupation at Lyon was as a teacher of humanities at the Collège de la Trinité where, since 1538, the distinguished humanist and poet Barthélemy Aneau had been attached as lecturer. On the formal appointment of Aneau as principal (1540), there were changes of personnel, but it is notable that Volusenus, unlike certain others, was retained as regent (Biot 1996: 125). In addition to the Scot's scholarly and educational skills, it has been said that he impressed his fellows with his piety and mysticism (de Groër 1995: 24–6). Among his colleagues was the poet Gilbert Ducher, whose *Epigrammaton libri duo* (1538) contained a wealth of tributes to the *littérateurs* of Lyon. In this volume, a poem paraphrasing and adapting Psalm 120/121 is addressed to Volusenus and may have been intended as a welcome to the new colleague (Appendix: A; Ducher 2015: 220–1, 486–7). One of his most interesting students was Sebastian Castellio (1515–63), famous in later life as a Bible translator, as a critic of Calvin, and as a proponent of religious tolerance (Guggisberg 2003: 17). However, shocked by religious martyrdoms at Lyon, Castellio in 1540 decamped to Strasbourg to join Calvin, whom at that point he still admired (Biot 1996: 87).

The Collège de la Trinité, founded as a municipal institution in 1527 and not formally a university, was staffed by 'des régents de grande érudition, tels Jean Pélisson, Florent Wilson, Claude Bigothier, Gilbert Ducher, Charles de Sainte-Marthe et surtout Barthélemy Aneau' [deeply erudite regents, such as Jean Pélisson, Florentius Volusenus, Claude Bigothier, Gilbert Ducher, Charles de Sainte-Marthe and especially Barthélemy Aneau] (Biot 1994: 446). It was the centre of intellectual life in the city, not least on account of its impact in the area of religion: 'Centre de culture où s'exprime le talent des régent-poètes, centre d'études où s'épanouit l'intelligence des jeunes Lyonnais, le Collège est peut-être bien aussi dès ces années 1535–1540, et du fait même de la présence de ces éminents régents, un terrain par où "s'infiltre" la Réforme' [A centre of culture in which the talent of the regent-poets finds expression, a centre of learning in which the intelligence of the youth of Lyon develops and expands, the Collège, perhaps even already from the years 1535–1540, and from the very fact of the presence of those eminent regents, is a place in and through which ideas of Reform gain entry] (Biot 1996: 121). It seems very likely that the Gryphius / Trinité cluster of scholars, poets, humanists and religious reformists – the renowned *sodalitium Lugdunense*, to which Sadoleto also belonged (Ducher 2015: 61) – would have constituted most of the initial readership of the *Commentatio*. The 1540 meeting of Volusenus with the erudite polymath Conrad Gesner occurred within this same cultural context, and it may have been the latter who was responsible for arranging the reissue of the *Commentatio* by Hieronymus Curio (Basel, 1544) – the only reprint of a complete work by Volusenus during the author's lifetime (Appendix: C). Copies are held at Münster, Universitätsbibliothek, and Paris, Bibliothèque Nationale.

It was in Lyon that Volusenus composed his *chef d'oeuvre*, the *De animi tranquillitate*, published in 1543 by Gryphius. Whereas the *Commentatio*, as will be seen below, owed a profound debt to the Psalms, the genre model for the later work was that of the philosophical dialogue, as practised by Plato and Cicero and continued by many Renaissance scholars, such as Erasmus and Sadoleto. The scene-setting was modern: three friends – Francesco Michele, Demetrio Caravalla and Volusenus himself – resort to a pleasant grove on the hill of Fourvière, overlooking the city and its rivers, and there they discuss the topic of tranquillity of mind. The location is significant, given that an alternative name for the *sodalitium Lugdunense* was the 'Académie de Fourvière' (Ducher 2015: 33–82). Tranquillity of mind, though a venerable and ever relevant topic, had for several reasons become newly urgent. One reason was the victory of an English Protestant army over that of Catholic Scotland at Solway Moss in November 1542. Another, of greater significance, was the death of James V on 14 December, which opened the way for Henry VIII to interfere directly in the affairs of Scotland (Cameron 1998: 314–25). A third was the formal establishment of the Roman Inquisition in June 1542, which prompted the flight from Lucca to Switzerland of a group of Italian intellectuals sympathetic to reform: these included Peter Martyr Vermigli, Paolo Lazise/Lacizi and Celio Secondo Curione; another important refugee at this time was the Capuchin Bernardino Ochino, who left to join Calvin in Geneva. These events constituted a double blow to the Church at the hands of heresy and apostasy, as Volusenus, from considerations religious, political and patriotic, would have been acutely aware. His whole career had been predicated upon the existence of harmonious relations between Scotland, England and France. In addition, via his friendship with Bonvisi he had become *au fait* with the situation in Lucca. The *Commentatio* had been dedicated to Francesco Turretini from that city, whose father, Regolo, was a business associate of the very Francesco Michele of the *De animi tranquillitate*. The Turretini – merchant bankers like the Bonvisi – were further associated through their links with the prior of the church of San Frediano, Peter Martyr Vermigli (McNair 1967; Baker-Smith 1984, 2006: 104). The warm greeting sent by Volusenus in 1539 to the younger Turretini, together with his friend Bernardino Ciono (another citizen of Lucca) and the entire *familia* of Bonvisi, is confirmation of this strong Italian connection.

The first third of the dialogue is preoccupied with the issue of how tranquillity of mind may be attained through the study of moral philosophy. This entrains a long discussion of the affections, which the author does not (like the Stoics) view as bad, but rather evaluates in as much as such affections promote or disturb balance in the mind: in the end, tranquillity comes with the realisation of the beauty and excellence of virtue. In the main part of the work, Volusenus goes on to illustrate the foregoing discussion with reference to the dream elicited by his youthful perambulations by the Lossie. A scene is evoked, with a temple atop a hill, and over the entrance is the inscription *Tranquillitatis aedes*. Guided by the gate-keeper Democritus, the dreamer observes that the whole edifice is supported on eight pillars, each of which is inscribed with its respective moral maxim. Yet this structure of wisdom fails to satisfy, since there is no mention of any afterlife. Democritus, as the representative of Ancient (and *ipso facto* non-Christian) philosophy, is found to be limited, in his stressing of the dual nature of man as being merely a combination of dignity and wretchedness. Resolution, happily, comes with progress to a second and better temple, presided over by St Paul, who draws attention to two further pillars, bearing the legends '*Nosce teipsum*' [Know thyself] and '*Agnosce Deum tuum*' [Acknowledge thy God]; this is accompanied by a vision of the crucified Christ, bringing in the possibility of salvation. It is evident that the *De animi tranquillitate* moves toward a fideistic conclusion akin to that of the *Commentatio*; one may therefore be sure that the text (*DAT*: 361) that is inscribed over the Pauline temple – '*Beati qui habitant in domo tua*' [Blessed are they that dwell in Thy house] (Psalm 83/84; cf. Isaiah 32:18) – indicates the same temple in which the speaker of the *Commentatio* (§§347–50) longs to find his ultimate rest.

This is a very brief outline of what is an extensive work, and the reader may be referred to the helpful formal analysis supplied by John Ward in his edition (1751: xxiii–xxxii), the discussion in Baker-Smith (1969), and the online transcription and translation of Sutton (2008). It is possible to discern a line of development in the oeuvre of Volusenus, whereby the exegetical and philological approaches characteristic of the works of his Paris years can be seen to bear fruit in those of his maturity, composed at Carpentras and Lyon. The taste for the poetry of Horace, shared in the days of his youth with John Ogilvie at Elgin, bears its own specific fruit in the Horatian ode with which the dialogue is concluded. Although the reputation of Volusenus is likely still to rest principally on the *De animi tranquillitate*, the aphorisms of the *Commentatio* deserve recognition as containing *in nuce* the essence of his view of the world – involving the combination of humanist learning and faith founded on Catholic tradition, for the sake of achieving a healthy balance of mind in an age of spiritual and intellectual anxiety.

LATER YEARS

As far as is known, the last published work of Volusenus is the *Latinae grammatices epitome*, duly printed by Gryphius in 1544. A late testimony to a career spent tutoring, it clearly derives from the author's responsibilities as a teacher at the Collège de la Trinité. It is a succinct summary of Latin accidence, but, despite the fact that the title page describes it as '*supra quam credas utilis*' [more useful than you might think], it does not range much beyond the practical and pedagogical. Nonetheless, this grammar book bears further witness to Volusenus's links with Lucca, since, in his prefatory remarks, the author recommends it to one Giovanni Sandino from that city. Volusenus calls the latter a '*nobili indole puer*' [youth of noble talents], who, once he has mastered the rules of grammar, will be able quickly to move on to access the Muses, and in later life pluck the sweet fruits of wisdom (Appendix: B). This harvesting image perfectly encapsulates the rationale of a lifetime dedicated to humanist scholarship, and it corresponds perfectly with – for example – that outlined in 1537 by Ferrerio to Robert Reid, in the preface to the *Historia abbatum de Kynlos* (Holmes 2008: 108–9). Volusenus – the tutor of Gregory Cromwell, Francesco Turretini and Giovanni Sandino, among others – always had the younger generation at the forefront of his mind. Though there is no documentary record of a meeting between Volusenus and Ferrerio, such an event would have been entirely possible, and could have occurred at Kinloss during Volusenus's 1535 return visit to Scotland – or conceivably in France, where Ferrerio spent much of the years 1537–41 (Durkan 1981: 183–6). The two scholarly contemporaries – the Italian teaching in Scotland, and the Scot teaching in France – shared the vision of the benefits of a humanist education.

Although Volusenus may have enjoyed many aspects of life in Lyon, he could hardly have failed to be alarmed at the news reaching him from Scotland, from the surrounding French region, and not least from his former base at Carpentras. Each of his successors in the grammar school there, who all to varying degrees sympathised with the movement for reform, stayed only a short time in post. Of them, the most outstanding was Claude Baduel (c.1499–1561), who had studied at Louvain, Liège, Marburg and Wittenberg; he was on his arrival at Carpentras already an associate of Johann Sturm,

Bucer and Melanchthon, and would eventually be ordained a preacher at Geneva. His ideas on a reformed programme of education were set out in his *De collegio et universitate Nemausani*, published by Gryphius in 1540. Four years later, while suffering persecution from the clergy at Nîmes, Baduel applied through Sadoleto for the position once held by Volusenus; however, he was dismissed after a year and, back in Nîmes in 1548, was officially denounced as a heretic (Douglas 1959: 183–5). Sadoleto himself, despite his tolerant attitude towards humanist reformers in general and to the series of reform-minded grammar masters whom he had helped to appoint, had now come under pressure from François I and the regional Catholic authorities to act against the Waldensian heretics. This led in 1545 to the massacres at Mérindol and Cabrières perpetrated by Jean Maynier d'Oppède, acting with the approval of Pietro Ghinucci, bishop of Cavaillon, and of Sadoleto's nephew Paolo who, by then, had become coadjutor-bishop of Carpentras (Douglas 1959: 186–91). Scotland had also been suffering, though in a different way. There the 'Rough Wooing', intended to secure a marriage alliance between the infant Queen Mary and Edward, son of Henry VIII, resulted in May 1544 in the city of Edinburgh being looted and burned by an English army under the earl of Hertford (Merriman 2000: 143–9).

Volusenus, who would have abhorred all such violence, may have contemplated a return to Scotland. However, there too the Church, under David Beaton, had become increasingly repressive in its response to heresy. This trend led to the trial and burning of George Wishart (1 March 1546), an event that precipitated the assassination of Beaton on 29 May. It was presumably against this widespread and general background of religious and political upheaval that Volusenus wrote to his mentor Sadoleto in 1546 (the letter has not survived, and its date cannot be more precisely determined), asking for advice as to how he should comport himself. In his reply, sent from Rome, Sadoleto declared his revulsion at those who were '*impulsi odio, et furore quodam rapti, tam temere ac nefarie ab Ecclesia desciscere*' [driven by hate and carried away by a kind of mad passion, to secede so rashly and abominably from the Church] (Laing 1827: 337–8). The venerable cardinal's reaction to schism in the Church, therefore, remained essentially the same as in his 1539 *Epistola* to the Genevans, even if he now expressed himself in sharper tones. His advice to his *protégé* was to remain within the faith, the '*vna rectissima ad aeternam salutem via*' [the one straightest path to eternal salvation], and, as it turned out, Volusenus followed the advice, did remain within the faith, and did not return to Scotland. Had he done so, one may speculate that he might have envisaged for himself some role within the post-Beaton context of the more conciliatory religious policies pursued by the regent of Scotland, James Hamilton, second earl of Arran (after 1548, duke of Châtelherault) and the latter's half-brother John Hamilton, the new archbishop of St Andrews. One critic has suggested that, after 1547, Volusenus might have returned to Carpentras (Péricaud 1850: 3–4), but such a *démarche*, with its possible implication of a search for tranquillity of mind in formerly familiar surroundings, cannot be confirmed.

Having opted to stay in France, Volusenus next makes an appearance in connection with the French translation (Lyon, 1549) of the enormously popular *Emblemata* of the jurist and humanist Andrea Alciato (1492–1550). This version was the work of Barthélemy Aneau, principal at the Collège de la Trinité, and the latter goes out of his way to speak in glowing terms of Volusenus's mastery of a range of languages (Greek, Latin, Scots, French, Italian, Spanish) as well as of his personal goodness (Laing 1827: 330; Bath 2003). The volume was dedicated to James Hamilton (1537–1609), son of the Regent Arran, and Aneau reveals that it was actually Volusenus who had suggested the idea of the French translation itself, as well as the dedication. After the assassination of Beaton, Hamilton junior had joined the supporters of the fiery Reformer John Knox in the castle of St Andrews, and the youth's subsequent zeal for Protestantism doubtless stemmed from that experience. A decade later, he would be found as the guest at Zürich of Peter Martyr Vermigli and, after Hamilton's return to Scotland, and before (in 1562) he became insane, he was a conspicuous figure in the kirk faction (Durkan 1986: 164; Dawson 2015: 41, 187). From 1548, however, he was detained in France as a guest-hostage of Henri II (Durkan 1986: 156). It has been suggested that Aneau's tribute to Volusenus might imply the eulogy of a man with secret Protestant sympathies from another similarly inclined (in 1561 Aneau would be murdered in the Collège de la Trinité by a Catholic mob), but that is not necessarily the case. It would seem more likely that Volusenus was as he had ever been – a humanist scholar and talented educator, and ultimately a loyal, if perhaps not in every respect a perfervidly loyalist, Catholic. The whole initiative of the Alciato volume fits well into the context of the 1548 arrangements for the future marriage of Mary Queen of Scots to the dauphin, when great political effort was being invested in the promotion of Franco-Scottish solidarity (Bath 2003; van Heijnsbergen 2004: 199–204). The fact that Hamilton was the son and nephew of the two currently most important political figures in Scotland would, in itself, have been an important consideration in the cultural relations between the two countries. Volusenus, who had a rich experience of acting as tutor to the sons of important men, may have been seen as an ideal person to give direction to the education of the young man, and the *Emblemata* may have been recommended mainly for the moral lessons in that work. Nonetheless, in the end, and for whatever reason, Volusenus was not appointed as tutor to James Hamilton.

In the light of Aneau's laudation of Volusenus, it is no surprise that in 1551 the Scot was chosen to deliver the annual oration at Lyon on the feast day of St Thomas (21 December), a commission for which he received 9 *écus* as reward. These were grand occasions, held in the centrally situated church of St Nizier in the presence of the king's lieutenant, the archbishop, the local aristocracy and the city authorities (de Groër 1995: 26; Biot 1996: 141). No record of the content of the oration is known, but it is at least clear that Volusenus was esteemed by both the notable and the knowledgeable. Despite this civic acclaim, however, he must have been aware of the deteriorating religious situation in the Rhône valley. Although three *luthériens* had been put to the stake at Lyon in 1540 (precipitating the departure of Castellio), a Protestant church was established in the city by 1546. Yet tensions remained and, following religious riots in the summer of 1551, there occurred the public burning of Claude Monier, who had been sent as pastor by Calvin himself (Biot 1996: 87).

Even while such events were taking place, the poetic talents of Volusenus were beginning to be made known to the world beyond Lyon. The Horatian ode, *Quid vos, O superi boni*, from the end of the *De animi tranquillitate*, was reprinted in *Pii graves, atque elegantes poetae aliquot [Several serious and elegant religious poets]* (pp. 431–6), published at Basel by Johannes Oporinus. The volume, undated, has been assigned both to 1548–50 (Baker-Smith 1991: 189–91) and to 1550–1 (Guggisberg 2003: 43). In this collection of high-quality neo-Latin verse, the stanzas by Volusenus find themselves together with the *De partu Virginis* of Jacopo Sannazaro, the *Christiados* of Marco Girolamo Vida, the *De animorum immortalitate* of Aonio Paleario, and poems, including psalm-versifications, by Marcantonio Flaminio and Sebastian Castellio. Ironically, the idea of such a volume had in principle been floated much earlier by none other than Sadoleto, who in 1535 had written to Gryphius in recommendation of the poetry of Sannazaro, Vida, Paleario and Flaminio, as being able to achieve a reconciliation of Christian teaching and Classical forms. The editorial figure behind the *Pii graves* was probably Castellio, who, after leaving Geneva and Calvin in 1545 for Basel, had worked for Oporinus, a publisher noted (as was Gryphius in Lyon) for printing literary works that combined the virtues of Christianity and humanism (Buisson 1892: I.35; Steinmann 1967: 62–3; Davis 1983: 263–4; Guggisberg 2003: 20).

Although it is always possible that Castellio included the poem by Volusenus simply as a tribute to his former teacher, other considerations may have been involved. Paleario and Flaminio were among those commonly reputed to be associated with the highly influential, notably reformist, and accordingly well-nigh totally suppressed book, the *Beneficio di Giesu Christo* (Venice, 1543). Already in the 1530s the sympathies of both poets had lain with the so-called *spirituali*, a movement that included such as Sadoleto, Pole, Contarini, and the not yet Protestant Pier Paolo Vergerio, men who, like Luther, favoured 'the central role of grace by faith in the Christian life' (MacCulloch 2004: 214) and hoped for reform to come from within the Church itself (Morpurgo 1912: 323–36; Caponetto 1972: 469–96; Fenlon 1972: 21–3, 69–88; Caponetto 1979: 23–31, 46–54). In Scotland too, many significant figures have been identified with views typical of the *spirituali* (Somerset 2018). The presence of Volusenus's ode in the *Pii graves* can be taken as a sign that Castellio must have considered the Scot as meriting a position alongside those greater and much better-known poets, as being comparable with them in both literary skill and religious orientation.

The Basel anthology is the first of several publications wherein the poetry of Volusenus could come to have a literary reception independent of his prose writings. The final ode and some other verses in the *De animi tranquillitate* were excerpted by the Scottish advocate Thomas Wilson (who claimed a family relation with Florentius and applied the name of Volusenus to himself) at the end of his edition of the works of his own father-in-law, Archbishop Patrick Adamson (1619: fols. 74–8). The poems subsequently found a place in the important anthology of Scottish neo-Latin verse, the *Delitiae poetarum Scotorum* (1637: II.539–44). The ode was also separately translated into English – for example, by Ninian Paterson in his book of epigrams (1678: 238–49), and more famously by Robert Blair in *The Grave* (1747: 31–9) – with the paradoxical result that, by the time of the Enlightenment, the name of Volusenus was perhaps more widely known than it had been during the Renaissance.

The date and circumstances of the Scot's death are as uncertain as those of his birth. Some libraries report the year 1546; in their exhibition catalogue, Cadell and Cherry opt for 1547 (1983: 27). Against that, there is a tradition that Volusenus died in 1551 near Vienne, south of Lyon, though the now known fact of the 21 December oration makes this dating, though not necessarily the placing, as good as impossible. Long ago it was stated, although it is unclear on what grounds, that Volusenus died in 1557 (Buisson 1892: I.36), and this date has been repeated (de Groër 1995: 26; Ducher 2015: 27). If, as Thomas Wilson and Dempster report, Volusenus did indeed die near Vienne, and in whichever year that was, it is possible that his final journey began in Carpentras. Yet, whatever his starting point, it remains uncertain whether, as has been claimed, he was planning to return to his native country (Laing 1827: 330; Péricaud 1850: 4), or was merely heading back to Lyon. The epigram on Volusenus (quoted in the preface to the present volume) composed by his friend, compatriot, and later committed Protestant, George Buchanan, speaks merely of '*ripam ad Rhodani*' [by the bank of the Rhône] (1725: II.379). It has been conjectured that Volusenus was the unnamed Scot scorned by Calvin in 1553 for supporting Castellio in connection with the latter's repudiation of the burning at Geneva of Michael Servetus (Durkan 2004). This unnamed individual, however, would seem perhaps more likely to be a current disciple of Castellio's rather than his erstwhile teacher. If that is indeed the case, such a person would most probably have been living in Basel and not at Lyon (Buisson 1892: II.112), with the result that the supposed reference to Volusenus would be unsafe. Moreover, Durkan's earlier (1982: 131) characterisation of Volusenus as 'a man of solitude' would rather suggest someone inclined to shun engagement in public controversy.

By way of summary, it can be said that the position of the Scottish scholar Volusenus within the larger literary culture of the Renaissance depended on three main factors: his skill in the international scholarly language of Latin; his personal contacts with leading humanist intellectuals within the British Isles and on the Continent; and his professional experience of tutoring at several important centres of learning. Like some of his famous contemporaries – for example, Erasmus, Sadoleto, Contarini – Volusenus could gain plaudits from both sides of the religious divide. In 1574 the *De animi tranquillitate* was expanded into an Italian-language treatise (recast into four books with many chapters, and often dismissed as merely a translation) by the humanist and pedagogue Orazio Lombardelli and published at Siena. On the other hand, reprintings of the Latin text were an affair of Protestant territories – the Netherlands (1637 and 1641), Scotland (1707 and 1751), Saxony (1760). Such a binary reception (cf. MacDonald 2009a), however, was already the fate of the earlier *Commentatio*, with its appearances at Lyon and Basel. The publishing history of the works of Volusenus's maturity reflects both the author's position as an evangelical humanist and the eirenic disposition of his mind. The *Commentatio*, for all its brevity, is a remarkable work of early modern Christian literature: suitable for all seasons, while simultaneously and eloquently witnessing to the contemporary crisis of faith.

APPENDIX

A: Gilberti Ducherii Vultonis Aquapersani epigrammaton libri duo
(Lyon, 1538), p. 50

[Epigram: To Volusenus]

Auxilii cupiens, erecta mente leuaui
  In montes oculos terque quaterque meos.
Sed solum a Domino auxilium, Volusene, uidebam,
  Qui nulla solus cuncta creauit ope.
Sedulus hic custos nunquam dormitet, ut errans
  Huc illuc pedibus commoueare tuis.
Non dormitabit, neque dormiet optimus ille
  Pastor, Idumaei cura salusque gregis.
Custodit Dominus tua te protectio, ne unquam
  Luceue sol urat, lunaue nocte sua.
Quantum hic mortalis uiues, custodiet omni
  Exitum, et egressum sedulitate tuum.

[Desirous of help, with mind erect have I thrice and four times raised my eyes
to the hills. But, Volusenus, I saw that help comes only from the Lord, who
alone with no assistance has created everything. This watchman is careful that
he should never slumber, since by your feet you may be carried astray hither
and thither. He will not slumber, neither will that best of shepherds fall asleep,
the guard and salvation of his Jewish flock. The Lord, your protection, watches
over you, lest ever either the sun burn by day or the moon by night. For the
length of this your mortal life, He, with perfect carefulness will watch over
your goings-out and your comings-in.]

B:Volusenus, Latinae grammatices epitome *(Lyon, 1544), p. 3*

[Advice to Giovanni Sandino]

Nunc celer ad Musas i per compendia, longae
  Ducere quo potuit uix labor antè uiae.
Curaque cùm desit nusquam generosa parentum:

Tu, tibi ne desis, chare caueto puer.
Sic uiridem ingenij plantamque rigabis, ut inde
    Dulcia iam senior carpere poma queas.

[Now go swiftly to the Muses by these short cuts, to where, previously, the
labour of a long journey could scarcely bring you. Although the generous care
of your parents may in no respect ever fail, take care, dear boy, that you never
be failing towards yourself. In this way, you will be watering the green plant of
understanding, from which you, when older, may pluck sweet fruit.]

C: Commentatio theologica *(Basel, 1544), p. 4*

Ad pium lectorem Epigramma

Minutus ut sit hic liber,
Amice Lector, non tamen
Minutus usus illius,
Nec est minuta dignitas.
Nam uerba fundit ignea,
Et pectus inflammantia
Ad sempiterni numinis
Syncerum amorem, et gloriam.
Proinde, cordi, est sanctitas
Cuicumque, curet maximè
Sibi ut libellum hunc comparans
Noctu diuque lectitet.[1]

[Epigram: To the pious reader.

This book, dear reader, small though it may be, is small in neither its use nor its
value. For it is a fount of words of fire, igniting hearts to a sincere love of the
everlasting God, and to His glory. Accordingly, whosoever takes holiness to
heart, let him take care to get himself this book and pore over it night and day.]

---

[1]   The author of these iambic dimeter verses is unknown.

EDITION AND TRANSLATION

TREATMENT OF TEXT

Copytext

The *Commentatio quaedam theologica* (Lyon: Sebastian Gryphius, 1539) — 8°,
A-G⁴H²— is here edited from the Vienna, Österreichische Nationalbibliothek
copy (online) and (by autopsy) from that in Edinburgh, National Library of
Scotland (RB.s.296). There are no differences between these in either textual
content or layout. However, they represent different states of the print: while
many pages in the Vienna lack their numbers, the pagination is complete in
the Edinburgh, which is thus doubtless the later, improved copy. The Vienna
copy is free of any manuscript markings; in that of Edinburgh, many passages
are marked by underlining, sidelining and, at two places (pp.7, 91), by marginal
annotation, and the practice of using double quotation marks in the margin
to indicate quoted sources has been greatly increased with manual insertions.

EDITORIAL PROCEDURE

The title page is reproduced photographically as the frontispiece. The aphorisms
appear in the original work as a continuous stream of brief paragraphs; in the
present edition, these are individually numbered. Page numbers and signatures
pertaining to the recto pages of the 1539 print are added in square brackets, to
allow the aphorisms as edited to be easily located in relation to the original.

Spelling, capitalisation and punctuation are in principle preserved, though
the following points should be noted. The floriated initial capital **E** in the
first aphorism is ignored, as are all accents (except in Greek words). Marginal
quotation marks are not reproduced. Superscript marks indicating nasals
are rendered as **n** or **m** as appropriate. The digraphs **æ** and **œ** are rendered
in separated letters; **ę** becomes **ae** or **oe** as appropriate; **ij > ii**; **& > et**; the
word-final abbreviation **q** is expanded as **que**; as an independent word, **o > O**.
Very few textual emendations are needed: minor cases are signalled locally by
asterisks; new material is supplied between square brackets; all emendations
are discussed in the relevant notes.

TRANSLATION

At a few places, the punctuation used in the translation may not correspond precisely with that of the Latin; Volusenus's addiction to parentheses, for example, is restrained. It is nonetheless hoped that the translation reflects the meaning intended by the author.

REISSUE

The reissue of the *Commentatio* (Basel: Hieronymus Curio, 1544) adds nothing to the text beyond printing errors and is therefore disregarded; the new liminary epigram is reproduced as Appendix C of Introduction.

THE TEXT

Florentius Volusenus Francisco Tur[retino] Civi Lucensi S[alutationes] D[at].

Nuper, mi Francisce, duo celebres uiri, Ioannes Bortiuicus regiae custodiae praefectus, et Panagius Hocedius amplissimi Principis Cardinalis Lothoringi a secretis, mihi persuaserunt, ut ineptirem: id est, ut Commentationem hanc, uel si mauis, precationem, quam amici cuiusdam rogatu obiter conscripseram, in uulgus edi permitterem. Eis ipse eo minus inuitus sum assensus, quod ea, nec ornatissimo Antistiti Vintoniensi, cuius doctrinam ingeniique excellentiam etiam docti suspiciunt, nec illius a secretis Germano Gardinero, iuueni insigniter cum docto, tum pio displicuit. Hanc tibi in praesentia, mi Francisce, nuncupo: qui me singulari tua humanitate, et liberalium disciplinarum cultu, tui cum primis studiosum reddidisti. Non tanti ea est (scio) ut nobis ingenii opinionem (nam neque in hoc comparata est) lucrifaciat. Satis superque mihi erit, si hinc fructus aliquis ad lectorem perueniat. Etenim illud ea gratia fieri posse confido: quod statuam, illum ualde improbum esse non posse, cuius mentem crebro subeunt generosae cogitationes, et sententiae. Eiusmodi / enim est τῶν νουθετικῶν λόγων (ut Socrates apud Xenophontem disserit) uirtus et efficacitas: quam cum prophanis concedamus, non possumus non copiosius, et cum accessione eandem sacris attribuere. Ea de causa nos hic passim sacra admiscuimus, quod libelli margo notis (ut uides) interpunctus indicat. Vale una cum nostro Bernardino Ciono, totaque ista Bonuisiana familia.

Florentius Volusenus sends greetings to Francis Turretini, citizen of Lucca.

Recently, my dear Francis, two distinguished men, John Borthwick, captain of the King's Guard, and Panagius Hocedius, secretary of his Princely Highness, the Cardinal of Lorraine, persuaded me that I should do something foolish: that is, that I should allow this Meditation (or, if you prefer, Prayer) to be published, which I had in passing drawn up at the request of a friend. I agreed to them with the less reluctance, since the thing had displeased neither the most illustrious bishop of Winchester, whose doctrine and excellence of understanding are admired even by the learned, nor his secretary Germain Gardiner, a young man remarkable both for his learning and his devotion. This I now dedicate, my dear Francis, to you, who, by your exceptional humanity and cultivation of the liberal arts, have made me one of your first admirers. It is not of such value, I realise, as to win us the reputation of wisdom, for to this end it has not been composed. It will be more than enough for me, if from this some benefit should come through to the reader. I am confident that that may well happen for this reason, that I am sure that a man cannot be very wicked, whose mind is filled with generous thoughts and opinions. For that is the virtue and efficacy of 'words of good counsel' (as Socrates asserts, according to Xenophon); and while we may concede it to profane words, we cannot fail to attribute it in fuller measure and with increase to sacred ones. Here throughout, for that reason, we have mingled in words of Holy Writ, which (as you will observe) are indicated by punctuation marks on the margin of the booklet. Farewell, together with our friend Bernardino Ciono and the entire Bonvisi family.

Flor[entius] Vol[usenus], COMMENTATIO THEOLOGICA.

[1] Expergiscere anima mea, expergiscere: Exurge gloria mea, exurge: Exurge psalterium et cithara, exurge diluculo.

[2] Noctis se tenebrae condunt: Lucifer formosos (de more) uultus exerens, rorem spargit in gramen: Ales, uicinae lucis nuntia, officii iandudum me admonet.

[3] Antistes magno huic, quod coelum, terrasque complectitur, templo datus sum: Nunc debitum sibi in hoc lucis reditu laudum carmen, de me lucis autor, idemque templi numen expectat.

[4] Consurge itaque Hierusalem, consurge: Excutere de puluere, et tanquam in die inclyti sacrarii tui, induere uestimentis gloriae tuae.

[5] Pone anima mea humiles has, indignasque tuo genere curas, teque ad tuum munus, pensumque reuoca: id est, ad conditoris tui laudes, et coelestium rerum commentationem te conuerte.

[6] Nonne deo subiecta es anima mea? Nonne ab ipso salus tua? Nunquid non ipse est pater tuus, qui possedit, fecit, et creauit te?

[7] Quod si foedum, atque indignum (ut re uera est) existimas, si quis beneficiis aliunde acceptis se assidue oblectet, totosque in ea defigat oculos, nulla interea autori gratia habita: expende tecum, quantum tu in praesentia sustineas officii, qui nihil habes, quod non acceperis.

[8] Quare age, expergiscere anima mea: Lauda anima mea dominum: et aeternum illum coeli regem, prona, supplex, omnique, qua datur obseruantia, ac religione (ut par est) adora.

[9] Scis, alme parens, nihil a nobis pro dignitate tua fieri posse. Vincit enim meritorum tuorum magnitudo omne cum linguae, tum mentis officium.

[10] Desistendum itaque in praesentia hoc conatu, atque incepto esset: nisi tu, qui non minus bonus, quam magnus es, officiosos huiusmodi conatus ubi uires desunt (in tanta etiam indignitate nostra interea conniuens) boni semper consuleres.

Florentius Volusenus, A Theological Meditation

[1] Awake, my soul, awake; arise, my glory, arise. Arise, psaltery and lute, arise with the dawn.

[2] The darkness of night is sinking away; Lucifer, raising (as ever) his beauteous countenance, is sprinkling dew on the meadow; the wingèd one, herald of the approaching light, summons me long since to my duty.

[3] I have been given as a priest to this great temple, which embraces heaven and earth. The author of the light, likewise the Godhead of the temple, now expects from me the praise-song due to him at this return of light.

[4] Rise up, therefore, Jerusalem, rise up; shake off the dust, and, as in the day of your glorious temple, be clad with the vestments of your glory.

[5] My soul, lay aside these lowly and trivial concerns, unworthy of your descent. Call yourself back to your function and to your task: that is, apply yourself to the praise of your creator, and to consideration of heavenly things.

[6] My soul, are you not subject to God? Is not your salvation from him? Is he himself not your Father, who has taken possession of you, made and created you?

[7] And if you think it disgusting and shocking (as indeed it is), that anyone should take continual delight in benefits accepted from someone else and keep his gaze entirely fixed on them and in the meantime feel no gratitude to their originator, think to yourself what an obligation rests at this moment on you, who have nothing which you have not received.

[8] Wherefore, my soul, bestir yourself, arise. Praise the Lord, my soul, and, bowing down in supplication, worship the eternal king of heaven with every possible obedience and devotion, as is proper.

[9] You know, loving Father, that nothing can be done by us that accords with your honour, for the greatness of your merits overwhelms every service of both tongue and mind.

[10] And so, this attempt, this endeavour, would have to be abandoned right now, were it not that you, who are no less good than great, will always take in good part dutiful attempts of this kind where our powers are inadequate, while closing your eyes to our very great unworthiness.

¹¹ Salue ergo magne deus: Salue arcana trias: Salue sacrosanctum coeli numen: Salue rerum omnium princeps et domine.

¹² O exuperantissime mundi conditor: O immensi olympi sempiterne regnator: O ingentis huius operosaeque molis dux ac rector sapientissime.

¹³ Tu uita, tu salus, tu communis omnium spes: Tu rerum flos, tu rerum decus: tu rerum delitiae, tu summum, imo unum uniuersi orbis bonum.

¹⁴ Nos mortales, et ex crassa hac, uisibilique materia, magna ex parte, constantes, te inuisibilem, seculorumque potentem regem, dilucide quidem non cernimus, hoc tamen nobis minime obscurum est, nos omnes, et quod sumus, et quicquid sumus tibi soli debere. Quamobrem, tibi regi seculorum immortali, inuisibili, soli deo, omnis sit honos, omnis sit gloria.

[p.9/A5] ¹⁵ Sed quid ego, O ineffabilis princeps, speciosis huiusmodi titulis adhibitis, te inuoco? Nam etsi hi uere in te quadrant, si tamen quicquam usquam in tantam excellentiam quadrare potest: illa tamen a me praetermissa appellatio est, quae non paulo prae caeteris popularis est et plausibilis.

¹⁶ Dicam ergo, O humani generis ignoscentissime pater. Tantum enim abest, ut ad confidentem hanc, atque audacem appellationem indignere, ut tute (quae tua est bonitas) quo miseros desperatione fractos, metuque exanimatos erigeres, ad eiusmodi appellationis, ac nomenclaturae formam nos institueris, atque informaris.

¹⁷ Secede iam, secede, reconde te, reconde: quantuncunque tamen secedas, quantuncunque te recondas, prorsus latere non potes. Visendum nimirum hoc tuum te prodit opificium: non obscurum ingenio tuo testimonium, dat artifex haec, atque incomparabilis structura.

¹⁸ Praestantiam tuam exquisitissimus hic apparatus loquitur: regni tui gloriam, et opes, admirabilis haec rerum magnificentia praedicat.

¹⁹ Es etenim tu reconditissimae maiestatis numen, intra ardua coelorum penetralia, in excelso isto aeternitatis domicilio, lucem habitans inaccessam.

[p.11/A6] ²⁰ Imo uerius ipse lux es, et quidem purissima: sed cuius fulgor etiam coelitum aciem praestringat: cuius radios ne diuorum quidem lumina perferant, nisi per te aduentitia quadam, ac precaria uirtute confirmentur.

¹¹ Hail, therefore, great God; hail, mystic Trinity; hail, most holy, heavenly Godhead; hail, King and Lord of all things.

¹² O most excellent creator of the world; O eternal ruler of this immense Olympus; O leader and most wise governor of this huge and elaborate structure,

¹³ You are the life, the salvation, and common hope of all; you are the flower and beauty of all things; you are the delight of all things, you are the highest, and indeed only, good of the universal world.

¹⁴ We mortals, being composed in great part of this gross and visible matter, do not clearly perceive you, the invisible and mighty ruler of the ages – yet this at least is not at all unclear to us, that all of us owe to you alone both that we are, and what we are. Wherefore to you, immortal ruler of the ages, invisible and only one God, be all honour and glory.

¹⁵ But why do I, O ineffable prince, call upon you, applying splendid terms like these? For, even if they truly fit you – if indeed anything anywhere can befit such great excellence – I yet have left out that title, which, far above all others, is popular and pleasing.

¹⁶ So I will say: O most forgiving Father of humankind. For far from being angry at this confident and bold address, you yourself (such is your goodness), in order to raise up wretched creatures broken with despair and nearly dead with fear, have established and shaped us for this kind of address and naming.

¹⁷ Withdraw, then, withdraw; hide, hide yourself away. Yet however much you withdraw, however much you hide, you cannot be concealed absolutely. This wonderful piece of work betrays you and brings you out to be seen; this cunningly wrought and incomparable structure gives no obscure testimony to your nature.

¹⁸ This most exquisite fabrication bespeaks your excellence; this wonderful magnificence of creation declares the glory and richness of your kingdom.

¹⁹ For you are a Godhead most mysterious in majesty within the lofty halls of the heavens, in that highest dwelling-place of eternity inhabiting light inaccessible.

²⁰ Rather, more truly you yourself are light, and indeed the purest light – the brilliance of which may blunt even the sight of the heavenly host, and the beams of which not even the eyes of holy men may endure, unless strengthened by you with some occasional and fleeting force.

²¹ Coelestibus enim illis animis, quia pene tot mentes toti sunt oculi, naturale uelut pabulum est illa ingenii lux, absoluta naturae cognitio.

²² Iisdem pro deliciis est, si tu, tu inquam qui omnis naturae autor, atque opifex es, ipsis obiter, sublustrisque duntaxat, et uelut per transennam intermicas.

²³ Quod si palam, et serenus irradias, nec te iam in se, aut aliena specie (quo naturae uis perducit) sed coram, atque ut es conspiciunt, ipsa felicitas est, et clarissimus ille aeternitatis dies.

²⁴ Dies inquam, quam nox consequens non excipiat, quam tenebrae non opacent, quam nullae unquam molestiarum nebulae infuscent, nulla angoris interturbet caligo.

²⁵ Tu simplex es, et inconcreta puritas: quicquid tamen intra immensos illos, atque inexplebiles τοῦ ὄντος sinus cadere potest, citra puritatis iacturam complectens.

²⁶ Apud te unum est uitae fons: Apud te unum uera gaudia: Apud te unum delitiarum flumina, et reconditae dulcedinis plenissimi amnes exundant.

²⁷ Nihil hic in terris solidae, nihil est syncerae uoluptatis: Semper laetis solicitum aliquid admiscetur: et si quid est (ut est) quod male cautis dulce appareat, praeterquam quod exile id est, et confuso uiciatum amaro, dictum factum euanescit.

[p.13/A7] ²⁸ Praestabilius quiddam, dignamque homine uoluptatem, naturae contemplatio promittere uidetur: quod sane re ipsa praestaret, nisi nox tanta non tam rebus, quam ingeniis nostris offusa esset, ut ueri uerius uestigatio quam inuento, sit haec nostra tantopere iactata philosophia.

²⁹ At apud te omnes sapientiae et scientiae thesauri sunt repositi. Tu scrutaris profunda fluuiorum: tu in lucem abdita pandis: tu sedes super cherubim, et intueris in abyssum: tu maris dinumeras arenam: tu coeli stellis nomina imponis.

²¹ For those heavenly spirits, since their minds are almost all eyes, their natural nourishment is as it were that light of the intellect, the absolute comprehension of nature.

²² And for them, it is their supreme delight if you – who, as I say, are the author and fashioner of all nature – should shine for them occasionally and with a faint gleam at least, as through a lattice.

²³ Because, if you blaze out clear and unclouded and they behold you, not as they are now or in some different state (to which their natural force is taking them), but in your actual presence and as you are, that is felicity itself and the utterly clear daylight of eternity.

²⁴ Daylight, I say, which no succeeding night may follow on, no shadows obscure, no clouds of troubles darken, nor blackness of misery disturb.

²⁵ You are purity unmixed and immaterial, and yet without loss of purity embracing whatever can fall within those immense and insatiable gulfs of existence.

²⁶ With you alone is the fount of life, with you alone is true happiness; with you alone do the rivers of delights and the swelling streams of hidden sweetness flow forth.

²⁷ Here on earth, there is nothing of lasting, nothing of unmixed joy; a disquieting element is always mixed in with things pleasant, and if there is anything (as there is) which might seem sweet to the ill-advised, besides the fact that it is meagre and spoiled by a bitter admixture, no sooner said than done, it vanishes.

²⁸ Contemplation of nature appears something more estimable and a pleasure worthy of man, and indeed it would really be superior, if such darkness had not been poured out, not so much over physical matter, as over our minds, with the result that our so vaunted philosophy is more truly the search for, than the discovery of, what is true.

²⁹ But in you all the treasures of wisdom and knowledge are stored up. You search the watery deeps; things hidden you bring into the light; you sit above the Cherubim and plumb the abyss; you number the sands of the sea; you appoint names to the stars of heaven.

³⁰ Nihil tibi praeteritum est: nihil item futurum. Etenim tu, uno eodemque praesente obtutu, ex editissimo isto, stabilique aeternitatis uertice simul prospicis, quicquid angusti temporis fluxus separatim edit, et tanquam in transcursu, obiterque contuetur.

³¹ Tu summus ille rerum coryphaeus, in ipsa uniuersitatis arce consistens, cuncta administras arbitrio procurationis tuae: quae eo usque efficax est, ut nihil sit in tanta rerum uarietate, et copia tam exile, aut tam minutum, quod iniussu tuo oriatur, aut fiat.

³² Casus procul a finibus tuis exulat: fortunam consilia tua excludunt, quorum summa cum firmitate ac constantia, mutabile hoc rerum, suum cuiusque ingenium, necnon et deliberationis quoque nostrae libertas, arcano quodam, nondumque satis explorato nexu cohaerent.

[p.15/A8] ³³ Auribus, animisque pariter absurdum est illud, imo impium est, Non uidebit dominus: non intelliget Deus Iacob: Tenebrae occultabunt me: nox illuminatio mea in deliciis meis.

³⁴ Num tu, qui plantas aurem, non audias? Num qui fingis oculum, non consideres? Num tu rei alicuius nescius esse queas, qui doces hominem scientiam?

³⁵ Eodem apud te loco sunt nox et dies, lux et tenebrae: tibi uel cordium tacitae patent cogitationes: imo tu penitissimos, et saepe ne nobis quidem ipsis perspectos, pectorum nostrorum recessus excutis.

³⁶ Hos tuos oculos, quisquis assidue ob oculos habet, non temere proponit ante oculos rem iniustam: et cum illo dilecto tibi rege, perambulat in innocentia cordis sui, in medio domus suae.

³⁷ Hanc numinis tui praesentiam, quisquis reueretur (papae quis non reuereatur?) solicitus cauet, ne unquam uel secum in animo turpiter, aut indecore instituat: officium, aut fidem, ut nemo hominum conscius sit, nunquam prodet.

³⁸ Sed oppido profecto excors, et inscitus ueri uenator sum, qui scientiae tuae opes, ex eorum, quae ipse unus uel nutu fabricatus es, agnitione aestimo.

³⁰ Nothing for you is past, neither is anything future. For, in one and the same present view, from that most high and fixed pinnacle of eternity you behold at one and the same moment whatever the flux of brief time brings forth separately and observes incidentally as it passes, so to speak.

³¹ You are the supreme director of all things; stationed in the citadel of the universe itself, you regulate all things through the decisions of your governance, which is effective to such a degree, that, in the great variety and abundance of things, there is nothing so trivial or slight that it originates or happens without your bidding.

³² Accident is banished from your realm; your counsels exclude fortune, and through the great firmness and constancy of these counsels, this changeable part of creation, the inborn nature of each man, and our liberty of decision-making, through some secret and not yet sufficiently investigated bond accord with the rest.

³³ Absurd equally to the ears and minds, and, in fact, impious, is this: The Lord will not see, the God of Jacob will not perceive; the darkness will hide me, night will be my light in my pleasures.

³⁴ You who place the ear, are you not to hear? You who make the eye, are you not to see? Are you, who teach man knowledge, capable of not knowing something?

³⁵ With you, night and day, light and darkness count the same; to you even the silent thoughts of the heart lie open; in fact, you examine the deepest, and often even to ourselves unviewed, recesses of our inmost being.

³⁶ Whoever constantly has these eyes of yours before his own eyes, does not readily set injustice in his sights, and with the king, beloved of you, he walks in the innocence of his heart, in the midst of his house.

³⁷ Whoever reveres this presence of your Godhead (good heavens, who would not revere?) habitually guards lest he propose anything corrupt or improper even secretly in his mind; he will never betray duty or good faith, even though no one should know of it.

³⁸ But, undoubtedly, I am absolutely a senseless and stupid hunter after the truth, if I assess the richness of your knowledge according to my perception of the things which you yourself alone have created even by a nod.

[39] Nihil est quod dixi: Nam tu unus uel hoc uno absolutae sapientiae laudem obtines, quod ipse tibi plene, et quoad eius fieri potest cognitus sis: tua solius laus haec est, quaeque in alios diffundi ac deriuari minime potest.

[p.17/B1] [40] Neque tamen in causa est ulla naturae tuae obscuritas. Siquidem quo praestantior es (nam ita natura passim comparatum est) hoc tuapte natura es illustrior. Verum ad immensi splendoris exuperantiam, omnis, quae non ipsa pariter immensa est, acies caligat quodammodo, et hebescit.

[41] Quid, quod te architectum ex operibus duntaxat, et eis, quae ipse architectatus es, effectis discimus? quae cum immenso interuallo infra te posita sint, potius quid non sis, quam quid sis, ostendunt.

[42] Nam si nobis constaret, quid tu sis, teque absque inuolucro, aut integumento etiam citra illam cumulatae compraehensionis laudem conspicere daretur, rationi uela (quippe portu inuento) complicanda forent.

[43] Ad has philosophandi metas ubi peruentum erit, huc ubi perductus fuerit commentationis cursus, praeter sempiternas illas ferias, et altissimum beatitudinis otium nihil sane restabit.

[44] Sed quid dixi, te omnia scire, te unum plene sapere? Aptius quidem tu, atque appositius, ipsa diceris sapientia. Non enim in te aliorum more ea cadit distinctio, ut aliud sit qui sapit, aliud ipsum sapere. quo fit, ut solus, neque inter cognoscendum, neque inter agendum labi possis, aut errare.

[45] Decorem tuum nullum carpit aeuum: pulchritudinem tuam sol et luna admirantur: Sereni tui uultus, coelum pariter, et terras quoque exhilarant.

[p.19/B2] [46] Caeterum alterius, et praestantioris generis est iste tuus decor, quam ut corporeis hisce oculis cerni possit: animi acies est, quae te uidet: eaque non nisi purgatissima.

[47] Nos tantisper, dum in caeco hoc carcere positi, perturbationum uinculis constringimur, umbras circunfusas, circumque uolitantes admiramur: illis inexhausta auiditate inhiamus: quippe rerum aspectui insolentes, atque insueti.

[39] I have said nothing of any worth. For you only hold the praise of absolute wisdom even for this reason alone, that you yourself are known fully to yourself, and to the fullest extent; this praise is yours and only yours, and it can in no way be diffused and diverted to others.

[40] There is no question of your nature being obscure. The more outstanding you are – and this is the way things normally go – the more obvious by your own nature you are. But, before the superabundance of measureless glory, every eye which itself is not equally measureless becomes somehow darkened and cloudy.

[41] What of the fact that we discover you as the great designer, from your works at least and from those effects which you have designed. But they, since they are set by an immense gulf below you, demonstrate rather what you are not, than what you are.

[42] For should it become clear to us what you are, and were it permitted to behold you without any mantle or covering, even if short of that excellence of total understanding, reason would have to fold her sails, the harbour surely being reached.

[43] When these goals of our philosophising are attained, the place where the course of our meditation will reach its end, there will indeed remain nothing but those everlasting holidays and the most deep rest of beatitude.

[44] But why did I say that you know all things, and that you alone are wise? Indeed, more fittingly, and more relevantly, you are called wisdom itself. For to you, unlike others, that distinction does not apply, whereby he who knows is one thing, and the act of knowing is another, from which it comes about that you alone can neither slip between understanding and doing, nor go astray.

[45] No passage of time takes anything away from your glory: sun and moon marvel at your beauty, at the sight of your serene face, heaven and earth rejoice together in equal measure.

[46] For the rest, that glory of yours is of a sort too different and too surpassing to be glimpsed by these bodily eyes; it is the eyes of the mind that see you, and of those only the most purified.

[47] We ourselves, as long as we are held in this blind dungeon, are bound by the chains of perturbation, and wonder at shadows surrounding us and flitting around; we yearn for them with never-exhausted greed, being unaccustomed and unused to the sight of reality.

⁴⁸ At ubi hinc ad lucem, ad res, et potissimum ad te, rerum florem abducemur, detectis continuo praestigiis, peregrinisque formis, formoso isti tuo ori loco cedentibus, sordebit nobis protinus quicquid antea charum, aut in deliciis fuit.

⁴⁹ Hinc est haud dubie, quod sacri illi tui uates, quos uberiore coelestium rerum cognitione impertiri dignatus es, proximas tibi mentes, quibus amplior est conspectus tui facultas, peculiari uoce Seraphim, hoc est, meros ardores appellarunt.

⁵⁰ Nam etsi totus ille coelitum coetus communiter incredibili quodam amore tui flagrat, expleri mentem nequeat, ardescatque tuendo: sunt tamen (ut credere par est) hic ignium gradus, sunt in amore discrimina.

⁵¹ Tantum enim abest, ut aliquando tui copia fastidium pariat, ut quo propius, quoque diutius conspiceris, hoc maiora exuscites incendia: hoc acrius, hoc dulcius spectantis te pectus aduras.

⁵² Quod si uisus, sic eos afficere soles, qui ipsi propemodum species et formae sunt (sic autem afficis proculdubio) quis me, bone Deus, cum ad conspectum tui admittar, ardor habiturus est? qui adeo a forma inops sum, et quem tam uehementer formae permouere solent.

[p.21/B3] ⁵³ Etenim et fugaces hae formarum umbrae, mihi mentis robur subinde labefactant: saepe ab instituta animi magnitudine, in leues quasdam curas deiiciunt: et (ut semel dicam) me pene surripiunt mihi.

⁵⁴ Si qua ex philosophiae studiis praesidia comparata sunt, quibus animus ad officium confirmetur, ea illae ipsae umbrae de loco depellunt. Ad haec tui memoriam, qua nihil debet tenacius in animo inhaerescere, obliterant: eamque denique rationem omnem, quae sapientiam attingit, fallaci sua specie eblandiuntur, atque expectorant.

⁵⁵ Quos igitur tu mihi sic φιλοκάλῳ spirabis amores? quantos ista tua forma, quam amare non solum laus est, sed etiam felicitas, suscitabis ignes, si semel diuinitatis tuae ualuis patefactis, decoris tui diuitias explices?

[48] But when we are led out of here into the light, to things solid, and especially to you, the flower of all – once all illusions and strange shapes have been revealed, yielding place before that beauteous face of yours – that which previously was attractive or our favourite delight will straightway seem of no account to us.

[49] Assuredly it was for this reason that those your holy prophets, whom you have thought worthy to have a share in a fuller knowledge of things heavenly, have called the intelligences closest to you, who have a richer capacity for seeing you, by the special term of Seraphim – that is, pure burning lights.

[50] For even though the entire company of celestial beings is in concert aflame with an incredible love of you, it could not be satisfied in mind and would wax hotter by gazing; there are here, as we may well believe, degrees of fires and distinctions in love.

[51] Far from the abundance of your presence ever giving rise to aversion, the more closely and continually you are seen, the greater are the fires that you ignite, and the more fervently and sweetly do you burn the heart of the person who gazes upon you.

[52] If when you are seen you habitually so affect those who themselves are almost ideas and forms (for indubitably you do so affect them) – what ardour will overcome me, good God, when I shall be admitted to sight of you, I who am indeed lacking in form, and whom forms habitually agitate so strongly?

[53] In fact, these fleeting shadows of forms again and again shake the firmness of my mind; they regularly cast me down from any established mental greatness into various trivial preoccupations, and, to say it once for all, they almost steal me away from myself.

[54] If any defences from philosophical studies have been acquired by which the mind might be strengthened to do its duty, those same shadows dislodge them. In addition, they destroy the memory of you, than which nothing should more tenaciously stick in the mind, and finally, by their deceptive appearance, they wheedle away and expel all that line of thought which relates to wisdom.

[55] And so, what feelings of love will you inspire within me, who am so much a lover of the beautiful? How great will be the fires which you kindle through that form of yours, which to love constitutes not only praise but also felicity, if the gates of your divinity are once thrown open and you lay out the riches of your glory?

[56] Vires tuae metas non habent: potentia nescit terminum. Tu totum nutu tremefacis olympum: Tu fera terribili iacularis fulmina dextra.

[57] Tu coelos digitulo appendis: tu palmo concludis orbem: tu montes in statera ponderas: tu irrequietum hunc et immani mole globum, paribus undique libratum ponderibus, tanquam per inane suspendis.

[58] Irae tuae obsistere nemo neque audet, neque ualet: Ante te incuruantur qui portant orbem: nutus tuos obseruat infatigabilis illa naturae uis, quae elementa coercet, quae syderum orbes incitatissimis cursibus usque conuoluit.

[p.23/B4] [59] Tu montes et colles humilias: praecipites das, quos cordis erigit superbia. Deturbas de sedibus potentes, et a puluere usque ad gloriae principatum humiles subuehis.

[60] Nihil te infenso tutum: Nihil te propicio extimescendum. Si populorum insurgant milia, si proelium ingruat, sub alarum tuarum umbra, hosti medium unguem ostendam.

[61] Altissimum enim posuisti refugium tuum: illo usque malum non pertinet, et flagellum non appropinquat ad tabernaculum tuum.

[62] Beatus cuius deus Iacob adiutor eius, spes eius in domino deo ipsius, cui superi, cui inferi, cui coelum, cui tellus, et maria parent.

[63] Tu pensilem hanc molem, et quicquid eius ambitur finibus, assidue fulcis. Tua solius uirtus est, quae cuncta cohibeat: te penes est unum uasti custodia mundi.

[64] Frustra enim collegam, aut muneris socium habet, qui ipse per se abunde, quod ex usu sit, praestare potest, sed nec in tanti numinis maiestatem, auxilii aliquando cadat egestas.

[65] Multitudinem ac sui partitionem ea natura non admittit, quae nullis perfectionis terminis circumscripta, omniaque complectens, nullam notam, nullum insigne alteri paris naturae relinquit, quod τῆς οὐσίας differentiam efficiat.

[56] Your power has no limits, its potential knows no end. With a nod of your head you cause all Olympus to tremble; with your terrible right hand you hurl devastating bolts of lightning.

[57] You hang the heavens with a little finger, you hold the world in your palm, you weigh mountains in the scales; this restless globe with its enormous mass you hold suspended in the void, balanced on every side with equal weights.

[58] To resist your wrath no-one either dares or has the power. Those who hold up the world bow before you; the indefatigable force of nature, which controls the elements and which rolls the circling stars all the way along their swift paths, watches for your nod of command.

[59] You bring mountains and hills low; you send headlong those whom pride of heart has elevated. You put down the mighty from their seats, and you raise the humble up from the dust to the highest position of glory.

[60] Nothing is safe when you are hostile: nothing is to be feared with your favour. If peoples should rise up in their thousands, if battle should be joined, I, under the cover of your wings, shall give the enemy the gesture of defiance.

[61] For you have made the Most High your refuge; evil does not reach there, and no scourge comes near your dwelling-place.

[62] Blessed is the man who has the God of Jacob as his helper, whose hope is in the selfsame Lord God, whom angels, demons, heaven, earth and seas obey.

[63] This massive hanging structure, and whatever is within its bounds, you support without intermission. Yours alone is the power which can hold everything together; in your hands alone is the custody of the vast world.

[64] Anyone who of himself and through himself is able to provide abundantly what is needful has no use for colleague or associate in his task, and neither at any time does a need for help befall the majesty of so great a Godhead.

[65] That nature does not permit of multiplication or division of itself, which is circumscribed by no limits in its perfection, which embraces all things, and which relinquishes no mark or badge of office to any other of equal nature, which would bring about a distinction of essence.

⁶⁶ Sunt tibi tamen legionum myriades, innumera coelitum turba, sic ordine decuriati, atque in stationes digesti, ut pars te assidue stipet, pars extra orbem hunc pro potestate regat et obtineat, principatus, dominationes, uirtutes, praefecti, procuratores, dioecete, nuntii, suum quisque munus obeuntes.

[p.25/B5] ⁶⁷ Verum hi omnes seruitium sunt, quorum opera uicaria non necessitatis, sed decoris causa est adhibita, ne scilicet quid in hoc opere, uel quod ad ornatum pertinet, desideretur.

⁶⁸ Tam pusillum uero est, quod illi absque te possint, ut si uel tantillum tu manum subducas, orbis continuo soluantur compagines, totaque naturae soliditas euestigio euanescat.

⁶⁹ Etenim ut riui non possunt non arescere, si fons undas neget: ut terra nequit non opacari, si sol se nubibus uestiat: sic tu, nisi uirtutem tuam longe, lateque diffundas, uani, irritique forent subiectae potentiae conatus.

⁷⁰ Nec tellus pondera sustineret, nec tellurem raucisona circumlamberet Amphitrite, nec luna coelum scanderet: imo ne tu quidem Phoebe, cuius gloria illustrior, radioso isto amictu niteres, si uel ad temporis punctum princeps illa causa opem suam subtrahat.

⁷¹ Vnum te superbus ille coelitum splendor indignantem exhorrescit, pronusque se tuis aduoluit genibus. Ad maiestatis tuae pedes, omnes diuorum ordines supplices se abiiciunt: Ad minimam nominis tui mentionem, profunda contremiscunt Tartara: Venerandum tuum numen medius hic orbis pauidus adorat.

[p.27/B6] ⁷² Extendis ad coelum manum, et dicis, Viuo ego inaeternum. acuis ut fulgur gladium, et iudicium arripit manus tua.

⁷³ Incendis in furore ignem, qui ad inferorum usque nouissima desaeuiat. Deuorat is terram cum germine suo, et montium exurit fundamenta.

⁷⁴ Telluris illi quidem, non coeli germen, qui usquedum uitam hic in terris incolerent, nihil praeclarum aut homine dignum moliti, nullum coelestis originis specimen dederunt, nullam patriae nobilitatis, tanquam coelo orti non essent, significationem fecerant.

⁶⁶ There are nonetheless with you myriads of legions, a numberless throng of heavenly beings, so ordered in ranks and distributed in their appointed positions, that part continually press close round you, part outside control and maintain this world as deputies for your sovereignty – principalities, dominions, powers, prefects, procurators, officials, messengers – performing each his individual service.

⁶⁷ Truly, all these are a body of servants whose vicarious work is applied not to supply a need but for beauty's sake, so that nothing of course in this work, even something for adornment, should be lacking.

⁶⁸ Indeed, it is but very little that they could do without you, so that, were you to take away your hand, even a tiny bit, the framework of the world would immediately dissolve and the entire physical reality of nature vanish on the spot.

⁶⁹ For, as brooks cannot fail to dry up should the source deny its flood, as the earth cannot but grow dark should the sun veil itself with clouds, so, unless you should far and wide pour out your might, vain and ineffectual would be the efforts made by any inferior power.

⁷⁰ The earth would neither sustain its weights, nor roaring Amphitrite wash it round, nor would the moon ascend the sky, nor indeed would you, Phoebus, whose glory is the greater, blaze in that radiant garb, if that first great cause were even for a moment to take away his rich store.

⁷¹ The magnificent splendour of the angels dreads only you in your wrath; falling down, they prostrate themselves before your knees. At the feet of your majesty all the orders of divine beings cast themselves in supplication; at the slightest mention of your name the depths of Tartarus tremble; this middle earth, fearful, adores your awesome Godhead.

⁷² You stretch your hand to the heavens and say: I myself live for all eternity. You sharpen the sword like lightning, and your hand takes hold on judgement.

⁷³ In your wrath you ignite such a fire as will rage right down to the furthest depths of hell. It engulfs the earth together with its produce, and burns up the foundations of the mountains.

⁷⁴ Those people, indeed, the produce of earth and not of heaven, who, as long as they were living their life here in the world, undertook nothing excellent or befitting humanity, gave no evidence of their heavenly origin, and had done nothing signifying their native nobility –

⁷⁵ Hos aliquando eousque tum irae tuae formido, tum degeneris impiaeque uitae conscientia percellet, ut fugam nequiquam meditati, montibus dicturi sint, Cadite super nos: collibus, operite nos.

⁷⁶ Quis nouit potestatem irae tuae? quam impatibilis sit furor tuus, documento est Tartareus ille tyrannus indignationis tuae fulmine, una cum asseclis ex summo coelo in ima Tartara praecipitatus.

⁷⁷ Clementissime parens, propter bonitatem tuam fac, ut ne unquam experiamur quid possis iratus: Ne, amabo, filios in furore arguas. Nam si tu iniquitates obseruaueris, si nos pro meritis tractaris, hei mihi, quis perferat? quis sustineat?

⁷⁸ Ignosce nobis parens, ignosce. Nescimus proculdubio, nescimus, quid facimus, cum te nobis iratum, te nobis inimicum facimus. Non animum aduertimus, quam atroces eos maneant poenae, qui maiestatem tuam procaciter lacessunt.

[p.29/B7] ⁷⁹ Nos quorsum ista tua lenitas atque expectatio euadat, non expendimus. Abutimur patientia tua: atque, quod non statim sceleratos ulcisceris, impune nos in te (ut uidemur) illusuros putamus.

⁸⁰ Sed longe secus est. Nam quo tardior, quoque inuitior ad uindictam descendis, hoc grauius suo tempore in facinorosos animaduertis: quippe quos tandem igni nunquam intermorituro tradis excruciandos.

⁸¹ O calamitosos, O terque quaterque miseros eos, quos tam amara sors expectat, quos tam acerba excipient fata. Quanto praestitisset nunquam lucem hanc aspexisse, quam post breuem, eandemque aerumnosam eiusdem lucis usuram crudelibus flammis escam obiici sempiternam?

⁸² Verum culpa omnis, nostra est parens: Nos soli in noxia sumus. Quanquam enim sors ea tam dura est, ut animus meminisse horreat: ita tamen fieri aequum est, quandoquidem a te, qui ipsa aequitas es, iniquum nihil proficisci potest.

⁸³ O sancte parens, quod ego te per diuinitatis tuae genium oro, per eum quo filium complecteris amorem obsecro, per paternam istam dextram obtestor, ut ne nos, qui numen tuum agnoscimus, qui nomen ueneramur, inter illa, quae in iram apparasti, uasa coniicias.

⁷⁵ These people the fear of your wrath and the awareness of their degenerate and impious life will so strike with terror, that, having vainly thought of flight, they will cry to the mountains: Fall upon us, to the hills: Cover us.

⁷⁶ Who knows the power of your anger? How unendurable your wrath can be, is shown by that tyrant of Tartarus, together with his minions cast down by the thunderbolt of your indignation from highest heaven to the lowest depths of Tartarus.

⁷⁷ Father most clement, by your goodness ensure that we never experience what you could do in your rage; neither, I beg you, accuse your children in your fury. For, if you should closely examine our sins, if you should treat us according to our merits, woe is me, who may endure, who may sustain it?

⁷⁸ Forgive us, Father, forgive us. We know not, forsooth, we know not what we do when we make you angry with us, make you hostile towards us. We do not turn our minds to consider what dreadful punishments await those who insolently provoke your majesty.

⁷⁹ We give no thought as to where that mildness of yours, your waiting, may end. We abuse your patience, and, because you do not immediately punish the wicked, we think that we will with impunity (as we seem to be doing) make mock of you.

⁸⁰ But it is far otherwise. For, the more slowly and reluctantly you descend to vengeance, the more severely do you, when the time comes, punish the wicked, those, indeed, whom you at last dispatch to the torture of never-relenting fire.

⁸¹ O unfortunate, O thrice and four times wretched are those whom such a bitter destiny awaits, whom so harsh a fate will overcome. How much better had it been never to have beheld this light than, after the enjoyment – brief and full of troubles – of that very light, to be thrown as perpetual food to the cruel flames?

⁸² Truly, Father, all the guilt is ours; we alone are to blame. For although that fate is so harsh, that the mind shudders to think of it, it is only just that it be so, seeing that nothing unjust can proceed from you, who are justice itself.

⁸³ O holy Father, as I beg you through the Spirit of your divinity and beseech you through that love wherewith you embrace the Son, and entreat you by that fatherly right hand of yours, do not cast us, who recognise your Godhead and venerate your name, among those vessels which you have prepared for your wrath.

[84] Pessimi sumus, fateor: pessime de te meriti, fateor: extrema omnia commeriti, fateor. O utinam haec uere negare possem. Verum quantuncunque malitiosi simus, ut malitia omnis nostra est, sic certe ipsi tui sumus, manuumque tuarum opificium.

[p.31/B8] [85] Itaque parens, etsi nos meritissimo perdere potes, longe tamen maiori gloriae tibi fore speramus, si eo, quod nostrum est, perdito, nos, qui tui sumus, serues incolumes.

[86] Sed enim ex nostro interitu, ac calamitate, quae poterit existere uirtutis tuae laus? Tu ne tantus rex, cuius opes immensae, qui uel nutu omnem mundum in nihilum, unde profectus est, redigis, contra folium, quod uento rapitur, ostendes potentiam tuam, et stipulam hanc siccam ad internetionem persequere?

[87] Nec mihi hic quisquam obstrepat, importunusque obiiciat, iustitiam ipsam nihil flagitiosum impunitum, aut inultum relinquere solere, eamque nos ad eiusmodi poenas deposcere. Tantum tu seruare uelis parens. Nam id demum iustum est, quod tu fieri uis.

[88] Poteris tu quidem nos quantuncunque immerentes nullo negotio seruare, quia es omnipotens. Voles autem, quia ipsa est bonitas. Hanc uero bonitatis tuae conscientiam, qua me consolor, qua me sustento, nemo mihi neque uiuo, neque mortuo eripiet.

[89] Sed quid ego de magnitudine tua uerba facere ingressus sum? Quid te lucem, quid uitam, quid speciem, quid sapientiam, quid potentiam, quid delicias, aut si quid aliud amabile est, aut praestabile, dicam?

[p.33/C1] [90] Nos quidem his, atque his uocabulis, nostro more loquentes te esse facimus, cum tamen nulla ne mentis quidem notio sit, quae naturae tuae proprietatem assequatur.

[91] Tu re ipsa neque hoc, neque illud es: sed uniusmodi quadam atque incogitabili simplicitate, et procul a uulgari ratione remota, bonorum omnium pelagus es immensum.

[92] Mosi famulo tuo, tui olim facturus copiam, teque coram uidendum exhibiturus, non minus uere, quam liberaliter ais, Veni, et ostendam tibi omne bonum.

[84] We, I confess, are the very worst; we, I confess, have deserved the worst from you; we, I confess, have all deserved every extreme punishment. O would that I were able truly to deny it. But however wicked we may be, to whatever extent the wickedness is all ours, so are we assuredly also yours and the work of your hands.

[85] Therefore, Father, even if, most deservedly, you can bring us to ruin, we nevertheless hope that it will bring you far greater glory, if that which is ours is lost, and you preserve us, who are yours, safe and sound.

[86] For, from our ruin and disaster, what praise of your virtue can there possibly be? Will you, that great king, whose rich resources are immense, and who with a mere nod of the head can take the entire world back to the nothing whence it came, show your power upon the leaf which is carried off by the wind, and harry the dry stubble to destruction?

[87] Nor is anyone to cry out on me and persistently object, that justice itself does not leave anything sinful unpunished or unavenged, and that she claims us for such fitting punishment. Only let it be your will to save, Father, for what you will to come to pass is ultimately just.

[88] In fact, you will be able to save us without any trouble, however much we do not deserve it, since you are omnipotent. Moreover, you will wish to do so because you are goodness itself. Indeed, this consciousness of your goodness, by which I console myself, by which I support myself, no-one will snatch away from me, whether alive or dead.

[89] But why have I started finding words to talk about your greatness? Why call you light, life, beauty, wisdom, power, delight, or anything else that is lovable or excellent?

[90] We indeed, speaking in our human fashion by these or those words, make you exist, though there is no notion even in our mind which might succeed in grasping the true quality of your nature.

[91] In fact, you are neither this nor that, but of a certain unique and unfathomable simplicity, and far removed from common understanding; you are an immense ocean of all good things.

[92] To your servant Moses, when once you were about to grant access to your presence and make yourself visible before him, you say no less truly than generously: Come, and I shall show you every good thing.

⁹³ Est et illud sane perquam appositum, quod maximus ille sacri carminis artifex Palestinus rex, cum nomen tuum de more celebrare adornans, quantus esses expenderet, ineffabilis maiestatis fulgoribus obrutus, Tibi, inquit, (tanquam proloqui superuacaneum foret) silentium, laus Deus in Syon.

⁹⁴ Ergo laudis loco, erit tacita quaedam magnitudinis tuae admiratio, cum religioso ac uenerabundo stupore coniuncta. Officium erit, id quod est, ingenue fateri, nos scilicet non esse praestando.

⁹⁵ Sed et has beatitudinis opes, intra inconcussa diuinitatis moenia, et ante aeuum conditum, solus possides, securus hostium, securus senii, securus iacturae.

⁹⁶ Nihil in te uarium, nihil concretum, nihil pensile, nihil aduentitium, nihil mole extensum, nihil qualitate affectum, nihil adhaerescens, nihil aliunde mutuatum, nihil alienae opis indigum, nihil duplum, nihil coactum, nihil diuiduum, nihil labefactabile, nihil ulla ex parte mobile.

[p.35/C2] ⁹⁷ Motus enim omnis, accessionis gratia fit: accessio defectum, qui in te non cadit, semper arguit. Quicquid igitur in te est, puritas est, diuinitas est, imo ipsum esse est. Quo fit, ut mutationis undique expers, potentissimo quodam et inuicto aeternitatis robore, perpetuo uegetus, florensque consistas.

⁹⁸ Hei mihi, quia commoratio mea prolongata est: quando ueniam? quando apparebo ante faciem dei mei? Quis mihi dabit pennas sicut columbae? et uolabo, ut requiescam in monte sancto tuo.

⁹⁹ Nunc procul a patria, extorrem me detinent haec tabernacula Cedar: nec per barbarum hunc, tumultuos[or]umque affectuum populum, pacato esse animo licet.

¹⁰⁰ Intra animi uallum est haec malesuada carnis lex, domestica atque intestina hostis, foecunda malorum sementis, quae ab penitissimis usque medullis per omnia membra diffusa, in actiones quoque ipsas proserpit.

¹⁰¹ Foris, mendaces fuci nusquam non molesti, nusquam non occursantes, pulchritudinis tuae aspectum, adeoque et amorem impediunt. Solidae uoluptatis spem cogitatione animoque temere praeceptam, inani sensuum ludificatione frustrantur.

⁹³ And indeed especially apposite is what the king of Palestine, that greatest maker of sacred song, says, when, preparing as was his custom to celebrate your name, he thought how great you are, and was overwhelmed by the blinding rays of your ineffable majesty: For you (as speech would be superfluous), silence is praise, O God, in Sion.

⁹⁴ Accordingly, in place of songs of praise there shall be silent worship of your greatness, combined with a devout and venerating wonderment. Our service will be that which it is: frankly to confess that we, actually, are not able to perform it.

⁹⁵ But you alone possess this wealth of bliss, within the unshaken walls of your divinity, from before the foundation of time, safe from enemies, from ageing and from wasting.

⁹⁶ In you is nothing different, nothing coalesced, nothing dependent, nothing extraneous, nothing extending in mass, nothing determined by any quality, nothing attached, nothing borrowed from anywhere else, nothing wanting outside help, nothing double, nothing combined, nothing divided, nothing destructible, nothing moveable in any part.

⁹⁷ All motion is for the purpose of acquisition: acquisition, which does not apply to you, always argues a defect. Therefore, whatever is in you is purity, is divinity, is very Being itself. From which it results that you, exempt from change in all respects by some powerful and unconquered force of eternity, exist forever full of life and vigour.

⁹⁸ Alas for me, for my sojourn here goes on; when shall I arrive? When shall I appear before the face of my God? Who will give me wings as of the dove, and I shall fly to take my rest on your holy hill.

⁹⁹ Now, far from my fatherland, these tents of Kedar hold me an exile; nor is it permitted to live with peace of mind among this barbarous people of raging passions.

¹⁰⁰ Within the rampart of the mind is this seductive law of the flesh, an enemy intimate and internal, a fecund sowing of evils, which, dispersed through every member right from the deepest marrow, creeps its way out into actual actions.

¹⁰¹ Outside, lying deceits – nowhere not troublesome, nowhere not assaulting – impede the sight and even the love of your beauty. By the empty trickery of the senses, they frustrate the hope of solid pleasure too easily anticipated by the imagination and the mind.

[102] Induci, trahi, et tanquam captiuum denique cupiditatum uinculis constrictum, abduci me miserum sentio ab his corporum exuuiis, quorum tamen, quod speciosissimum est, quodque praestantissimum tecum compositum, ne exilis quidem umbrae locum implet.

[p.37/C3] [103] Etenim ea quae sub aspectum et sensus cadunt, ut illustrem uisum habeant, concreta tamen cum sint, fragilique coacta natura, quantulum id est, quod tecum commune habent, qui simplicissima es οὐσία?

[104] Quae uero procul a sensibus positae res sunt, maiorem quidem obtinent dignitatem, atque quod mortalis concretionis exortes, intelligentiaeque participes sunt, propius quidem a te absunt, sed neque illae nisi extremis lineamentis, non habitu solido te referunt.

[105] Vtraque ergo mendica sunt. Vtraque precario tuoque munere subsistunt. utraque non modo non speciosa, sed si tibi conferantur, ne esse quidem censenda sunt.

[106] Tu uero qui ne sub intelligentiam quidem nostram cadis, adeo aliorum omnium splendorem restinguis, ut illa ipsa aperte testificentur et doceant, se pene nihil, te unum omnia esse, atque intra interminatos magnitudinis tuae fines, quicquid uspiam boni aut pulchri est, aut esse potest, complecti.

[107] Illa quidem mutantur, magnaque ex parte, sicut uestis, usu ueterascunt, diuturnitate extabescunt, aut certe uniusmodi perpetuo non consistunt. Tu uero idem ipse es, et anni tui non deficient.

[108] Itaque ubi ex densis hisce tenebris, atque undique circumfusa caligine, in lucem istam, et rerum puritatem emersero, fore certo scio, ut me harum, quae nunc me habent, curarum poeniteat.

[p.39/C4] [109] Ora rubor obducet, facies a fletu madescet, quod non te unum perpetuo respexerim: quod aliunde quicquam boni, quam ex te perenni, et uberrimo bonorum omnium fonte petierim.

[110] Ipse mihi iure irascar: ipse me tum pugnis caedam, capillum mihi uellam, pectus contundam: ipse de me supplicium sumam, quod tam serus speciem istam adamarim, quae una ab ipsis aeternitatis primordiis (si tamen hic primordia dicenda sunt) in infinitum aeuum illibata perseruerat.

[102] Wretched, I feel myself seduced, betrayed, and finally ensnared by the chains of desires, led away captive by these trappings of corporeal things, and of these the most beautiful, the most splendid, compared with you, does not even fill the place of an empty shadow.

[103] For those things which fall under sight and sense, though they have a brave appearance, yet, since they are compounded and essentially friable, how little do they have in common with you, who are the most unalloyed Divine Essence itself?

[104] And indeed, those things which lie remote from the senses do in fact acquire a higher rank and, because they have no share of mortal concrescence and do share intelligence, they are a shorter distance away from you, but not even they, except in bare outline, represent you in solid form.

[105] Both sorts, therefore, are beggars. Both subsist by provision, dependent on your favour, and both are to be judged not only not beautiful, but, if compared with you, not to exist at all.

[106] Indeed you, who do not even fall within our understanding, so eclipse the splendour of all other things, that those same things openly testify and teach that they are almost nothing and that you alone are everything, and embrace, within the boundless limits of your greatness, all that is, or can anywhere be, good or beautiful.

[107] Those very things are indeed subject to change; and, to large extent, like a garment, they grow old through use and wear away over a long period of time, or certainly do not constantly remain in one condition. But you yourself are indeed always the same, and your years will not run out.

[108] And so when, from out of these dense shadows, and from the darkness all around me, I shall emerge into that light and world of purity, I know for sure that I shall repent of those preoccupations, which at present detain me.

[109] Redness will suffuse my cheeks, my face will be moist with weeping, because I have not at all times looked to you alone, and because I have sought some benefit elsewhere than from you, the everlasting and overflowing fount of all good things.

[110] With justice, I shall grow angry at myself; I shall strike myself with blows, shall tear my hair, shall beat my breast. I shall myself exact my own punishment, because I have fallen so late in love with that beauty, which uniquely, from the very beginnings of eternity (if, that is, one may here speak about first beginnings) persists unimpaired till the end of time.

¹¹¹ Quodnam misero mihi in ignotas illas oras migraturo solatium afferat ignaua haec uita, tota in sordibus, tota in coeno posita? Quid laetabile ea mens habitura est, quae nullius honesti studii conscia est: quaeque non meminit se, in ullam uitae partem se praeclare dedisse?

¹¹² Si quidem quamuis animum usque in futuram uitam intentum habere per praesentis uitae conditionem non liceat: foede tamen, turpiterque degenerat, qui non ad diuina illa (queiscum cognationem habet) crebra mentis exultatione subinde sublimem se tollit.

¹¹³ Quare igitur appendimus argentum, et non in panibus? laborem, et non in saturitate? Cur prudentes, scientesque, quae nocuere sequimur: fugimus, quae profore scimus?

¹¹⁴ Quae, malum, insania est, peritura bona tam ardentibus uotis appetere, tot parare sudoribus: et ad immortales illas spes, ne tantillum quidem commoueri? putre et cadauerosum hoc corpus tantopere curare: animum, qui diuinus est, negligere?

[p.41/C5] ¹¹⁵ Quid iuuat eos haurire latices, qui poti, sitis molestiam adaugeant, non restinguant? Quorsum attinet tam auide eum uorare cibum, qui ad famem nihil faciat?

¹¹⁶ Qui bibit ex hac aqua, sitit iterum. Copia fastidium gignit: Fastidium noua sequuntur uota, et nouae curae: quo sit, ut curae, cupiditatesque in immensum abeuntes, nusquam ubi consistant inueniant.

¹¹⁷ Huc, illucque discurritur, gestitur, trepidatur, doletur: mille tempestatum conflictationes, mille curarum difficultates oboriuntur, ac ne multa, inanis sane tumultus frustra suscipitur, et in sterili uita labore perit.

¹¹⁸ Et profecto ita habet, nec priusquam ad te felicitatis fontem, et beatitudinis portum recursum sit, quisquam turbulentos hos animorum motus, iactationumque fluctus tranquillauerit.

¹¹⁹ Eo nimirum ingenio est animus noster, ut omnis boni capax sit. Omne bonum usque sitit, quod cum alibi quam in te non sit, tantisper dum tu abes, nec εὐθύμια ulla, nec laudabilis illa ἀπάθια ulli contingit.

¹¹¹ What solace may this sluggish life, entirely sunk in corruption and filth, bring to me, a wretch about to depart for those unknown shores? What gladdening thought is that mind to have, which is not aware of any honest ambition and does not remember having applied itself with any distinction in any area of life?

¹¹² Yes indeed, though it may not be permitted through the condition of this present life to keep the mind firmly focused upon the future life, yet that man falls away foully and shamefully, who does not often by the frequent exultation of his mind raise himself up high to those things divine, with which he has an affinity.

¹¹³ Why, therefore, do we spend money and not for bread, expend labour and not for satisfaction? Why, as men of prudence and knowledge, do we follow those things which have caused harm, and flee those things which we know will benefit us?

¹¹⁴ Out upon it! What folly it is, to yearn with such ardent prayers for goods that will pass away and to procure them with such hard efforts, and in fact to make not the slightest move towards those immortal hopes; to expend so much care on this putrid and moribund body and neglect the soul, which is divine?

¹¹⁵ What good does it do, to gulp down fluids, which when drunk do not quench but add to the pangs of thirst? What is the point of greedily gobbling the sort of food which does nothing for hunger?

¹¹⁶ He who drinks of this water thirsts anew. Overabundance of anything makes one disgusted with it, and that disgust is succeeded by new desires and new concerns, and so it comes about that concerns and desires, advancing into the boundless, can nowhere discover where they might come to a stop.

¹¹⁷ Hither and thither there is rushing, desiring, anxiety and unhappiness; a thousand colliding tempests, a thousand perplexing cares arise, and, to say no more, vain tumult is taken on to no purpose and life perishes in sterile labour.

¹¹⁸ And indeed, this is the case, and not until he has made recourse to you, the fount of felicity and haven of beatitude, will anyone calm these turbulent motions of the mind and storm-floods of turmoil.

¹¹⁹ Our mind, by its very nature, is indubitably capable of apprehending the Supreme Good. It constantly thirsts after the Supreme Good, but since that does not exist anywhere but in you, as long as you are absent, neither that calm cheerfulness nor that praiseworthy indifference to passion can be experienced by anyone.

¹²⁰ Simul uero ac tu ades, atque ex tuis fontibus uel libare contigerit (nam pleni illi haustus ante uitae huius finem negantur) cupiditatum deferuescit flagrantia, tempestates silent, et insani ponunt murmura fluctus.

[p.43/C6] ¹²¹ Ades uero tu proculdubio ei, qui tibi fidit, qui te ex animo amat, qui pietatem, qui humanitatem, qui denique officium rebus aliis (ut par est) omnibus anteponit.

¹²² Huic honesto incolumi, nulla grauis est iactura. Hic dummodo abs te gratiam ineat, studiaque sua tibi probet, susque deque fert ut reliqua succedant. Hic se in portum appulit, unde securus eos respicit, quos undantes curarum aestus absorbent.

¹²³ Hic turba in imis relicta uallibus, in edita uirtutum iuga euasit, ubi perenni collium uirore, id est, deliciis non perituris, animum exaturat. Hic alta mentis ab arce despicit errantes, humanaque gaudia ridet.

¹²⁴ Itaque quando praesentia tua tantum secum commoditatum affert, mirum uideri non debet, si quisquis pius est, quoties se a te destitui sentit, lachrymosis singultibus, ardentibusque animi uotis, cum sacro illo palmiferae Idumee principe, te sibi reddi exoptet.

¹²⁵ Quis mihi det (inquit) ut sim iuxta menses pristinos, secundum dies quibus Deus custodiebat me, quando splendebat lucerna eius super caput meum, et ad lumen eius ambulabam in tenebris?

¹²⁶ Sicut fui in diebus adolescentiae meae, quando secreto erat Deus in taber-naculo meo: quando erat omnipotens mecum, et in circuitu meo pueri mei: quando lauabam pedes meos butyro, et petra fundebat mihi riuos olei.

[p.45/C7] ¹²⁷ Redactus sum in nihilum: Abstulisti quasi uentus desiderium meum, et uelut nubes pertransiit salus mea. Nunc autem in memetipso marcescit anima mea, et possident me dies afflictionis: interiora mea efferbuerunt absque ulla requie.

¹²⁸ At nos miseri eiusmodi desideriis uacui re derelicta fugaces umbras nequicquam consectamur. Graue nobis cor est, pronum est, in ima tendit. Nihil altum, nihil erectum, nihil magnificum meditatur: diligimus uanitatem, et quaerimus mendacium.

¹²⁰ But as soon as you are present, and one gets the chance even to sip from your fountains (for those deep draughts are denied before the end of this life), burning desires cool down, tempests grow still, and the raging flood quiets its noise.

¹²¹ And you indeed are present without doubt to the one who trusts in you, who loves you from his soul, and who puts faith, brotherly love, and in short his duty before all other things, as is right to do.

¹²² To this man, honourable and unshaken, no loss is heavy. He, provided that he finds favour with you, and makes his efforts acceptable in your eyes, cares nothing as to how the rest turn out. He has brought himself into harbour, from where in safety he looks back upon those whom raging tides of cares are swallowing down.

¹²³ He, leaving the disordered throng in the deep valleys, has escaped into the high peaks of virtue, where, with the everlasting verdure of the hills – that is, delights that will not perish – he replenishes his spirit. Here, from the lofty citadel of the mind, he looks down upon those who wander, and laughs at human joys.

¹²⁴ And so, when your presence brings with itself so great a mass of benefits, it ought not to be seen as marvellous if any devout person, whenever he feels himself forsaken by you, should, with tearful sobs and burning prayers from the soul, long for you to be restored to him – together with [Job] that holy prince of Idumaea, the land of palm trees.

¹²⁵ Who will grant me, he says, that I may be as in months past, according to the days wherein God looked after me, when his lantern shone over my head, and by his light I walked in the dark?

¹²⁶ As I was in the days of my youth, when God was secretly present in my dwelling-place, when the Almighty was with me and my children around me, when I washed my feet with butter and the rock poured me out streams of oil.

¹²⁷ I am brought to nothing. Like the wind, you have taken away my desire, and like the cloud my good fortune has passed away. Now, indeed, my soul grows feeble within me, and days of affliction take hold of me; my inner organs have burned within me, without any rest.

¹²⁸ But we, wretched people, devoid of such desires, abandon substance, and move fruitlessly after fleeting shadows. Our heart is heavy, it lies prostrate, it heads towards the depths. It contemplates nothing lofty, nothing noble, nothing magnificent: we love vanity and seek what is false.

¹²⁹ Siquidem omnis caro foenum, omnis gloria eius tanquam flos agri: diluculo efflorescit, ante uesperum decidit, et arescit. Sola perpetuo manent mentis atque animi bona: florem decoris singuli carpunt dies.

¹³⁰ Nunc, mi anime, si uis ut te uotorum tuorum nunquam poeniteat, ut ignium nunquam pudeat, conditoris tui uultus intra te penitus reconde. Et quando ille solus semper formosus est nunquamque de te benemereri cessat: ille solus tuos amores auferat: ille habeat secum, seruetque sepultos.

¹³¹ Ille est, quem in sacro epithalamio ex tot milibus selectum, prorsusque et ab omni parte desiderabilem, formosa illa sponsa praedicat, cuiusque amore illa ipsa tantopere ardet. Ille speciosus forma prae filiis hominum, ille rerum flos illibatus.

¹³² Ille thesaurus in agro reconditus: ille preciosa illa margarita fortunarum omnium, imo lucis, imo uitae, et si quid luce ac uita charius esse potest, et illius quoque dispendio comparanda.

[p.47/C8] ¹³³ Talis igitur, et tantus eras, tu rerum parens, priusquam montes fierent, aut formaretur terra et orbis, in isto diuinitatis tuae regno florens, natiuis pollens opibus, gloriosus, omnique beatitudinis laude intra temetipsum ante aeuum conditum cumulatus.

¹³⁴ Nouo etenim rerum ortu tu ne hilo quidem auctior futurus eras: quemadmodum etiam ne hilum quidem tibi decedat, quamuis omnia in pristinum nihil redeant: quippe quod immensus sis undique, et immobilis.

¹³⁵ At tibi tandem, quae tua est bonitas, uisum est has magnitudinis tuae opes expromere, et spectabilem hanc rerum molem, cum antea extra te nihil esset, admirabili plane artificio architectari.

¹³⁶ Vis enim effectrix, et causa, quae hoc, aut illud est, hoc aut illud efficit. Tu, qui non hoc aut illud es, sed ipsum ὄν, adeoque totum ὄν es, totum hoc ὄν, nulla eius parte praeuia, nulla quae praecedat subiecta materia, e nihilo producis, atque effingis.

¹³⁷ Nec mora, productum, atque in partes aptissime distributum, ornamentisque idoneis undique expolitum, ea lege, ac ratione gubernas, ut facile appareat, summo consilio, non incerto casu molem hanc constare.

[129] Indeed all flesh is grass, and all its glory is as the flower of the field; it blossoms with the dawn, and before evening falls and withers. Only the good things of the mind and the spirit remain forever; one by one the days pluck the flower of beauty.

[130] Now, my soul, if you wish never to repent of your desires, and never feel ashamed of burning passions, conceal deep within you the face of your creator. And, since he alone is always beautiful, and never ceases to deserve your gratitude, let him alone capture your feelings of love; may he hold them with him and keep them buried there.

[131] He it is, whom in the holy bridal song that beautiful bride proclaims, chosen from so many thousands and absolutely and in every respect desirable, with love of whom that bride so burns. He is in form beautiful beyond the sons of men, he the untouched flower of all things.

[132] He is the treasure hidden in the field, he is that precious pearl to be bought at the expense of one's whole fortune, of light, indeed of life, and, if anything can be dearer than light and life, at the expense of that too.

[133] Such you were and so great you were, Father of all things, before the mountains were made or the earth and the world took shape, flourishing in that kingdom of your divinity, mighty in your inherent richness, full of glory, within yourself laden with every praise of beatitude, before the birth of time.

[134] For indeed you were not going to be one whit enriched by the new beginning of things, just as indeed not a jot would fall from you, even though all things returned to the original nothingness; inasmuch as you are in all respects measureless, and never to be changed.

[135] But to you, ultimately, such is your goodness, it seemed good to exhibit these riches of your magnitude and, though previously nothing existed outside of you, to construct with the most admirable artistry this impressive mass of matter.

[136] For an efficient power or cause which is 'this or that' brings about this or that effect. You, [Truth] — who are not this or that, but are being itself, and therefore the whole of being — you produce and form all *this* being from nothing, from no previous part of it.

[137] And this Being, straightway created and most fittingly distributed into its parts, embellished on all sides with suitable adornments, you govern by such law and reason, that it is quite apparent that this mass of matter exists by supreme design and not by uncertain chance.

¹³⁸ Etenim exquisitus hic apparatus, et decentissimus seculorum ordo ab infinita pene uetustate cursus sui uestigia nusquam inflectens, eximiae cuiusdam tum sapientiae, tum potentiae opus sit necesse est.

[p.49/D1] ¹³⁹ Nam cum fluxum, errabundum, casuique obnoxium sit pene quicquid hic orbis complectitur, non posset tantae molis nauis inter hos fluctus ratum hunc cursum retinere, nisi tu nauarchus clauum peritissime moderareris.

¹⁴⁰ Nihil in tanto opere temere est, nihil otiosum: nihil monogrammon, nihil non omnibus suis numeris aptum, et expletum. Omnes partes tales, ut neque ad usum meliores, neque ad speciem pulchriores esse potuerint.

¹⁴¹ Porro autem ut sapienti potentia omnem mundum et condidisti, atque exornasti, sic eundem perpetua benignitate alis, et foecundas. Das enim tu escam et pullis coruorum, qui et ipsi opem tuam, suo more crocitando, implorant.

¹⁴² Aperis enim tu manum tuam, atque omne animal liberaliter exaturas. Simul uero ac tu faciem auertis, spiritus ea deficit, et in pristinum puluerem, quantumcunque caeteroquin uiuacia, redeunt.

¹⁴³ Sed et per singulas molis huius partes tu permeas, sed non permixtus: in ima descendis, nec summa, nec media relinquens: extima ambis, sed non exclusus: Omnia moues, ipse requietus: Omnia moderaris, ipse non solicitus.

¹⁴⁴ Tu totus totum orbem imples, et totus es in singulis orbis partibus: ubique praesens es, sed nemini, nisi si cui tibi uisum est, conspicuus: ingens quoque animis illaberis, sed tacitus: abis rursus, studiorum indignitate offensus. Si ueneris ad me, non uidebo: si abieris, non intelligam.

[p.51/D2] ¹⁴⁵ Si ascendero in coelum, tu illic es: si ad inferos demigrem, ades. si sumptis diluculo pennis ad extremum usque mare deferar, manus tua est, quae et ducit, et detinet.

[138] For this most carefully thought out construction and this most seemly procession of the centuries, from almost infinite ages past never bending the line of its course, must of necessity be the work of some exceptional wisdom and power.

[139] For, since almost everything which this world embraces is in flux and liable to go astray, and the plaything of chance, it would not be possible for a ship of such great mass to maintain this steady course among these waves, if you, as master, were not most expertly controlling the tiller.

[140] Nothing in this mighty work is for nothing, nothing without function; nothing sketched out, nothing not perfect and complete in all its numbers. All the parts are such that they could not have been either better suited for use or beauty.

[141] Moreover, just as you created and adorned the whole world through your wise power, so you nourish it and make it fertile through your perpetual benevolence. You give food even to the young of ravens, which themselves beseech your bounty in their natural way, with their croaking.

[142] For you open your hand and liberally satisfy every creature. But, if you turn away your countenance, at that very moment the spirit departs from them, and they return to the original dust, however full of life they were before.

[143] But you permeate the various parts of this earthly mass, though without mixing with it; you descend to the depths, while not leaving the heights or the middle; you circle the outermost perimeter, but not as one shut out; you move all things, while yourself in rest; you control all things, while yourself without disturbance.

[144] In your entirety you fill the entire world, and in your entirety you are in each and every part of the world; you are everywhere present, but are visible to nobody, unless to one to whom you choose to be visible. Mighty in size, you also glide into men's minds, but silently; you depart again, displeased at the inadequacy of their ambition. If you come to me, I shall not see it; if you go away, I shall not mark it.

[145] If I ascend to heaven, you are there; if I travel down to hell, you are present. If I were to put on wings at dawn and be carried to the uttermost parts of the sea, it is your hand which both guides and holds me.

¹⁴⁶ Tu unus ille hominumque deumque pater, summus Iupiter, cuius numine omnia sunt plena. Tu spiritus, qui coelum, terram, camposque liquentes intus alit. Tu mens illa, quae per magni huius corporis artus infusa totam molem agitat.

¹⁴⁷ Attamen non te locus, cum immensus sis, sed tu locum concludis, qui quo longius naturae dignitate a corporibus abscedis, hoc uirtutis, adeoque et hypostaseos propinquitate rerum, quas moderaris, ingenio ita exigente, iisdem praesentius ades.

¹⁴⁸ Tu rerum omnium principium: tu item omnium finis, utriusque tamen iuxta exors. Tu forma, sed libera, ac ab omni materiae conditione multo alienissima. Tu simplicissima quaedam idaea, sed quam tot, tamque diuersae res pro rata quaeque portione imitantur.

¹⁴⁹ Nihil enim est in hac rerum innumerabilitate tam paruum, quod non magnitudinis: nihil tam malum, quod non bonitatis tuae, tanquam uestigia quaedam, seruet impressa.

¹⁵⁰ Itaque ut ex te omnia manant, sic ad te omnia moliuntur, tanquam in portum, recursum; omnia te usque referre student. Neque id ab re: quandoquidem quo quodque tibi uicinius est, tuique similius, hoc absolutius est, et perfectius.

¹⁵¹ Inest nimirum in ipsis rebus, uelut quaedam originis suae recordatio, ac bonitatis tuae sensus aliquis, ut tu plane sis illa communis omnium uoluptas, suaui quodam, ac arcano assuctu, perinde ac magnes ferrum, aut succinum paleam, si paruis magna componere fas est, omnia sursum ad te trahens, ac subuehens.

[p.53/D3] ¹⁵² Vnde nec nos etiam interea, dum deprauatis abripimur affectibus, nisi boni species adeoque tui quaedam similitudo permouet: sic, ut quicquid nos inescat incautos, quicquid stupidis imponit, quicquid imperitos in fraudem illicit, te aliqua ex parte ementiatur.

¹⁵³ Non enim uaferrimus hic hostis, ueterator serpens, qui nos secum humi repere cogit, quique omne naturae nostrae corpus malarum cupiditatum ueneno penitus infecit, prius infelicis mali esum miseris persuadet, potioremque nostri partem non pessime conari solitam a recto abducit, quam spem aliquam similitudinis ostendat: illud subinde inculcans, Eritis sicut Dii.

[146] You are the sole Father of men and of gods, the supreme Jupiter, with whose Godhead all things are filled. You are the Spirit which from within nourishes the heaven, the earth, and the watery plains. You are the mind which, poured in among the joints of this huge body, moves the entire massy world.

[147] Nevertheless, since you are immense, place does not enclose you, but you enclose place – who, the more distinct you are from corporeal things by the dignity of your nature, the more present you are with them by the proximity of your power as the essential underlying substance, the inherent quality of the things which you govern requiring this to be so.

[148] You are the first principle of all things; you likewise are the end of all, yet having no share in either. You are form, but without restriction, and utterly alien from any condition of matter. You are a kind of purest idea, but one which so many and so diverse things imitate, each in its own degree.

[149] For there is within this innumerability of things nothing so tiny but that it preserves certain traces, like footprints, of your greatness, nothing so bad but that it has traces of your goodness.

[150] And so, just as all things proceed from you, so do all things work towards a return to you, as if back to harbour, and strive always to reflect you. And not without reason, for the closer something is to you, the more it is similar to you, so it is the more absolute and the more perfect.

[151] There is of course in actual things a sort of recollection of their origin and some sense of your goodness, so that you are plainly that common desire of all things, which, through a certain sweet but mysterious power of attraction, draws and transports all things upwards towards you – just as, if one may compare small things with large, a magnet draws iron or amber chaff.

[152] It follows that we too meanwhile, as we are being dragged away by our perverse desires, are not swayed unless by a vision of the good and actually a certain likeness of yourself – it being the case that whatever catches us when we are off our guard, whatever imposes upon us in our stupidity, whatever entices us in our inexperience into guilty action pretends to be you in some way or other.

[153] For this most cunning enemy, the slithery trickster who makes us crawl with him on the ground and who has deeply infected the whole body of our nature with the poison of evil passions, does not press upon us wretched creatures the eating of the cursed apple, and lead away from the right our better part which does usually try not to do the worst, until after he has held out some hope of similitude, insinuating constantly: You shall be as gods.

154 Absolutus iam erat reliquus (ut ad rerum seriem redeam) orbis: leges acceperat idem, quibus in omne aeuum deinceps uteretur: restabat operi imponere fastigium. Igitur ne templo huic tam augusto deesset Antistes, uel theatro tam magnifico spectator, homo a te conditus est, atque in totius operis meditullio collocatus.

155 Quorsum enim attinuerat tam pulchram condere molem, cuius fructum nemo sentiret, cuius rationem nemo intelligeret? quod sane munus iccirco solus ipse inter animantes fungi possum, quod uni mihi a te animus, mensque data est.

[p.55/D4] 156 Facile uero admirabilis haec orbis designatio atque apparatus ad tui agnitionem animum excitet: agnitio ad amorem, ac uenerationem perducat: cuius praecipue muneris efficiendi colendique causa nati atque in lucem editi sumus.

157 Sed cum permulta sint in hoc opere contenta, quae sapientiae tuae testimonium dent locupletissimum: cum tamen omne coelum, terrasque cogitatione perlustro, ipse mihi praecipuum operis miraculum uideor.

158 Quam operosa est haec corporis huius compages, quam apta cum ad usum, tum ad uenustatem haec lineamentorum conformatio, quam ingeniosa haec structura, quae diuinam mentis naturam cum corpore sic commisit, ut inde absoluta quaedam totius orbis imago consurgat, quicquid maiore illo mundo cohibetur liquido repraesentans.

159 Verum tu, mi anime, hic principem locum obtines: atque hoc ipso, quod animus, quod mens es, id est, intelligendi ui praedita, brutis, rationisque expertibus rebus omnibus ingente interuallo antecellis.

160 Tu etenim, etsi mole uacas, omnem tamen, et immensam hanc molem sine mole complecteris: ut tu plane immensum quiddam, adeoque deus quidam (si dicere fas est) corpusculo conclusus uidearis.

161 Tu a crassis hisce rebus corporum etiam extima ora transmissa ad tenues illas, et incorporeas res, a sensilibus ad insensiles, a creatis denique et uisibilibus ad inuisibilia Dei creatoris ascendis.

¹⁵⁴ The rest of the world (to return to the sequence of things) was now complete; this same world received the laws, which henceforth it would use in all ages. It remained to impose a crowning glory upon the work. Therefore, that there should lack no chief priest for so august a temple or spectator for so magnificent a theatre, man was created by you and placed right in the middle of the whole creation.

¹⁵⁵ For what would have been the point of creating such a beautiful world, of which no-one would experience the fruit, no-one understand the purpose? I alone can uniquely perform this function among living creatures, because to me alone has soul and mind been given by you.

¹⁵⁶ In truth, the admirable design of this world and its ordering may easily excite the mind to the recognition of you, recognition lead on to love and veneration, and for the sake of performing and observing this duty above all have we been born and brought out into the light.

¹⁵⁷ But, while in this work of creation so very many things are contained, such as to provide the richest testimony to your wisdom; yet while in my thought I survey all heaven and the lands of earth, I myself seem to myself to be the chief miracle of that work.

¹⁵⁸ How elaborate is the frame of this body, how well adapted both for use and for loveliness is this harmony of parts, how ingenious is this structure which so conjoins the divine nature of mind with body, that a sort of absolute image of the entire world arises therefrom, clearly representing whatever is contained within that larger world.

¹⁵⁹ Truly, my soul, you here occupy the chief position, and by that self-same fact, that you are both soul and mind, which is to say are endowed with the power of understanding, you are by a huge interval superior to the brute beasts, and all things which have no share of reason.

¹⁶⁰ For, even though you have no mass, you nonetheless, without mass, embrace all this immense massy world, so that you certainly seem to be something immense, and (if one may say such a thing) even a sort of god contained within a tiny little body.

¹⁶¹ Away from the gross matter of these corporeal bodies, crossing even the outermost frontier, you mount up to those abstract and incorporeal things, from those which can be sensed to those which cannot be sensed, and finally from things created and visible to the invisible things of the creator God.

[p.57/D5] ¹⁶² Diuina plane est haec facultas, nec a corporea aliqua radice manare potest: est enim corpus omne suo sibi ingenio brutum: necesse est altiorem habeat originem, ut corporeae concretionis, sic et mortalitatis quoque expertem.

¹⁶³ Intelligens enim omne, hoc ipso, quod intelligit omnia, alia est: illa quidem, quae per se inesse, aut inhaerescere non possunt, uicariam supponunt speciem: haec uero, quae per se conuenire possunt, re ipsa insunt. Atqui ex hoc numero uel maxime est immortalitas, dos uel in primis intellectus dignitati congruens.

¹⁶⁴ Tu rursus, mi anime, temporum superatis angustiis, spes et cogitationes in omnem immortalitatem propagas: tantoque sempiterni aeui, et earum, quae sensibus non subsunt, rerum (cum uales, affectusque caecos in consilium non adhibes) amore flagras, ut prae illis, quae praesentia adsunt, pili non facias.

¹⁶⁵ Ad hanc certe immortalitatis laudem non tantopere aspirares, non tanto impetu contenderes, si earum rerum affinis, imo si ὁμογενές non esses. Etenim ut nihil nutu suo pronum fertur in terram, quod ipsum nihil habet terrestre: sic nihil in aethera aeternum subuolat, quod nihil possideat aethereum, aut aeternum.

¹⁶⁶ Itaque, mi anime, quanquam ipse tibi ad unguem exploratus non es, ex his tamen colligas licet, te superioris, diuiniorisque cuiusdam esse ordinis, adeoque si quis animus est, qui tam absurde, tamque abiecte ipse de se sentiat, ut se pari cum belluis aetatis spatio circumscribat, ac metiatur, profecto τοῦ νοῦ, id est, suam ipsius dignitatem non satis expendit.

[p.59/D6] ¹⁶⁷ Intellectuine nos, et animis rerum praestantissimis eam aeui perpetuitatem excordes negabimus, quam plerisque corpulentis rebus naturam concessisse manifestum est? hac scilicet ea est prudentia, ut in deterioribus conseruandis sit solicitior.

¹⁶⁸ Vtcunque cadat, certe rei magnae iacturam honesta uita facere non potest: et si quam faceret, esset illa plane non ignobilis. Siquidem praestat uirum aliquando fuisse, quam nunquam. Nunquam uero is fuit, qui rationem, qui fas usque aspernatus, se totum libidini permisit.

¹⁶² Clearly, this faculty is God-given, and cannot proceed from any corporeal root, for every bodily thing is brutish in its essential nature; it must have a higher origin, one not sharing in corporeal formation, and so also not sharing in mortality.

¹⁶³ For understanding everything, by the very fact of understanding all things, it is a thing different from them. Those things which by themselves are not able to have either independent existence or consistency, present an appearance not their own, but those things which of themselves have the power of forming a consistent whole, have real existence. And indeed, immortality above all is of this number, a gift especially suited to the dignity of the intellect.

¹⁶⁴ Again, my soul, surpassing the narrow bounds of time, you extend your hopes and thoughts into complete immortality. You burn with such great love of time everlasting and of those things which are not subject to the senses (while you are well, and do not pay heed to blind passions) that, compared with these, for things which are immediately present, you care not a straw.

¹⁶⁵ Certainly, you would not so forcefully aspire to this splendid immortality, not strive for it with such enthusiasm, if you had no affinity with those things or, indeed, did not share an origin with them. For, since nothing by its own volition is carried down to the earth which itself possesses nothing of earthliness, so there flies up to the everlasting heavenly world nothing that does not possess something of the heavenly and the eternal.

¹⁶⁶ And so, my soul, although you have not investigated yourself in scrupulous detail, you may nevertheless gather from these things that you are of a superior and somewhat more divine order; and moreover, if there is any rational spirit such as to feel so absurdly and so contemptibly about himself that he limits and measures himself to a lifespan equal to the beasts – assuredly, he does not sufficiently weigh the worth of his mind, his own worth in fact.

¹⁶⁷ Shall we in our stupidity deny to the intellect and to minds, which are the most outstanding things in existence, that length of time which it is obvious that nature has bestowed on the majority of material objects? By this way of thinking it becomes 'wisdom', to be too concerned with preserving the 'less good' things.

¹⁶⁸ However things fall out, it is clear that the honourable life cannot suffer the loss of the [really] great thing [i.e. virtue]; but, if it did so at all, that would not make it ignoble. Indeed it is better to have been a man at some time than never. Truly, that man was never a man, who, disdaining reason and the divine law, has surrendered himself totally to sensuality.

¹⁶⁹ Adde, quod improbae uoluptates semper in amarum deficiant, quibus, uelimus, nolimus, tandem carendum erit, quarumque amissionem hoc aegrius feremus, quo easdem impotentius amauimus.

¹⁷⁰ Caeterum quantum insit in honesto operaeprecii, si euentus expectationi (ut haud dubie faciet) respondebit: praeter illum, qui accipit, nemo ne diuinare quidem poterit. Improbitas quid expectet, ipsa uiderit.

¹⁷¹ Mihi sane, uel una natura hac in parte magistra, nunquam uerisimile fiet, munificentissimum illum orbis moderatorem non uiridiora et solidiora, quam in hac uita appareant, praemiorum genera pietati, recte factis, officiisque adferuare.

[p.61/D7] ¹⁷² Quamobrem, mi anime, iam dispice quid decorum postulet et postquam ipse tibi autor non es (nihil enim est, quod ipsum se efficiat: Ipse enim fecit nos, et non ipsi nos) autori tuo, a quo eam naturae excellentiam consecuta es, grates pro uiribus age.

¹⁷³ Tibi igitur, O magne rerum parens, qui mihi tot, tantorumque munerum autor es, gratias ago. Ego, qui parua mens sum, tuam magnitudinem, tuum numen, O magna, O immensa mens, agnosco, profiteor, supplexque et ex animo adoro.

¹⁷⁴ Supremus enim ipse fui in illa nascentis mundi origine tuus labor, et tanquam coronis, imo uero finis. Nam etsi tu, qui omnium es principium, idem es et finis: singula tamen, quae hic orbis cohibet, tam manifestam afferunt utilitatem, ut tota ipsa apparatio hominis causa suscepta uideatur.

¹⁷⁵ Mihi agri segetem, arbores item fructus in uictum, animalia foetus in uarios usus edunt: lucis, et densis syluis se montes uestiunt, frondosaque inter tesqua canorae accinunt auiculae.

¹⁷⁶ Mihi tellus uiridi gramine, uarioque flore tecta, sensus detinet: gelidi passim fontes erumpunt, et herbosis conclusi ripis, nitidi decurrunt in uallibus amnes.

¹⁷⁷ Mihi se maritimi inflectunt cursus: mihi tonat coelum, mihi uenti spirant, mihi decidunt imbres: omnis denique illa, quae in aethere fit, operosa uarietas inseruit.

[169] Besides, wicked pleasures always end in bitterness, and them we will eventually have to do without, willingly or unwillingly, and the loss of them we shall suffer with the greater pain, the more immoderately we have loved them.

[170] On the other hand, how much satisfaction there is to be found in what is honourable, if the outcome corresponds to the expectation (as it will doubtless do), no-one, apart from the man who experiences it, will have any idea. What vice may look forward to, she may herself consider.

[171] To me indeed, with nature perhaps alone as my teacher in this matter, it will never seem likely that the most generous controller of the world does not keep kinds of rewards, too rich and substantial to appear in this life, for piety, for deeds and duties rightly performed.

[172] Wherefore, my soul, consider what proper behaviour demands, and as you yourself are not the author of yourself (for there is nothing that may cause itself to be: for he created us, and not we ourselves), to your own author, from whom you have acquired that excellence of nature, give thanks according to your powers.

[173] To you, therefore, O great Father of all things, who are to me the author of so many and such great gifts, I do give thanks. I, who am a tiny mind, acknowledge, proclaim, and humbly from my soul adore your greatness, your Godhead, O great, O measureless mind.

[174] For I myself was your supreme work in the creation of the new-born world, and, a kind of finishing touch, the end in fact. For though you, who are the beginning of all things and are even also the end, the many things which this world contains nevertheless so testify to their manifest utility, that this entire construction seems to have been undertaken for the sake of mankind.

[175] For my benefit, fields produce crops, trees fruit for sustenance, animals their progeny for many uses; hills clad themselves with groves and thick woods; amid leafy glades, little songbirds warble.

[176] For my benefit, the earth, bedecked with its fresh grass and with many a flower, captivates my senses; chill fountains gush out everywhere, and within their grassy banks gleaming streams run down in the valleys.

[177] For my benefit, the tides of the sea bend their courses, for me the sky thunders, for me winds blow, for me showers fall; in short, all the elaborate variety generated within the ether serves my interest.

[p.63/D8] ¹⁷⁸ Mihi uer tepet, aestas feruet, grauidatur autumnus, bruma riget: mihi rutili Solis, mihi blandae Lunae, reliquorumque astrorum multiplices obsequuntur anfractus: sed et tu quoque, O uenusti oris Lucifer, stertentem me ad lucis munia uocas.

¹⁷⁹ Quid, quod et aetherei proceres, rerum secundum te longe praestantissima, studiose huc operam suam conferunt: quippe quibus tu, cui et in ipsos quoque imperium est, nostrae salutis procurationem credis, ac demandas.

¹⁸⁰ Ac, ut ne longius euager, frustraque infinitatem persequar, totus rerum orbis huc tendere apparet, non contentus necessaria uitae supeditasse praesidia, nisi etiam quae ad elegantiam, amoenitatemque spectant sufficiat.

¹⁸¹ Plane omnia pedibus nostris subiecisti, terreni orbis reges nos creasti: omnium in nobis, non modo usumfructum, sed etiam quodammodo dominatum, esse uoluisti.

¹⁸² Iam uero mihi, quem tot insignibus, tantisque honoribus amplificasti, quid tandem das negotii, aut quod statuis benignitati pretium? sane non auarum, aut iniquum. Nempe, ut te autorem agnoscam, tibi pareamuni, idque nullo tuo interim, sed meo solius, eoque non mediocri, commodo.

¹⁸³ Tantum enim abest, ut tibi gratiam referre, meque hoc officiorum onere liberare ualeam, ut quoties illud ipsum efficere enitor, toties tu me nouo tibi beneficio deuincias, nouumque accipiam in humeros onus: quandoquidem et sancti istiusmodi conatus beneficia tua sunt.

[p.65/E1] ¹⁸⁴ Nemo enim uenit ad te, nisi tu illum trahas: nemo sufficit ex se sancte uel destinare: nemo tanti est, ut sibi iure uel honesti propositi laudem uendicare possit. Tu unus es, qui omne bonum in omnibus operaris: tibi uni recte factorum laus princeps, laus media, laus denique postrema debetur.

¹⁸⁵ Sed neque intra hos munificentiae terminos tibi consistere uisum est: quin obseruantiam hanc, atque seruitium, multis iandudum nominibus debitum, totque ante redemptum praemiis, meriti loco habes, noua scilicet laborum mercede proposita, eaque sane non exili.

[178] For my benefit, the spring brings warmth, summer its burning heat, autumn its fecundity, winter its rigour; for me the multiple and regular revolutions of the radiant sun, the gentle moon, and the other stars do service. But you especially, O Lucifer of the lovely face, you summon me from my snorings to the duties of the light.

[179] What of the fact that the lords of the heavens, second to you by far the most excellent of things, eagerly bestow their labours on this task, as it is to them that you, who have authority even over them, entrust and delegate the provision of our safety.

[180] But, not to stray too far and pursue infinity in vain, the whole created world appears to proceed to this end, that, not content with having furnished the necessary supports of life, it should also provide the things which contribute to refinement and comfort.

[181] You have clearly put all things under our feet, you have created us as kings of the earthly world; it was your wish that not only the usufruct, but also as it were the lordship of everything should lie with us.

[182] So now, what is the task which you then give me, whom you have made great with so many distinctions and such great honours, and what price do you set on such benignity? Certainly not an excessive one or unfair, but just this, to acknowledge you as the author, to obey you alone and so benefit you not at all but only myself alone, and that in no small way.

[183] So far am I from being able to thank you and release myself from this burden of duties, that, however often I endeavour to achieve that very thing, you bind me to you with a new favour, and I take a new burden upon my shoulders, for indeed even holy efforts of this kind are favours from you.

[184] For no-one comes to you, unless you should draw him; no-one has the ability of himself even to purpose in a holy way; no-one is of such worth that he may justifiably claim for himself even the praise for virtuous resolution. You are the one and only, who bring about all goodness in all things: praise for good deeds – beginning, middle and end – is due to you alone.

[185] But neither is it your plan to remain within these boundaries of munificence; but rather, you count this observance and service – long owed to you on so many counts, and already paid back with so many rewards – as something requiring recompense, and you propose a new kind of reward for labours, and one certainly not negligible.

¹⁸⁶ Quantas tu nobis, bone Deus, spes ostendis? Quae promittis gaudia, modo hoc temporis punctum, hoc incertum fugacis uitae momentum, praepostero, atque intempestiuo praesentium bonorum fructu, seculis infinitis, ac aeternitati non anteponamus.

¹⁸⁷ Ad summum istuc aethera nos inuitas, ubi perpetuus spirat ueris honos, mulcet et elysias aura beata rosas: ubi iuuentae flos non marcescit, ubi corpus hac sordium obscuritate posita, patibilique prorsus exuta natura menti negocium non facesset.

¹⁸⁸ Vbi animus securus intercessurae aegritudinis, aut molestae interpellationis, interuentusque malorum securus, proprias fore, ac sempiternas has uoluptates, quas conspectus tui parit, certo sciet: ubi nihil quod ad decus, uerasque delitias attinet, desyderet: ubi immortali aeuo, ut semel dicam, summa cum pace fruatur.

[p.67/E2] ¹⁸⁹ Non enim oculus uidit, neque auris audiuit, sed nec humanae mentis coniectura assequitur eius mercedis amplitudinem, quae nos expectat, modo uiuamus ex dignitate nostra, et sapientiae, uirtutumque munera fungentes, nosmetipsos a belluarum uilitate uindicemus.

¹⁹⁰ Atqui ad hanc uitae rationem, ad gloriosam hanc palmam, etiam ut nullum aliud propositum sit praemium, praeter nudae uirtutis laudem, cupidissime contendere, totisque (quod aiunt) habenis ferri debemus.

¹⁹¹ Siquidem ipsa uirtus sibimet pulcherrima merces est: ipsa una, quamuis uniuersus fieret interitus, et a funere nihil superesset, natiuis suis illecebris ad uerum decus trahere debet.

¹⁹² Pudet me, fateor parens, quoties eorum uirorum, in quibus, praeter hanc naturae scintillam, nihil luminis inerat: quibus tu extraordinariam hanc religionis lucem non concesseras, praeclara de uirtute iudicia lego, cum statuunt in ea una tantum inesse decus, ut etiam unus dies, ex ipsius praescriptis actus, cum ipsa possit immortalitate contendere.

¹⁹³ At ipse, cui non tantum de hac uirtutis dignitate constat, uerumetiam pulcherrima praemia, certissimae spes sunt ostensae, supinus sterto, nec ad tam gloriosae laudis cursum accingor.

[186] What great hopes, good God, do you show us? What joys do you promise, provided only that we should not put this point of time, this uncertain moment of fleeting life, with its absurd and untimely enjoyment of present good things, before untold centuries and eternity.

[187] You invite us thither to that highest heaven, where breathes the perpetual beauty of spring and where a blessed zephyr soothes the heavenly roses; where the bloom of youth does not fade away, where the body, laying aside the darkness of its filth and completely throwing off its suffering nature, will cause no trouble to the mind.

[188] Where the mind, safe from intervening sickness and annoying interruption, and safe from intrusions of evil things, will indubitably know that these joys which the sight of you produces will be its own and will last for ever; where there is nothing that it might still desire by way of glory and true delight; where, to say it once for all, it may enjoy time immortal with greatest peace.

[189] For eye has not seen, nor ear heard, neither does the conjecture of the human mind comprehend the fulness of that reward which awaits us, provided that we live in accordance with our dignity, performing the duties of wisdom and virtue, and assert our freedom from the vile state of brute beasts.

[190] Nevertheless, towards this principle of living, towards this splendid palm of glory, even if no other reward were set before us, beyond the praise of unadorned virtue, we ought to struggle most eagerly and be carried along, as they say, at full tilt.

[191] For indeed, virtue herself is her own most beautiful reward. She alone, though there should be universal extinction, with nothing surviving that death, should draw the mind by her own intrinsic enticements towards true distinction.

[192] I confess, Father, I am ashamed, when I read the splendid opinions about virtue of those men, in whom there was no light further than this little spark of nature, to whom you had not granted this extraordinary light of religion – when they declare that such great distinction exists in her alone that even a single day lived according to her principles could compete with immortality itself.

[193] But I myself, for whom not only is this concept of virtue's worth well established, but to whom the most beautiful rewards and most assured hopes are displayed, lie supine and snoring, not girding myself for the race for such glorious praise.

194 Et profecto generosis animis non exiguae mercedis loco est recte facti conscientia: neque uera uirtus magnopere peregrinum aliquod moratur operaepretium.

[p.69/E3] 195 Ea demum probitas est, quae gratuita est: non quae tanquam utilitatum mercatura lucrum sectatur, uenalis, mercenaria, extrinsecusque ex praemio pendens.

196 Is tibi probatur, qui te, propter te, quoad eius fieri potest, non prorsus propter se, quaerit: quanquam, nescio quomodo, utilitate sublata, languemus ad officium, gratisque nos probos esse poeniteat: sic immodice φιλαῦτοι sumus.

197 Syngraphane et tanquam obsignatis tabellis tecum quisquam agat? nos, qui mali sumus, benignius eos habemus, quos existimamus amore potius, quam lucri spe impellente nobis inseruire: Et tu qui bonitas es, nihil tale praestabis?

198 Proinde nae ille mihi nunquam probus est, qui uno pene metu a malo temperat, qui tantisper iniuria abstinet, dum eam rescitum iri credit. Quis hic? quam nefarius fiat, si metu excusso, atque exempto, opinionis error impunitatem promittat? Oderunt sane peccare boni uirtutis amore.

199 Ergo hoc tu parens de filiis expectas, ut innocentia, et mutuis inter nos humanitatis certemus officiis: teque debitae pietatis honoribus afficiamus:

200 Vt natiuae nobilitatis memores, a corporis obsequio, indulgentiaque discedamus, carnis eiiciamus societatem: neque affines earum rerum simus, quae diuinam nostri partem degenerare cogant.

[p.71/E4] 201 Quae sursum sunt, sapiamus: quae sursum sunt, quaeramus: non quae super terram. Ad te fontem, unde riuuli: ad te unum, unde multa: ad te centrum, unde lineae, defluximus (nam alia ad felicitatem non itur) reditum sedulo adornemus.

202 Neque aliud fortasse fuerit uberius ingenui pectoris, teque parentem resipientis, argumentum, quam si ea, inter quae hic in terris uersatur, humilia, seque indigna iudicet: in te uero usque feratur.

[194] And to be sure, for noble minds the knowledge of something done aright takes the place of considerable reward; neither does true virtue very much care about any outside recompense.

[195] In short, real goodness comes free; she is not on the hunt for profit, as if bargaining for benefits, neither corrupt, mercenary, nor dependent on any reward from without.

[196] That man finds favour with you, who seeks you for your own sake, as far as is possible, and absolutely not for his own sake; though somehow or other, once 'advantage' is removed, we slacken in our duty and may regret being upright for nothing — so immoderately do we love ourselves.

[197] Is anyone to deal with you on the basis of a signed and sealed covenant, as it were? We, who are bad, consider more favourably those who, we think, serve our interests, impelled by love rather than by hope of reward. And you, who are goodness, will you do nothing similar?

[198] Accordingly, indeed, I can never consider that man upright, who from fear of punishment alone forbears from evil, who abstains from wrong for as long as he believes that it is going to be found out. Who is this man? What a heinous criminal he would become, if that fear were shaken off and removed, and mistaken public opinion were to promise impunity? Good men, in truth, hate to sin from love of virtue.

[199] Therefore, Father, you expect this from your children, that we should compete among ourselves in innocence and the mutual duties of humanity, and that we should grant you the honours of the piety which is your due;

[200] And that, mindful of our native nobility, we should step back from allegiance to, and indulgence of, the body, cast out companionship with the flesh, and not be attached to such things as cause the divine part of ourselves to degenerate.

[201] Let us set our affections on those things which are above; let us seek out those things which are above, not those which are on the earth. Let us carefully prepare our return to you the fount, from which as streams we flow, to you the One, from which as many we come, to you the centre, from which as radii we stream out, for there is no other route to felicity.

[202] And there would perhaps be no richer evidence of a noble spirit savouring of you, Father, than that it should judge those things among which it spends its time here on earth as base and unworthy of itself, and be constantly impelled towards you.

[203] Nonne et hac maxime ratione rem facio, ipse me perficio? si tanto semper meliores sumus (ut proculdubio sumus) quanto magis in illud imus, quo nihil est melius.

[204] Itaque cum affectu extra meipsum feror, si in te feror, bene est: necesse est enim sublime sit illud, quod intra te receptum, sublimitatis tuae fit particeps.

[205] Cum cogitando aliquid intra se mens admittit, si tu es, qui admitteris, aut aliquid quod te redoleat, bene est: necesse est enim, magnum sit illud, quod intra se rem immensam claudit.

[206] Hanc uiam nobis muniamus oportet, si uere magni, uere excellentes esse uelimus. Non aurum hoc, non sceptra praestant, neque quicquam eorum, quae stupidum uulgus in admirationem adducunt.

[207] Ex ea re una uera illa animi existit magnitudo, quae non ad imperitae multitudinis, sed ad conscientiae iudicium abunde amplum ingenuis mentibus theatrum se componit.

[208] Hinc inuictum mentis robur. Nihil eum, qui ita compositus est, de gradu deiiciat: Nihil non in meliorem accipiat, quisquis ita se comparauit. Hunc, si fractus illabatur orbis, impauidum ferient ruinae.

[p.73/E5] [209] Restat interdum fortuna: aduersae res saepius eos grauius premunt, quos maior uirtutis cura detinet: aliter saepe usu uenit, atque nobis stolidis in expectatione fuerat.

[210] Sed tu tum potissimum nobis consulis, atque hac ratione caues, ne uoluptatum Sirenes, quod bonae mentis est, si quid tamen est, excantent: et ne coelestium rerum studium praesentium male suaui dulcedine uicti ponamus.

[211] Neque dubium est, quin quoties ob corporis, aut fortunae bona accepta gaudemus, aut adempta dolemus, eo nos diui loco habent, quo nos iam cum matura aetate sumus, pueros habere solemus, cum ipsi propter scruta, puppas, trochos, poma, aliasque id genus pueriles delicias perturbantur.

[212] Nae ego, si saperem, haud paulo mallem hanc mihi fabulae personam, quae uirtutem, et decus sapit, atque una cum filio tuo crucem baiulare, quam perpetuo mollem uitae cursum, in quo nihil sane praeclarum, aut gloriosum inest.

²⁰³ Isn't this the way that I can best do myself good and achieve my goal – if we are always better (as doubtless we are) the more we move towards that than which nothing is better?

²⁰⁴ And so, when I am by a powerful surge of emotion transported out of myself, if I am transported into you that is good; for what is received within you, and shares in your sublimity, must necessarily be sublime.

²⁰⁵ When by thinking the mind admits anything into itself, provided it is you who are admitted, or something redolent of you, that is good, for that which encloses something immense within itself must necessarily be great.

²⁰⁶ This is the road that we must build for ourselves, if we would be truly great and truly excellent. Neither wealth nor power provides this, nor any of those things which win the admiration of the madding crowd.

²⁰⁷ From that one thing alone arises that true greatness of mind, which orders itself not to suit the judgement of the naive multitude but according to the judgement of conscience, a stage quite large enough for noble minds.

²⁰⁸ From this comes unconquered strength of mind. Nothing may throw the man, thus composed, off his step; there is nothing that the man who has so settled himself would not take for the better; if the world should break up and collapse, the ruins will strike this man still fearless.

²⁰⁹ Meanwhile there is still the question of fortune. Adversity often presses particularly heavily on those who are occupied by a greater concern for virtue. Things have often turned out differently to what we, in our dullness of mind, had expected.

²¹⁰ But it is in *this* situation particularly that you look out for us, to stop the Sirens of sensuality from singing away any element there is of a good mind, and prevent us from laying aside our passion for heavenly things, overcome by the seductive sweetness of present ones.

²¹¹ There is no doubt but that, whenever we rejoice at the gaining of the good things of the body or of fortune, or grieve at the loss of them, the divine beings view us in the same way as we, when now of mature age, are accustomed to view children, when they are distressed about worthless things – dolls, hoops, fruit, and other puerile pleasures of that sort.

²¹² Verily, if I were wise, I should greatly prefer for myself the role in the play of one who has a sense of virtue and honour, and together with your Son to shoulder the cross, rather than an always soft path of life in which there is nothing truly excellent or glorious.

²¹³ Etenim nos, quos totos sibi uendicat fracta haec, et desidiosa uitae ratio, non ab re gurgites, ac helluones, non laudi, ac gloriae, sed abdomini nati, tellurisque duntaxat pondera, frustra lucis huius usum accepisse uidemur.

²¹⁴ At is, qui glorioso laborum cursu, qui praestantium rerum studio ignauiam deuitarit, iure glorietur, se non frustra natum. Iure laetus, et fidens ad fabulae remigrat autorem, qui impositam personam bene gesserit.

[p.75/E6] ²¹⁵ Iure is in magnorum uirorum numerum uenit, qui inter paucos, in tanta somniantium turba (somniamus enim, qui species pro rebus amplectimur) saepius experrectus, ludificationem, et praestigias auersatus, somniare se depraehendit.

²¹⁶ Sed quid mirum est, omnem uitae rationem esse peruersam, eaque prima haberi bona, quibus iure uix postremus locus debetur: quandoquidem animum tam multiplex opinionis error ab ipsis protinus incunabulis inficit, quem maiorem in modum omnium ordinum pestifer et exitialis consuetudo confirmat.

²¹⁷ Sed ut ad bonitatem tuam, alme parens, redeam: Certe post tot, et tanta tua beneficia, si humanitas non potuit, certe pudor, aut saltem metus nos in officio retinere debuit.

²¹⁸ Verum nos nulla benignitatis tantae ratione habita, sic in te, cui par referri, aut merita persolui gratia nequit, cuique in omnibus morem gestum oportuit, fuimus iniuriosi, et noua scelerum accessione assidue prouocauimus, ut iam in ipsis foribus ingrati generis excidium foret.

²¹⁹ At tu parens, qui sine modo beneficia facere gaudes, non modo iram, et eam quidem iustissimam, refraenas, atque coerces: sed etiam eo denuo beneficio, atque honore afficis hostes, qualem nullum etiam amici summeque in te officiosi expectare potuissemus.

[p.77/E7] ²²⁰ Ipse Deus hominem induis, nostramque naturam incredibili generis nostri tum commodo, tum gloria ad diuinitatis tuae contubernium, copulationemque, quam fieri potuit arctissimam, euexisti.

²¹³ For we, whom this weak and effete lifestyle claims entirely for itself, veritable bottomless pits and gluttons, born not for praise and glory but for the belly, in short just burdens upon the earth, seem truly enough to have received to no purpose the enjoyment of this light.

²¹⁴ But the man, who via a glorious course of struggles, who by his devotion to excellent things has avoided sluggish inactivity, may rightly boast that he has not been born in vain. With justification happy and confident, he makes his way back to the author of the play, as one who has carried out well the role assigned to him.

²¹⁵ Rightfully, that man joins the number of great men, who, among few in this huge throng of dreamers (for we dream, embracing appearance as reality), often wakes up and, repudiating trickery and illusions, realises that he is dreaming,

²¹⁶ But what wonder is it, that the whole scheme of life is perverse, and those things are considered as the first of goods, to which the hindmost place is scarcely due, seeing that such a multiple error of opinion besets the mind right from the cradle, which baleful and deadly convention in all ranks of society reinforces in ever greater measure.

²¹⁷ But, gentle Father, to return to your goodness: assuredly, given so many and such great kindnesses on your part, if humane feeling has not been able to hold us to our duty, shame, or at the least fear, ought to have done so.

²¹⁸ But we, taking no account of such great goodness, towards you, to whom adequate recompense cannot be paid nor the thanks owed be given, whom it was fitting that we should oblige in all things, have been so disrespectful and have so constantly provoked you with a new access of wickedness, that the destruction of our ungrateful race will already be right at the doors.

²¹⁹ But you, Father, who without measure delight to confer benefits, not only curb and repress your anger, and anger indeed most justified; but even once more bestow such a favour and honour on your enemies, as we, even if we were your friends and most dutiful towards you, could not have expected.

²²⁰ You yourself, God, put on Man and, to the incredible advantage and glory of our kind, have exalted our nature to fellowship with your divinity, and to the closest possible union.

²²¹ Et nescio, parens, an de rerum principio, atque a naturae ortu ulla in re adeo diuinitatis uires intenderis: facile enim hoc inter opera tua palmam accipiat, quando nullum rei conditae decus maius excogitari potest, quam ut diuinitatis honore communicato cum Deo conditore communiter subsistat: eiusdem dignitatis socia, et in excelsissimo rerum fastigio posita, sub pedibus nubes, sydera, et diuos denique ipsos uideat.

²²² Ipse nobiscum hic agens, doctrina pariter et uita uniuerso orbi beatitudinis consequendae rationem clarissime exponis, passim te nostrae accommodans infirmitati, in his quae cum recto non pugnant.

²²³ Inops ipse, nostrique causa aerumnosus, monstrabas quam contemnenda sint illa, quae uulgo praeclarissima existimantur: quamque candide nos aliis impertiri debeamus, cum nostra illis opus est opera.

²²⁴ Ante Euangelium tuum omnis mundus densissimis laborabat errorum tenebris: et quod erat honoris, ac laudis, in te unum conferendum, id impia fraude, sacrilegaque impudentia in commentitiam quandam multitudinem est dispertitum.

²²⁵ Plane Deus eras absconditus, notus pene tantum in Iudaea Deus, et non temere alibi, quam in Israel, magnum, et celebre fuit tuum nomen.

[p.79/E8] ²²⁶ At Euangelii tui beneficio, ut alia passim non sit assecutus orbis, pene tamen totus te unum, ut es, rerum et parentem, et dominum ueneratur.

²²⁷ Neque profecto hoc in paruis ducendum est, orbem ipsum tantis purgatum esse erroribus, atque a nefario impietatis, et ἀχαριστίας quoque crimine mortales ad officium reuocatos esse.

²²⁸ Adde, quod tot, et tantis circunuallabamur undique malis, ut inde humanitus, et citra tuam opem emergi non posset: cum non tam ob communem originis labem, quam ob suum cuiusque crimen omnes capitales, mortique obnoxii sempiternae essemus.

²²⁹ At filius tuus dilectus Christus, unus, idemque tecum, et cum sacro spiritu Deus, peccata nostra in se transtulit, et iuxta crudeli, ignominiosoque mortis genere pro nostrum omnium sceleribus poenas abunde dependit: nostrique luxus sordes innocuo suo cruore eluit.

²²¹ And I know not, Father, whether, right from the first creation of things and the origin of nature, you have so applied the power of your divinity in any thing. This should easily take the prize among your works, as no greater glory for a created thing can be conceived than sharing in the honour of divinity and standing together with God the creator, beholding the clouds under his feet, the stars, and finally the company of heaven themselves.

²²² Living with us here, equally in teaching and in life, you set forth most clearly for the whole world the way of attaining blessedness, everywhere accommodating yourself to our infirmity – in things which do not conflict with the right.

²²³ Yourself poor and afflicted with suffering on our behalf, you showed how contemptible are those things which are commonly considered excellent, and how sincerely we should share with others when they have need of our assistance.

²²⁴ Before your Gospel came, the whole world laboured under the most profound darkness of error, and any honour and praise that should have been conferred on you alone was through impious fraud and sacrilegious impudence distributed among a host of falsehoods.

²²⁵ You were indeed a hidden God, fully hidden, almost only in Judea known as God; and in hardly any other place but in Israel was your name great and famous.

²²⁶ But through the benefit of your Gospel, granted that in places it has not acquired all the rest of it, the world nevertheless almost in its entirety venerates you the one Father and Lord of all, as you are.

²²⁷ Assuredly it is not to be considered a little thing that the world itself has been purged of such great errors, and that mortals have been called from the wicked sin of impiety and lack of charity back to their duty.

²²⁸ Add the fact that we were surrounded on all sides by so many and such great evils, that, humanly speaking, short of your generosity there was no possibility of escape, since we were under sentence and liable to an eternal death, not so much on account of the common failing of original sin, but rather on account of each man's individual sins.

²²⁹ But your beloved Son Christ – One God with you and the Holy Ghost – has taken our sins upon himself, and thereto with his cruel and shameful manner of death, has abundantly paid the penalty for the wicked deeds of all of us; he has washed away the stains of our excess with his innocent blood.

²³⁰ Quicquid enim tormentorum perpessus est, quicquid supplicii sufferebat, sua quidem sponte, sed nostri causa, sufferebat: ut non minus ille uere, quam pie cecinerit, paruulum natum nobis, filium datum nobis.

²³¹ Vnus enim ille agnus undique immaculatus, idonea inuentus est uictima: Vnus ille frugi filius, infensum nequam seruis patrem placare ualuit: unus nos reduxit tecum in gratiam, quam eandem sempiternam fore multiplici sacramentorum pignore spem nobis dedit certissimam.

[p.81/F1] ²³² Etenim et ipsum corpus, quod paulo ante tam indigne habitum erat, triumphata iam morte rediuiuum, non prius supra sydera ipsa scandere intermisit, quoad peruentum esset in eam sedem, quam omnipotens rerum parens ad dexteram filio apparauerat.

²³³ Sic quoties miseros scelerum conscientia ad desperationem adigit, quoties metus horrida minitatur tartara, ad filii tui crucem, tanquam ad asylum, receptumque tutissimum confugimus.

²³⁴ Tanta tu hominum charitate, gratiaque teneris, ut filium tuum, tibi unice dilectum, nobis clypeum dederis, qui nos ab ira, atque indignatione tua, quam assidue commeremur, protegat, ac tueatur.

²³⁵ Crucis enim haec impressio peculiaris nota est, et symbolum, eos, quorum misereri decreuisti, distinguens ab his, in quos ob mala facinora arcano quodam consilio inaeternum es saeuiturus.

²³⁶ Dedisti enim hanc metuentibus te significationem, ut fugiant a facie arcus, nec limina illa uis ultrix aut inimica contingit, quae pretiosus ille agni cruor illeuit.

²³⁷ Eo ipse te nobis misericordiae uinculo obstringis, ut nos pro meritis tractare, pene dixerim non possis: nos, inquam, qui in filii tui, nostra causa tam male accepti, tamque immaniter excarnificati, in tutela sumus, et fide.

[p.83/F2] ²³⁸ Fidem enim tu ita fore dedisti ei, qui tibi serio, et ex animo fidit, qui CHRISTI crucem amplectitur, non modo delictorum omnium gratiam fieri, imo ne iudicatum quidem iri eiusmodi.

²³⁹ Iam uero quis tam ineptus est, ut extimescat, ne tu, qui ipsa es ueritas, fidem fallas, aut promissum non facias: neque temere alia ratione grauius te offendimus, quam cum bonitati tuae, promissisque diffidimus, contantiusue fidem habemus.

[230] Whatever tortures he endured with patience, whatever punishment he suffered, he suffered of his own free will indeed, but for our sake; as the prophet proclaimed no less truly than faithfully: To us a child is born, to us a son is given.

[231] For alone that lamb, immaculate in every respect, is found the suitable victim; alone the worthy Son had the power to placate the Father, furious with his worthless servants; alone he restored us to grace with you and gave to us most certain hope, through the manifold assurance of the sacraments, that that grace would be eternal.

[232] For that very body, which shortly before had been treated with such indignity, restored to life with death now defeated, did not cease to climb above the stars themselves, until it arrived right at that seat which the all-powerful Father of the world had on his right hand, appointed for the Son.

[233] So whenever consciousness of sins drives us wretches to despair, whenever fear threatens the dreadful horrors of hell, so we take our flight to the cross of your Son, as to a sanctuary and most safe retreat.

[234] You are bound by such love and grace towards men, that you gave your Son, your uniquely beloved, as a shield for us, to protect and defend us from your wrath and indignation, which we constantly deserve.

[235] For this mark of the cross is a special sign and symbol, distinguishing those on whom you have decided to have mercy, from those towards whom, because of their evil crimes, you will by some secret counsel remain forever wrathful.

[236] For you have given this as a sign to those who fear you, that they may escape the face of the bowmen, and no avenging or hostile power touch those doorways which the precious blood of the lamb has smeared.

[237] You bind yourself to us with such a chain of mercy that you, I might almost say, cannot treat us as we deserve – we, I say, who are under the protection and guarantee of your Son, for our sakes so badly treated, so barbarously tortured.

[238] For you have given a guarantee to the one who earnestly and from his spirit trusts in you, who embraces the cross of CHRIST, not only that all his sins are forgiven, but that furthermore no such judgement will be instituted.

[239] Indeed, who is so absurd as to fear lest you, who are truth itself, would break your undertaking or not keep your promise; and there is no easier way to offend you gravely than by distrusting your goodness and your promises, or being doubting in our faith.

²⁴⁰ Quid sibi uult hoc, coelestis parens? Num tuae opes sine nobis non consistunt? Non praeuideras tam ingratos nos fore aduersus te? Quid est homo, quod sic illum magnificas, et apponis erga illum cor tuum?

²⁴¹ Profecto quamuis nobis, non tibi, tota haec laboret benignitas, nisi immensae bonitatis esset meritorum neglecta ratione nullis munificentiae finibus circumscribi, et nobis quoque, apud quos collocantur ipsa beneficia, male collocata uideri possent: cum nemo pene sit, qui magnopere studeat se gratum esse.

²⁴² Salue ergo chare IESV: salue fili dei uiui; salue aeterni patris uerbum: salue intemeratae uirginis proles: salue salutis autor: salue nostri generis decus: salue spes, salue praesidium, salue immensi orbis dominator, seruili habitu, ac figura contecte.

²⁴³ Quantopere tu mihi charus esse debes dulcis IESV, qui cum summo meo tempore ad tribunal tuum facinorosus homuncio sistar, nihil afferre potero, quod ab hoc capite aeternae mortis sententiam propulsare possit, praeter ista tua uulnera, in quae necesse est me abdam tantisper, dum causa dicenda erit, dum ira tua deferbeat.

[p.85/F3] ²⁴⁴ Quantopere mihi in hoc incumbendum est, ut abs te gratiam ineam, a quo uno non tam sempiterni doloris, ac miseriae depulsionem, quam uerae felicitatis cumulos expecto.

²⁴⁵ Punctum est quod uiuo. Cur non ad hoc temporis punctum abdicatis, reiectisque aliis rebus omnibus, nunquam a crucis tuae amplexu diuellor? Crucis inquam, in qua tot honestissimae spes collucent, quae intus uerum decus, et uera gaudia, etsi aliud fronte praefert, haud dubie recondit.

²⁴⁶ Atque utinam, parens, crucis hoc beneficium aliae quoque gentes communiter nobiscum agnoscant: sic enim omnes concordi religione, et communibus sacris te communem omnium deum coleremus.

²⁴⁷ Caeterum id ut fiat, optare quidem licet: cur autem non fiat, curiose indagare nefas est. Quis enim nouit sensum domini? quis arcanas consiliorum tuorum rationes scrutetur?

²⁴⁸ In infimis, et his quae ad manum sunt rebus, haeremus, fallimur, allucinamur: et miramur, si prouidentiae tuae mysteria nos fugiant?

²⁴⁰ What does this mean, heavenly Father? Surely not that your generosity would have no scope without us? Had you not foreseen that we would be so ungrateful towards you? What is man, that you so magnify him and set your heart upon him?

²⁴¹ Certainly, however much all this benignity may labour on our behalf and not for yourself, if it were not the mark of immense goodness to take no account of merits and not be restricted by any limits on munificence, even to us on whom they are bestowed those same benefits could seem to have been badly bestowed; for there is almost no-one who makes much effort to be grateful.

²⁴² Hail, therefore, dear JESUS; hail, Son of the living God; hail, Word of the eternal Father; hail, offspring of the immaculate Virgin; hail, author of salvation; hail, glory of our humanity; hail, hope; hail, our protection; hail, Lord of the immense world, concealed in garb and form of a servant.

²⁴³ How dear, sweet JESUS, should you be to me, who, when at the end of my days I, a sinful little mortal, shall be set before your judgement seat, shall not be able to adduce anything that could avert from this head the sentence of eternal death, except those wounds of yours, in which I must hide, while the case is being pled and until your anger subsides.

²⁴⁴ How hard I ought to be striving to enter into your favour, from whom alone I look not so much for removal of eternal death and misery, as for heaped up true felicity.

²⁴⁵ I live for but a moment. Why, at this moment of time, am I not, forswearing and rejecting all else, never torn from the embrace of your cross? Of the cross, I say, in which so many most praiseworthy hopes shine, which within itself, even if its outward appearance betokens something else, undoubtedly conceals true honour and true joy.

²⁴⁶ And, Father, if only other nations also would acknowledge this benefit of the cross together with us; for so would we all, in religious harmony and with shared sacraments, worship you as the common God of all.

²⁴⁷ However, one may indeed wish for it to happen. But why it does not happen, it is forbidden to investigate too closely. For who knows the mind of the Lord? Who may discern the secret purposes of your decisions?

²⁴⁸ In the lowest things, in things that are at hand, we stick, we are deceived, our minds wander; and then are we amazed if the mysteries of your providence escape us?

²⁴⁹ Praecipua sapientiae pars est, insipientiam suam non ignorare: nec temere hisce de rebus statuere, quas arcanas esse uoluit is, qui intelligentiae nostrae modum statuit, et quasi quibusdam limitum terminauit angustiis.

²⁵⁰ Ille, quem coelestis quidam mentis aestus ab terris ad tertium usque coelum ultra astra abripuerat, quique arcana uerba, quae proloqui nefas esset, audiuerat, simulatque terris redditus est, immensos esse diuini ingenii fines, uias imperuestigabiles, infinitas sapientiae opes non obscure testificatur.

[p.87/F4] ²⁵¹ Sed nec in cruce quidem IESV mei quicquam est, quod uel gentium philosophia, si modestiam adhibeat (ut in diuinis rebus praecipue par est) possit improbare.

²⁵² Huius meae crucis humilitas superba quaedam, et inconsyderata ingenia, et quae falsa doctrinae persuasio inflauerat, a religione deterruit. Nae illi tamen interea et ab ipsius philosophiae, cuius nomine gloriantur, praeceptis, atque institutis aberrasse, prudentiaeque inanes comperiuntur.

²⁵³ Etenim philosophorum, qui habiti sunt sanctissimi, ea quae ad luxum, fastum, corporisque uoluptates pertinent, bonorum nomine non sunt dignati: uidebant nimirum ea omnia nullius propemodum, prae animi uirtute, momenti.

²⁵⁴ Quid est, quaeso per deum immortalem, quod toties reges, populosque committit, quod mortales ad caedes, sceleraque facienda impellit, in summa, quod totam uitae, ac officiorum rationem perturbat, praeter immodicum eiusmodi rerum studium?

²⁵⁵ Itaque meus CHRISTVS, in cuius arbitrio positus erat rerum omnium fructus, cui tot legiones, tamque numerosum coelitum praesto erat, parebatque ad nutum seruitium: qui una uocula cohortem resupinarat, ista sua cruce, hoc est, insigni opum, fastus, uoluptatumque contemptu pene, si qua alia re, mihi diuinitatis fidem facit.

[p.89/F5] ²⁵⁶ Nos degener uulgus inuicem alii ex aliorum opinione pendemus, et stulti stultis stulte placere: uideri, non esse, magni studemus: illi uni patri omnipotenti uitam suam, quod et cumulate praestitit, probare curae fuit.

²⁴⁹ The principal part of wisdom is not to be unaware of one's own lack of wisdom, nor rashly to make decisions about the things that he wished to be secret, who set a limit to our understanding and restricted it as it were within tight bounds.

²⁵⁰ That man, whom a sort of celestial mental impetus had carried from the earth as far as the third heaven beyond the stars, and who had heard secret words which it was not permitted to speak aloud, immediately on his return to earth testified openly that the territories of the divine mind are immense, his ways unfathomable, his wealth of wisdom infinite.

²⁵¹ But neither in the cross of my JESUS, is there anything which the philosophy of the gentiles might find fault with, if it were to show humility (as is right to do, especially in things divine).

²⁵² The disgrace of this my cross has frightened away from religion some proud and injudicious minds, ones which the false persuasion of a philosophy had puffed up. Yet those very people are meantime nevertheless discovered to have strayed away from the precepts and commandments of the very philosophy in whose name they glory, and are found to be actually devoid of wisdom.

²⁵³ For indeed, those considered most to be revered among philosophers have deemed those things which belong to excess, conceit and the pleasures of the body not worthy of the name of 'goods'; they certainly saw all these as almost of no importance, in comparison with virtue of mind.

²⁵⁴ What is it, I ask by the immortal God, that so often sets kings and peoples against each other, that drives mortal men to murder and the committing of crimes, and which, in sum, throws into confusion the whole scheme of life and duty, more than the unrestrained passion for things of this kind?

²⁵⁵ And so my CHRIST, under whose control had been set the usufruct of all things, who once had so many legions, such a numerous throng of heavenly beings standing at the ready and obedient to his very nod, who had with one little word laid low an army, has, by that cross of his, that is, by his glorious contempt for wealth, conceit and pleasures, created within me, almost more than by anything else, faith in his divinity.

²⁵⁶ We, a degenerate crowd, depend on the opinion of others, each following a different one, and as fools endeavour foolishly to please fools. To appear, not to be, great is our aim. For him, his task was to make his life acceptable to the one Father almighty, and this he achieved in full measure.

²⁵⁷ Adde, quod nostrae salutis negotium sic transigendum erat. Nam cum mundus per suam sapientiam autorem suum male gratus non agnosceret, placuit mundi autori hac ratione in speciem ridicula salutis ac religionis scientiam per omnem orbem propagare.

²⁵⁸ Hac ratione retundenda erat nostra arrogantia, sic reprimendum supercilium, ut iam uel ludibriosa hac cruce magistra in obscuro esse non possit, quanto diuina, si ita loqui fas est, stultitia humanae praestet sapientiae.

²⁵⁹ Tibi, ut abiecta sis crux, humani tandem ingenii fasces se demisere: tu regum superasti potentiam: inferorum euertisti opes: atque triumphata morte, errorumque fugatis nebulis, obluctante orbe pene uniuerso, uitam et clarissimum ueritatis diem, patris nostri agnitionem, quae obliterata fuerat, perpetuamque delictorum amnestiam mortalibus reuexisti.

²⁶⁰ Quid? quod et si quid uerae religionis est, aut apud uicinas gentes, aut apud eas, quas montium excelsitas, aut aequorum uastitas a nobis disiunxit, id omne tibi, O sacra, O frugifera arbor, acceptum referendum est.

[p.91/F6] ²⁶¹ Est Christus munus te dignum, parens, immensum beneficium ab immensa bonitate profectum: Eius uita pariter et mors omnis praestantis uirtutis exemplum: Ille unus sanctitatis, officiorum, et coelestis philosophiae magister.

²⁶² Nostrum autem homuncionum hoc in primis interest, abs te, qui Deus dominusque es, imperia accipere: imperata impigre facere: eique doctrinae sine contatione assentiri: quam abs te profectam idonea argumenta demonstrant.

²⁶³ Sedenim si hic error est, tu profecto, qui ueritas es, erroris es (quod in intelligentiam non cadit) magister: quum talia passim doctrinae testimonia dederis, quae aliunde quam abs te existere non poterant.

²⁶⁴ Doces quae superant rationis captum, sed eiusdem ordinis argumenta adfers, nempe miracula, quibus etiam ipsa natura obstupefacta est, cum uideret suas refigi leges: quod ab alio fieri non poterat, quam a te, qui omnis naturae autor, et rex easdem in principio fixeras.

²⁵⁷ Moreover, the business of our salvation had to be transacted in this way. For, since the ungrateful world in its wisdom would not acknowledge its author, it pleased the author of that world to spread knowledge of salvation and religion throughout the whole world via this seemingly ridiculous plan.

²⁵⁸ By this plan our arrogance had to be beaten down, by this plan our pride had to be suppressed, so that now, with even this derisive cross as our instructress, it could not be unclear how much divine foolishness, if one may so speak, excels human wisdom.

²⁵⁹ Before you, O cross, despised as you may be, at last, the ensigns of human intelligence have lowered themselves. You have overcome the power of kings, you have overturned the powers of hell. And, having triumphed over death and dispersed the clouds of error, though almost the entire world resists, you have brought back for mortals life and the refulgent light of truth, the acknowledgement of our Father, which had been wiped out, and a perpetual amnesty for their offences.

²⁶⁰ What of the fact that, if there is anything of true religion either among neighbour nations or among those whom the towering height of mountains or the vastness of oceans has separated from us, all of that is to be ascribed to you, O holy, O fruit-bearing tree.

²⁶¹ Christ is a gift worthy of you, Father, an immense benefit proceeding from an immense goodness. His life, and his death equally, is an example of every excellent virtue; he is the only teacher of holiness, duty, and heavenly philosophy.

²⁶² It is the principal interest of our tiny human figures to receive commands from you, who are God and Lord, energetically to perform those commands, and to assent without reservation to that doctrine, which appropriate arguments show to have proceeded from you.

²⁶³ But in fact, if there is error here, you, who are truth, are certainly the teacher of error (and this is something which does not come within comprehension), since everywhere you have given such testimonies to the doctrine as could not have sprung from any source but you.

²⁶⁴ You teach things which are beyond the reach of reason, but you bring arguments of the same order, that is, miracles, by which even nature herself was astounded, when she saw her laws dismantled, which could not be done by anyone but by you, who, as the author and king of all of nature, had established those laws in the beginning.

265 Accedit, quod una hominum species, nescio quo infelici fato, tantum abest, ut suum finem, contra quam solent caeterae animantes, assequatur: ut uix e multis milibus unum inuenias, qui ita sit moratus, ita animo, ac uita constitutus, uel ut ipsa ratio postulat.

266 Belluisne igitur, aliisque rebus, etiam inanimis, et indignis, quae cum homine componantur, natura matrem: uni homini crudelem se praebuit nouercam: eiusque rei curam abiecit omnium, quas ipsa genuit, longe praestantissimae: cuiusque gratia caetera comparata uidentur?

[p.93/F7] 267 Absit, ut tam indigne de prouidentia, aut natura sapientissima, eademque optima rerum matre, existimemus: Sit nobis hoc argumento locupleti, alias esse, longeque diuiniores hominis rationes.

268 Hoc certo sit indicio, uera esse, quae una nostra philosophia Christiana de mali huius fonte, originis labe, foecunda malorum semente, deque futuro et meliore rerum statu, ubi decoro inseruietur, disserit: qui nisi esset, profecto uideretur homo a natura abiectus.

269 Accedit, quod quicquid praecipit meus Christus, pietas est absoluta, humanitas singularis: illud undique rotundum, ac candidum manhu est, quod nos dum in hac terra deserta, inuia, et siticulosa peregre erramus, pascit, et sustentat.

270 Neque enim honestiorem, aut optabiliorem felicitatis rationem, aut uiam eo perueniendi expeditiorem, quisquam excogitauerit, ea seruatoris nostri, quae nos erudit, ut abiecta impietate, et praesentis uitae desideriis, sobrie, iuste, et pie uiuamus: expectantes beatam spem, et aduentum gloriae magni Dei.

271 Sed et mihi quoque seruator, cum in crucem tuam intueor, sub primum aspectum horror es, ignominia es, et dolorum aceruus, res (ut apparet) cum ea, quam quaero felicitate, ex diametro pugnantes.

[p.95/F8] 272 At cum mysterium expendo, et nucleum nuce fracta, ut ualeo, contrecto, decus es, et deliciae: sed quas impertire non soles, nisi iis, qui omne suum studium in hanc crucis meditationem contulerunt.

[265] There is also the thought that the species of men alone, by some unlucky fate, is so far from achieving its end, contrary to what other living creatures usually do, that out of many thousands you may hardly find one who has such a character and is so constituted by his mind and life, as even reason herself demands.

[266] So, has nature shown herself a mother to wild beasts and to other things, even to inanimate ones and things unworthy to be compared to man, and to man alone shown herself a cruel stepmother, and thrown off the care of by far the most excellent thing of all that she herself brought forth, and for the sake of which the other things seem to have been provided?

[267] Far be it from us, to have such unworthy thoughts about providence or wisest nature, herself the best mother of things. We can see a really satisfying piece of evidence in that the thoughts of man are quite different and much more divine.

[268] Let this be a sure indication – the truth of those things which only our Christian philosophy teaches concerning the source of this evil, original sin, fecund in sowing evils, and concerning a future and better ordering of things, where what is honourable will be the guiding principle; were that not the case, it would surely seem that man is rejected by nature.

[269] In addition, whatever my Christ teaches is absolute mercy, is humanity extraordinary. [It is] that manna, round on every side and white, which feeds and sustains us, while we wander far from home, in this pathless and thirsty desert.

[270] And no one could think out a more honourable or more desirable scheme of felicity, or a more expeditious route for arriving there, than that of our saviour, which teaches us how, casting off impiety and the desires of this present life, we may lead a sober, righteous and godly life, looking for that blessed hope and coming of the glory of the mighty God.

[271] But, even for me too, saviour, when I contemplate your cross you are at first sight horror, ignominy and the accumulation of sorrows, things diametrically conflicting, as it appears, with that felicity which I seek.

[272] Yet, when I ponder the mystery, and, once the shell is broken, handle the kernel, as best I can, you are a thing of beauty and delights; but delights you do not usually share, unless with those who have focused all their endeavour into this meditation on the cross.

²⁷³ Hi exugunt mel de petra, oleumque de saxo durissimo: Hi hauriunt aquas in gaudio de fontibus seruatoris: Hi renuunt aliunde, quam ex te, consolationem admittere.

²⁷⁴ Hi eam sibi innocentiae legem indicunt, ut non modo extra rectum nihil uelint: sed etiam, quo filii tui similes euadant, a concessis uitae adminiculis, sine quibus aegre ea continetur, pertinaciter abstineant.

²⁷⁵ Hos nulla frangunt aduersa, nullae emolliunt libidines, nullae liquefaciunt uoluptates: quinetiam inter medios cruciatus pene effusa quadam laetitia exultant.

²⁷⁶ Quoties tui recordatio animum subit, lachrymae illis nectar et ambrosia: paupertas, opes: contemptus, laus: uita, dispendium: mori, lucrum.

²⁷⁷ Id unum sibi studio habent, id unum laudi sibi fore putant, si uitae conformatione filii tui, uel minima ex parte, similes euadant.

²⁷⁸ Pars in syluis, inter deserta ferarum lustra uitam agit, ubi uictum non iam infelicem bacchas, lapidosaque corna dant rami, et uulsis pascunt radicibus herbae, egeni, afflicti, in montibus et speluncis et cauernis terrae, quibus plane mundus dignus non erat.

²⁷⁹ Pars urbes incolit, et in communes descendit consuetudines: uerum omnes eo spectant, ut officium suum et operam commodius aliis praestare possint: lucrum magnum ducentes, si uel rei suae damno aliis commodent.

[p.97/G1] ²⁸⁰ Nunquam his fatum expectatione maturius superuenit: tantum abest, ut huius uitae amoenitatibus capiantur, ut consuetudinis tuae desyderio incensi, inuisam hanc cupiant quam primum abrumpere lucem.

²⁸¹ Quod si nunc haec horrida crux, si tenuis dulcedinis tuae gustus sic mentes inebriat, et naturae immutat ingenium, ut crudelem uitae huius amorem in odium conuertat, quid tum fore existimandum est, cum deliciarum tuarum fluminibus inundabis?

273 These suck honey from the stone and oil from the hardest rock; joyful, they drink in waters from the wells of the saviour; they decline to admit consolation from any source but from you.

274 These decree this law of innocence for themselves – they not only desire nothing outside what is right, but even, in order to become sons like to you, with determination abstain from even the permitted supports of life, without which it is hardly maintained.

275 No misfortunes break these men, no passionate desires enervate, no pleasures dissolve, but, even in the midst of tortures, they rejoice with a kind of outpouring of happiness.

276 As often as the recollection of you comes to mind, tears become to them nectar and ambrosia, poverty is wealth, contempt is praise, life is loss, death is gain.

277 This alone do they have for their intent, this alone do they think will be found commendable in them, if, through conformity of life, they may turn out sons even in the smallest part like you.

278 Some of them lead their life in the woods, among the wildernesses of beasts, where branches yield berries and stony cornel-cherries, by way of sustenance, miserable no more, and where they support themselves on plants they root up, living in hardship and affliction in the mountains, caves and hollows of the earth, men of whom the world clearly was not worthy.

279 Some of them dwell in towns, and stoop to common customs, but all of them with the intention of being able with greater convenience to discharge their duty and service to others, considering it great profit if they may oblige others, even by material loss to themselves.

280 For these men, death never arrives sooner than expected. So far from being captivated by the delights of this life are they, that, burning with longing for companionship with you, they are eager to break off this hated life as soon as possible.

281 Therefore, if this horror-inducing cross, if a tiny taste of your sweetness now so intoxicates minds and transforms their natural character that it turns fierce love of this life into hatred of it, what must we think will happen when you flood them with the torrents of your delights?

²⁸² Haec est Christianae philosophiae uis, haec sacrae huius persuasionis potentia, quae coelesti quadam metamorphosi homines uel ante diem, pene dixerim, deos efficit.

²⁸³ I nunc tu, cui humanae sapientiae confidentia cristas tollit, qui physicam ubique rationem requiris, qui oracularis disciplinae autoritatem eleuas, et ex tua ista, si potes, philosophia eiusmodi studiorum fructus in medium affer.

²⁸⁴ Plane ne humanitus quidem sapit, qui non haec omnia diuinitus constituta uidet: et ut ratio peculiaris rerum passim in promptu non sit, certe fidei, et assensionis ratio copiosa non deest.

²⁸⁵ Quare ut illi explodant quibus tu nondum oculos aperuisti, ipse tamen Christum meum arctissime semper complectar. In te domino gaudebo, et exultabo in Deo IESV meo.

[p.99/G2] ²⁸⁶ Proinde sacra haec fidei persuasio, haec fiducia, quae bonitate tua nititur, non carnis, non nostrae industriae, aut arbitrii, sed gratiae tuae peculiare munus est.

²⁸⁷ Abscondis enim haec a sapientibus et prudentibus, qui suo ingenio metiri se posse confidunt arcanas operum tuorum rationes.

²⁸⁸ Reuelas ea paruulis, quos modestia erudiuit ad pietatem, quos salutaris animorum demissio integros, idoneosque reddit discipulos, et alumnos disciplinae tuae.

²⁸⁹ Hinc ego te, parens, per teipsum oro, atque obsecro, ut sacer tuus spiritus usque praesens sic animum meum moderetur, ne sensus mei uanitatem aliquando secutus, aliud mihi persuadeam, quam in abs te datis ecclesiae tuae oraculis continetur.

²⁹⁰ Sed quid feci parens? quorsum haec benignitatis tuae recensio, beneficiorumque catalogus? quandoquidem uel arenae maris facilius fuerit, quam meritorum tuorum numerum inire.

²⁹¹ Nunquam tu intermittis boni aliquid nobis facere: nullum momentum uacat aliquo tuo munere: etsi eius sensum grauis hic ingrati animi, curisque superuacaneis implicati, ueternus impediat.

[282] This is the strength of Christian philosophy, this the power of this holy conviction – by a sort of heavenly metamorphosis, it makes men even before their time into – I might almost say – gods.

[283] Go then, you, whose cock's comb rises out of confidence in human wisdom, who demand everywhere a physical explanation, who set on high the authority of your 'oracular' school of thought, and out of that philosophy of yours produce, if you can, that kind of fruit from your studies.

[284] Forsooth, that man does not even have sense on a human level, who does not see that all these things are constituted divinely; and, though a particular explanation of things is not everywhere obvious, a full explanation from faith and belief is not lacking.

[285] Therefore, though those people whose eyes you have not yet opened may slow-clap me off the stage, I myself shall nonetheless always embrace my Christ with all my strength. In you, Lord, I shall rejoice, and shall exult in JESUS, my God.

[286] Accordingly this holy conviction of faith, this confidence, which is based on your goodness, is the particular gift not of the flesh, not of our doing or deciding, but of your grace.

[287] For you hide these things from the clever and the wise, who are confident that by their own lights they can measure the secret reasons behind your works.

[288] You reveal those things to children, whom humility has instructed into piety, and whom a healthy lowliness of mind has rendered upright and apt disciples and pupils of your teaching.

[289] Hence, Father, I pray and beseech you by yourself, that your ever present Holy Spirit may so control my mind, that I may not, pursuing the vanity of my own understanding, convince myself of any other thing than is contained in the pronouncements given by yourself to your church.

[290] But what have I done, Father? To what end this surveying of your benignity, this listing of your beneficence, since it would perhaps have been easier to count the grains of sand in the sea, than to attempt a tally of your merits.

[291] Never do you cease from doing some good for us; no moment is without something from your provision, even if here the heavy lethargy of an ungrateful mind, trapped in unnecessary cares, obstructs awareness of it.

²⁹² Caeterum simulatque animus a corpore diuorterit, atque ad formidolosum tuum tribunal uitae, ac uillicationis rationem reddam, tum demum aperte intelligam, quanto tibi, quam mihi ipsi charior fuerim.

²⁹³ Quoties sciens, prudensque, sed male profecto prudens, ea te spectante admisi, quae mille expianda crucibus, quae praesentaneo fuerant fulmine uindicanda?

[p.101/G3] ²⁹⁴ At tu toties contemptus, toties capitaliter offensus, quoties tamen ex animo turpitudinis nos poenitet, misericordiae gremium aperis, et indulgentia plusquam patria rursus in gratiam recipis.

²⁹⁵ Nihil tibi reliquum facis ad beneficentiam: nullum unquam in te nobis commodum clauditur: at nos nec magnitudine tua deterriti, iniuriis te onerare remittimus: nec bonitatis exuberantia pellecti, officium facimus.

²⁹⁶ Quae abs te condita sunt, et quae sua natura (nisi ferrei, et omnis humanitatis expertes essemus) nos ad eum amorem, atque obseruantiam, quae frugi filios decet, exuscitant, nostra culpa abs te abducunt.

²⁹⁷ Fallacia bona pro te uero, ima pro te summo, magno maiestatis tuae contemptu, magno etiam interea nostro et damno, et dedecore nequicquam consectamur.

²⁹⁸ Sordet nobis, quod dicere nefas est, tuus CHRISTVS, uilis illius crux. Hunc Deum atque unicum, ut est, immensi orbis regem confitemur: ueritas tamen cultus illius negligitur, species duntaxat retinetur.

²⁹⁹ Extrinsecus nonnihil elucescit industria nostra in caeremoniis: sed solidae pietatis munera, ardor ille fidei atque, quae tu in primis requiris, humanitatis officia desiderantur.

³⁰⁰ A funere communia cum illo in coelo praemia expectamus, cum tamen in uita nihil sit commune, neque quicquam sit, quod tantopere refugiamus, atque eius similes fieri: tenues aut inopes uideri nos pudet, improbos non pudet.

[292] However that may be, as soon as my mind has separated from the body, and at your terrible judgement seat I shall give an account of my life and my stewardship, then I shall at last fully learn how much dearer I have been to you than to myself.

[293] How often, knowing and aware, but certainly badly aware, have I committed things in your sight which should have been expiated by a thousand crosses, and punished by an instant thunderbolt?

[294] But you, so often treated with contempt, so often offended so grievously, nonetheless, whenever we repent from our hearts of our shameful conduct, so often do you open the very bosom of mercy, and, with indulgence more than that of a father, accept us back into grace.

[295] You leave nothing out when it comes to beneficence; nothing of advantage to us is ever kept back within yourself. But neither deterred by your magnificence do we cease from loading you with injuries, nor, enticed by the exuberance of your goodness, do we do our duty.

[296] The things which you have ordained and which by their very nature – if we were not iron-hearted and devoid of all human feeling – awaken us to the love and obedience which is proper to worthwhile sons, through our own fault lead us away from you.

[297] We vainly pursue false goods instead of you the truth, the lowest things instead of you the Highest, to the great contempt of your majesty, and incidentally also to our own great damage and dishonour.

[298] Your CHRIST, wicked as it is to say so, is of no account to us and his cross worthless. We confess him to be God, and the only king, as he is, of the immense world. Yet the truth of his worship is neglected, with merely the appearance maintained.

[299] Outwardly, our busy activity shines out well in ceremonies, but the functions of genuine piety, that ardour of faith, and – what you especially ask for – the duties of humanity are wanting.

[300] After death, we look forward to rewards in common with him in heaven, though in life there is nothing in common and nothing we flee so much as becoming like to him; we are ashamed to seem lowly or poor, but not to seem wicked.

[p.103/G4] 301 Desidiae nostrae ingenii prauitatem praeteximus, uirium causamur infirmitatem, culpamque naturae sedulo assignamus: uereor ut uel hic subsistere possimus, si tu pro tuo iure nobiscum agere uelis.

302 Quotus quisque nostrum est, qui uel illud praestat, quod in naturae uiribus positum confitemur, quod a philosophis de officiis traditum est, et praeceptum: ut de absoluta pietate taceam, quam tu, etsi supra naturae uires est, nunquam tamen negas iis, qui ex animo petunt.

303 Profecto, parens, nisi essent istae bonitatis tuae diuitiae, istud nunquam non patens miserationum tuarum asylum, de nobis actum esset: una foret miseris salus, nullam usquam sperare salutem.

304 Itaque propter istas bonitatis tuae diuitias, propter acerbissimos filii tui cruciatus, quos ille nostri causa, te ita ordinante, pertulit: propter sacrosanctam eiusdem mortem, parce nequitiis nostris.

305 Parce item propter gloriam nominis tui: quod non alia magis ratione illustratur, quam cum indignis, nobisque longe diuersum meritis, parcis. Nam tu solus mundum facere potes, quod ex immundo, et uenenato conceptum est semine.

306 Opificium tuum sumus, sed quod ipsi tamen uarie deformauimus, ac dissipauimus: serui sumus, sed nequam: imo filii, sed male frugi, et degeneres, qui amplissimum a te patre acceptum patrimonium, hoc est, corporis, animique dotes, cum his barbaris scortis, hoc est, malis cupiditatibus decoximus.

[p.105/G5] 307 Miserere nostri parens: nosti ex qua simus materia compositi: nosti quid cognati suadeant affectus. Noli perdere eos, qui tanti tibi constant, et quos tanti redemeris.

308 Porro autem si quid est in omni mea uita a me gestum, quod rectum appareat, et hic quoque culpam deprecor. Quid boni fructus ex hac mala arbore enasci ualet? Si quid est, ut aegre est, tuum est, non meum: tibi illud acceptum refero.

309 Non intres in iudicium cum seruo tuo. Nemo in conspectu tuo, si tu summo iure agas, iustus inuenitur. Si coner me innocentem ostendere, os meum condemnabit me: ipse conatus culpa est ingens. Causam non dicam, tibi eam trado: quando ne coeli quidem mundi sunt coram te.

[301] We make our inborn depravity an excuse for our idleness, we plead the infirmity of our physical strength, we are quick to assign the blame to nature. I fear we might not have any ground to stand on even here, should you wish to proceed against us according to your right.

[302] How few there are of us, who achieve even what we admit to lie within our natural strengths, that is, what has been handed down and taught by philosophers concerning our duties. To say nothing of absolute devotion, which, even though it is beyond our natural powers, you nonetheless never refuse to those who seek it from their heart.

[303] Certainly, Father, were there not those riches of your goodness, that ever open sanctuary of your compassion, it would be all up with us; the one salvation for the wretched would be to hope for no salvation anywhere.

[304] And so, on account of those riches of your goodness, on account of the most bitter torments of your Son, which he according to your plan endured for our sake, on account of his most holy death, pardon our iniquities.

[305] Spare us likewise on account of the glory of your name, which is most of all made splendid when you spare the unworthy, us, that is, who deserve far different treatment. For you alone have the power to make that thing clean which was conceived from unclean and poisoned seed.

[306] We are your creation, but one, nevertheless, which we ourselves have variously deformed and ruined; we are your servants, but worthless. Rather, we are your sons, but no good and degenerate, who have squandered the most plenteous patrimony received from you, Father, which consists of the gifts of the body and mind, on these foreign whores, that is, evil desires.

[307] Have mercy upon us, Father; you know from what material we are made, you know what the passions which come with it urge us to do. Do not let those be lost who are so valuable to you, and whom you have redeemed at such a price.

[308] Furthermore, if there is anything done by me in my entire life which might appear righteous, even here too I entreat pardon for my guilt. What in the way of good fruit can be born from this bad tree? If there is anything (there hardly is), it is yours, not mine; I attribute it to you.

[309] Do not enter into judgement with your servant. No-one in your sight is found righteous, if you should employ the strictest judgement. If I should try to show myself innocent, my own mouth will condemn me: the very attempt is a huge guilt. I shall not argue the case, I transfer it to you, since in your presence not even the heavens are clean.

³¹⁰ Arcana afflatus tui opera, caecos hos affectus, malorum fontem et fomitem radicitus euelle: ea manda animi solo semina, ea insere plantaria, quae uberes uirtutum fructus, et germen oculis tuis non ingratum afferant.

³¹¹ Deturbatis hisce, quae ipse me peruerse amans, in animo meo, templo tibi debito, suppono idolis: tuum tibi locum postliminio uendica: ab ore tuo nunquam lumina deflectam: in hoc unum mentis aciem assidue intendam.

³¹² Lucis tuae usque affulgentis ope, cum praeter te nihil dulce, aut decorum sit, interuenientibus (ut solent) quas uel malus daemon, uel caro offundit nubibus, ac praestigiis, nihil praeter te dulce, aut decorum appareat.

[p.107/G6] ³¹³ Religioni habeat, dolorem accipiat animus, tanquam contaminetur, ubi senserit aliquid intra se uel fortuito irrepsisse, quod decus, aut animi magnitudinem non resipiat.

³¹⁴ Eiusmodi cogitationibus, quae ad te tum cognoscendum, tum amandum non conducunt, mens extemplo nuntium, tanquam prophanis (ut sunt) remittat: eiiciat quam primum, ac eliminet, quicquid dignitatem suam uiolare possit.

³¹⁵ Multas tu laetitiae causas mihi suppeditas, inter quas sane non postremas tenet, quod siue domi, siue foris, siue in turba, siue in solitudine agam, animus secum libere bonitatem tuam reputare potest: sic, ut nihil sit, quod nos ab eo munere fungendo impedire possit, quo nemo praestantius excogitauerit.

³¹⁶ Perit haud dubie omnis ea aetatis pars, ex uitae albo expungenda est, quae cogitationem in res humiles atque contemptas abiecit; tantisper dum nos indigna studia detinent, belluae potius sumus quam homines.

³¹⁷ Hei mihi, si ita habet, ut profecto habet: Quota mihi uitae pars periit, imo pene tota frustra consumpta est: defecerunt plane in uanitate dies mei, et anni pudendi cum festinatione.

³¹⁸ Dehinc, amabo parens, fac tu unus sis amores, tu unus ignes: Te uigilans in oculis feram: te noctis somnia referant: tu semper in ore, tu semper sis in animo.

310 Through the secret working of your inspiration, uproot these blind passions, the source and kindling material of evil. Set those seeds in the soil of the mind, plant those saplings which will produce the plentiful fruits of virtues and a growth not unpleasing to your eyes.

311 Casting down these idols which I, perversely loving myself, substitute in my mind, the temple that is rightly yours, re-assert your rights, claim your place for yourself. Let me never turn my eyes away from your face: on this one thing let me constantly turn the gaze of my mind.

312 Nothing other than you is sweet or lovely, and so, when those clouds and deceptions intervene, as they do – put in the way by an evil demon or the flesh – let it be made clear, by the power of your light, everywhere refulgent, that nothing other than you is sweet or lovely.

313 The mind should have a sense of unease, should feel pain as if contaminated when it becomes aware that something has crept into it, even by chance, which does not accord with the honour or greatness of the mind.

314 To thoughts of that kind, which lead neither to knowledge or love of you, let the mind immediately send an order to get them hence, as being sacrilegious, as indeed they are; let it cast out and eliminate as soon as possible whatever could outrage its dignity.

315 You furnish me many causes of happiness, among which certainly not in the last place is that the mind, whether I be occupied at home or out of doors, whether in a crowd or in solitude, can freely within itself consider your goodness, so that there is nothing to prevent us from performing that duty, than which no-one has thought up one more excellent.

316 Without a doubt, all that part of our existence goes to waste and needs to be wiped from the record of life, that throws away our thinking on low and contemptible subjects; for as long as unworthy pursuits detain us, we are beasts rather than men.

317 Woe is me if that is so, as assuredly it is. What a large part of life has gone to waste, rather, almost all of it has been used up in vain; clearly my days have been consumed in vanity, and years of shame, as they hurried past.

318 For this reason, I beg you, Father, make sure that you alone be my love, you alone my passion. Waking, may I have you before my eyes; may nocturnal slumbers bring you back; may you be you always in my mouth, always in my mind.

[p. 109/G7] 319 Ipse me deseram, tibi uni fidam, totus ex te pendeam, me totum ad arbitrium tuum accommodem, quando etiam si liberum foret, prouidentiae tuae casses effugere, et mihi arbitrio meo fata fingere, conscius tamen sapientiae et bonitatis tuae libens, meritissimoque me totum tibi permitterem.

320 Spes meas omnes, opesque in te collocem, me totum in contemplatione maiestatis tuae ponam: et in his IESV mei uulneribus, tanquam columba in foraminibus petrae, perpetuo delitescam.

321 Ea semper mens uotorum puritate niteat, ut tibi illic, tanquam in grato recessu, diuersari libeat: tibi, inquam, qui pascis inter lilia, cui puritas unice grata, donec aspiret dies felicitatis, et inclinentur umbrae miseriae.

322 Quemadmodum desyderat ceruus ad fontes aquarum, sic ad te aspiret anima mea: et sicut uelis passis, plenoque cursu in istum sempiternae requietis portum contendat.

323 Sint interdiu, sint item et noctu mihi lachrymae panes, dum dicitur per singulos dies animae meae, Vbi est Deus tuus? Quo abiit dilectus tuus, O pulcherrima mulierum?

324 Fastiditis hisce uulgaribus, et minutis bonis, te immensum bonum studiose exquiram. Surgam, et circuibo magnam hanc, cui tu praees, ciuitatem per uicos, perque plateas, per omne rerum genus quaeram, quem diligit anima mea. Nihil enim est, quod bonitati tuae non det testimonium.

[p. 111/G8] 325 Percontabor de ipsis uigilibus, atque excubitoribus, qui hanc ciuitatem custodiunt, a quibus naturae perfectio ociosam uacationem remouit: de hisce, quod propius te referant, solicitius quaeram, an uiderint, quem diligit anima mea: neque operam intermittam, quoad aedes tuas subeam, donec te inueniam.

326 Nonne satius est in domo Dei abiectum esse, atque imum illic tenere locum, quam hic, inter tot scelerum sordes, in peccatorum commorari tabernaculis?

327 Adeo corrupta sunt hic omnia, ut uix ad horam intemeratum conseruare liceat honestum: istic tecum non est, quod timeamus, ne in turpitudinem aliquam delabamur: quae profecto non ultima felicitatis pars est: et propter quam uel in primis hinc migrare optandum est.

[319] May I abandon myself, may I trust in you alone, may I wholly depend on you, may I conform myself entirely to your decision, since, were I free to escape from the net of your providence and order my fate according to my own decision, I would nevertheless, conscious of your wisdom and of your goodness, gladly and most deservedly surrender myself entirely to you.

[320] May I place all my hopes and prosperity in you, may I set myself entirely to contemplation of your majesty; and in these wounds of my JESUS, like a dove in the clefts of the rock, may I forever hide myself.

[321] May my mind always shine with such purity of desire, that it is your delight to lodge there, as in a welcome place of retreat – you, I say, who feed among the lilies, and to whom purity alone is pleasing – until the day of felicity breaks and the shades of misery flee away.

[322] Just as the hart pants for the springs of water, so let my soul long for you, and, as with full sails and a straight course, make for that haven of perpetual rest.

[323] By day, and again by night, may tears be my bread, when each day it is said to my soul: Where is your God; where has your beloved gone, O most beautiful of women?

[324] Scorning these common and tiny good things, may I eagerly seek out you, the immense good thing. I shall arise and go round this great city, of which you are the head; through its neighbourhoods and through its streets, through every kind of things I shall seek out him whom my soul loves. For there is nothing that does not bear witness to your goodness.

[325] I shall ask from these watchmen and sentries who guard this city, from whom their perfection of nature has withdrawn idle freedom from service. From these, because they reflect you more closely, shall I enquire with anxious care, whether they have seen him whom my soul loves. Neither shall I cease my efforts until the time that I enter your dwelling, until I find you.

[326] Is it not better to be a person of no consequence in the house of the Lord, and there to occupy the lowest place, than to dwell here in the tents of sinners, among so much squalor of sin and wickedness?

[327] Here all things are so corrupt, that hardly for an hour is it possible to keep rectitude untarnished. There, with you, there is no reason for us to fear lest we slide into any turpitude. That is certainly not the least part of felicity, and for this it should be even our primary desire to quit this place.

³²⁸ Hisce studiis assuefacta haec animula, fata tarda, et mortem ut seram increpitet: ad aduentus tui mentionem gestiat: longum uideatur hoc exilium, cuius hei mihi nimium crudeli amore tenemur.

³²⁹ Viuam ego iam non ego: quod autem nunc uiuo in carne, in fide tua CHRISTE fili Dei uiui, uiuam: qui dilexisti me: qui tradidisti temetipsum pro me. In summa, tecum uiuere amem: tecum obeam libens.

³³⁰ Tu nunc, parens, sic hisce uotis faue, et generosos hosce, qui intercurrunt, conatus sic sufficias, ut in constantem uitae rationem coalescant: meque eo tua ope perducas, quo praeclari impetus tendunt.

[p.113/H1] ³³¹ Sic animula haec, hac rerum facie sublata, in abditas illas oras animoso, fidentique cursu peruecta, in uoce laudis, et exultationis ingrediatur in locum tabernaculi admirabilis.

³³² Mors, quae dicitur, si poenam habet, maiorem commerui: atque utinam sic defunctum sit. Verum poena haec nullius morae ad gaudia perpetua transmittit: ad te parentem deducit: cuius conspectus uel mille mortibus redimendus foret.

³³³ Vel hinc legitimos a nothis dignoscere licet: Hi non solum timide, sed etiam dolenter admodum hinc abeunt, obluctantur, eiulant, tanquam magnis spoliati bonis: quae sane degeneris animi sunt documenta.

³³⁴ Contra legitimi, etsi ipsis nonnihil trepidationis et lapsuum conscientia, et naturae infirmitas incutiant: animos tamen facile recipiunt, neque grauatim discedunt: quod sciant, bonitatem tuam omnem ipsorum malitiam infinitis partibus superare.

³³⁵ Verendum sane est, ne non agnoscas, ne tanquam spurios abdices, atque exhaeredes eos, qui dum in hac uita essent, se nunquam humo tollere sint conati: nec in laudem aliquam uindicare studuerint: quorumque animos nulla unquam huius ad te reditus cura subiit.

[328] This little soul of mine, once accustomed to such yearnings, would chide fate for delaying, and death for coming too late; at the mention of your coming it would jump for joy. This exile would seem long, but, woe is me, we are actually gripped by a most cruel love of it.

[329] May I now live, but not I; the life I now live in the flesh, may I live in your faith, O CHRIST, Son of the living God, who have loved me and have given yourself for me. In sum, may I love to live with you, may I willingly die with you.

[330] Look with favour now, Father, on these prayers, and may you so fill out these noble, intermittent attempts, that they coalesce into a steady purpose of life and through your aid bring me to the place which my beautiful impulses are aiming to reach.

[331] So may my little soul, with this outward appearance of things once removed, be swept along on a bold and confident course to those hidden shores, and with a voice of praise and exultation enter into the place of the wonderful tabernacle.

[332] If what is called death involves punishment, then I have really deserved punishment, and would that that were the end of it! But this immediate punishment transports one to perpetual joys; it leads, Father, to you, and the sight of you would be worth purchasing with perhaps a thousand deaths.

[333] Perhaps this is the way one may distinguish the true-born from the illegitimate. The latter depart from here not only in fear but in great sorrow, they put up resistance, they wail as if being robbed of great benefits, all of which are signs of a not true-born mind.

[334] The true-born, on the other hand, even though consciousness of failings and the infirmity of nature may shake them not a little, they nonetheless easily recover their spirits and do not depart unwillingly, because they know that your goodness overcomes all their own wickedness to an infinite extent.

[335] It is certainly to be feared that you will not acknowledge, that you will disdain as bastards and disinherit, those who, while they were yet in this life, never tried to raise themselves from the earth, did not strive to lay claim to any praise, into whose minds there never entered any thought of this returning to you.

336 Illa ipsa mors si naturae tributum est, sine querela pendatur: et quantulacunque haec lucis usura tibi *[lucis ab autore data est, haec] lucis autori alacriter, et cum gratiarum actione restituatur.

337 O faustum, O felicem eum diem, cum ex hac turba et colluuione, ex molesto hoc carcere in nobile illud animorum concilium, et felicitatis locum proficiscar.

[p.115/H2] 338 Absistite curae degeneres, procul hinc, procul este Circea pocula, exitiosum ueternum, nempe profundam patriae obliuionem, inducentia.

339 Si oblitus fuero tui Hierusalem, obliuiscatur mei dextera mea: renuat aliunde, quam ex te, consolationem admittere anima mea: dies illi antiqui, aeternique anni animum habeant.

340 Sic uos, filiae Hierusalem, sic uos coelestes animi nunciabitis dilecto meo. Adiuro uos filiae Hierusalem, nunciate quia amore langueo.

341 Nunciate in tenebroso corporis huius gurgustio mentem esse inclusam, quae terrena haec, quibus undique septa est, fastidiat, et ardore plane non ignobili ad coelestia aspiret.

342 Cernite ut in ea studia omni cura incumbat, quae uestri ordinis propria sunt: hoc est, ut plurima praestantium rerum commentatione usque se exerceat: eisque duntaxat uotis teneatur, quae uitae commutatio perficere, non extinguere solet.

343 Cernite ut uobis, quoad per debitam diuinae prouidentiae reuerentiam licet, istam rerum puritatem et decus, quod diuina affert consuetudo, tamque puram aetatis degendae rationem potius, quam nascenteis inde delicias, etsi summae sint, inuideat.

344 Haec sunt procul dubio uerae illius uitae praeludia, quam hoc ocyus corpore laxati consequemur, quo studiosius eam, dum in uitae huius ludo, atque palaestra sumus, didicerimus, ac uelut adumbratione quadam praesumimus.

[p.117/H3] 345 Hoc celerius hic animus, corporis pondere liber, in illud beatitudinis domicilium penetrabit, quo enixius nunc, dum corpore clausus tenetur, foras eum locum uersus eminebit.

[336] If that same death is a tax due to nature, let it be paid without complaint; and however small is this enjoyment of light given you by the creator of light, let it readily be returned to the creator of light, with the giving of thanks.

[337] O how auspicious, O how happy that day, when I shall set off from this uproar and slough of filth, out of this wearisome dungeon into that noble company of souls and the place of felicity.

[338] Be gone, unworthy preoccupations, away from here, away, you cups of Circe, inducing pernicious torpor and profound forgetting of our fatherland.

[339] If I forget you, Jerusalem, may my right hand forget me; may my soul refuse to admit consolation from anywhere but from you; may those days of old fill my mind and the years of ancient times.

[340] This, daughters of Jerusalem, this, heavenly spirits, will you tell to my beloved: I adjure you, daughters of Jerusalem, cry out, that I am weak with love.

[341] Tell that a mind is shut away in the gloomy hovel of this body, which disdains these earthly things with which it is hedged about, and with an ardour clearly not ignoble aspires to heavenly things.

[342] Observe how it devotes all its energies to those concerns which are proper to your rank: that is, how it exercises itself continually with many a meditation upon excellent things, and is in short held by those aspirations which exchange of life is wont to fulfil and not extinguish.

[343] See how, insofar as is allowed by the reverence owed to divine providence, the mind envies you that purity in daily life and the grace which constant association with the divine brings, envies you such a pure way of spending your life, rather than envying you the delights deriving therefrom, though they may be of the highest.

[344] These are without doubt the preludes to that true life, which we will acquire all the more quickly once loosed from this body, the more eagerly we have learned it in the school and exercise ground of this life and foreshadow in some sort of vague outline.

[345] This mind, free of the dead weight of the body, will the more quickly enter into that home of bliss, the more strenuously now, while held shut in by the body, it will reach out beyond it towards that place.

[346] Hanc facultatem si dabis: haec, coelestis parens, si exorauero (quidni exorem eiusmodi res a te optimo parente, per filium tuum petens, atque obsecrans?) quod a me requiris, utcunque praestabo.

[347] Perenni mentis studio in te, unde prodii, remigrabo. Spectator ero in hoc tuo theatro, etsi non tam, quam debeo, gratus: minus tamen quam soleo ingratus Antistes, itemque utcunque pius.

[348] Eam hic in terris transformationem incipiam, imo ipse in me incipies, quam pro sola tua bonitate istic in coelo feliciter absolues.

[349] Verum tantisper dum hic ago, in templi dumtaxat uestibulo uersor: procul a tuo conspectu, procul a maiestatis tuae adyto positus.

[350] At olim istic tecum in penitissimo diuinitatis tuae sacrario numen tuum coram contuens, canticum gloriae, carmen laudum, Misericordias domini inaeternum cantabo.

FINIS.

[346] If you enable me to do this, heavenly Father, if my prayers are answered – and why should I not win things like this from you, best of fathers, when I beg and beseech through your Son? – then what you require of me, I shall perform as best I can.

[347] By perpetual application of the mind, I shall return to you, from whom I came forth. I shall be a spectator in this your theatre, even if not so acceptable as I ought to be; yet less unacceptable than I usually am, a priest, and one faithful as best he can be.

[348] Here on earth I shall begin that transformation – or rather, you yourself will begin it within me – which, simply through your goodness, there in heaven you will successfully bring to completion.

[349] Truly, as long as I here live, I busy myself at least in the forecourt of the temple, set far from sight of you, situated far from the very shrine of your majesty.

[350] But one day there with you, in the inmost sanctuary of your divinity, contemplating your Godhead in your very presence, I shall sing a song of glory, a song of praise, and the mercies of the Lord forever.

FINIS

CRITICISM

1. The *Commentatio* as literature

It is easy to accept the description of the *Commentatio* as 'a remarkable work' (Baker-Smith 1996: 8), though less easy to determine just what makes it so, since any such attempt involves a consideration of content, genre, form and style, as well as a search for a potential literary model. However, the *Commentatio* is certainly remarkable by virtue of being unlike the other writings of Volusenus. It is not exegetical in method, as were his expositions of psalms and the commentary on the *Somnium Scipionis*; its structure is not determined by that of any prior text; it lacks any pedagogical purpose, like that of his epitome of Latin grammar; it is no philosophical dialogue in the manner of the *De animi tranquillitate* and, unlike the latter, contains no autobiographical detail; even its rather ostentatious Latin style sets it apart. The very form of the title is of interest: whereas the text proper begins under the header '*Commentatio theologica*' [Religious meditation], the 1539 title page inserts between these words a '*quaedam*' – making it into 'A kind of religious meditation' – before continuing '*quae eadem precatio est, de industria tanquam in aphorismos dissecta: lectori, praesertim erudito et pio, multum sane placitura*' [which at the same time is a prayer, purposely cut down into aphorisms – indeed most pleasing, especially to the learned and pious reader]. It would seem that Volusenus is fully aware that he is embarking upon a new genre, wherein the aphorisms comprise the distinctive feature.

Critics have found considerable difficulty in assessing the nature of the *Commentatio*. It has been called a 'petit livre mystique' (Buisson 1892: I.36), and, more prosaically, a 'rendering of passages of Scripture into prayers' (Cadell and Cherry 1983: 27). Baker-Smith offers several labels: 'this unusual work' (1969: 289); a 'handbook of suggestive materials' for meditation (1969: 290); a 'devotional manual' and a 'sequence of prayers' (2006: 101); negatively, he has characterised it as 'not a schematic work like Ignatius of Loyola's *Spiritual Exercises*' (1984: 91). Underlying these descriptions is the idea that, in the case of this work, the medium is in very large part the message. Accordingly, the most satisfactory label is perhaps that of '*theologia rhetorica*', which is said to have been 'a feature of humanistic activity since Petrarch, adapting the classical arts of persuasion to the urgent needs of a church in decline' (Baker-Smith 1991: 192).

In simple and purely formal terms, the *Commentatio* consists of 350 brief paragraphs. Normally between two and eight lines in length (in the format of the original print), these are often not discursive but exclamatory in nature, and many are only loosely connected with those immediately around them. Indeed, the frequent changing of topic and authorial voice is a salient rhetorical feature of the work, and it is notable that only at a very few places does a sentence continue grammatically from one aphorism into the one following (§§12–13, 74–5, 199–200). This is doubtless the result of the 'dissection' announced on the title page – though whether that image need imply that the meditation began as a unified prose work only subsequently to be chopped into individual fragments is doubtful. The aphorisms, as already discussed in the Introduction, seem rather to have been composed, collected and arranged during the time spent by Volusenus at Carpentras. Responsibility for the appearance of the published collection is assigned to the prompting of a group of friends, an account of origins attractive in its apparent straightforwardness; however, as an editorial strategy, it also serves to free the author from any possible charge of immodesty, in bringing into the public sphere material that might be deemed excessively personal. Indeed, the effect of the stream of aphorisms, which dispenses with any obvious logical organisation in favour of an accumulation of ostensibly spontaneous thoughts, inevitably creates a sense of immediacy and thereby adds to the personal character of the work. The resulting impression of rhetorical fragmentation has caused the *Commentatio* to be summed up as a 'scriptural mosaic in a classical idiom' (Baker-Smith 1969: 293–4).

The very use of the term 'aphorism' is itself not without interest. In some other contexts, it would denote the pithy statement of a principle or precept in any science – as with the famous medical aphorisms of Hippocrates. Alternatively, it might be applied to an anthology of short and lapidary extracts from some larger source-work or from the writings of some figure of authority – as, for example, the *Sententiae aliquot velut Aphorismi, ex omnibus Augustini ac aliorum libris* [*Some wise sayings or aphorisms from all the books of Augustine and others*] of Prosper of Aquitaine (fifth century), a theological collection published by Gryphius in the same year (1539) as the *Commentatio*. However, neither of these prestigious collections is 'through-composed', in the sense of being structured as an organic whole with a pre-conceived internal dynamic; instead, the arrangement of material is that imposed by an editor. A parallel of later days would be the *Pensées* of Pascal, where the end-result cannot be assumed to reflect the author's own design. On the other hand, there are also some literary works in which the author has chosen to present his material in a sequence of short passages; such is the case, for example, with the visions of Paradise in the *Centuries of Meditations* of Thomas Traherne, which give the impression of a series of emotional, and even ecstatic, reactions to the visualisation of what can hardly be grasped by the normal operations of the intellect.

One text that – in terms of both content and form – was available to serve as a model for Volusenus is the *Oratio de hominis dignitate* of Giovanni Pico della Mirandola (1463–94). This celebrated document, formed of 268 aphorisms, was composed in 1486 and printed in the following decade. Early in the sixteenth century there were printings in Italy, France, Germany and Switzerland

(Pico 2012: 6, 45–54) and from any of these the humanist Volusenus could have encountered the work. The very possibility thereof should not surprise, since an acquaintance with Pico is already manifested in the 1535 *Scholia*, in a reference (sig. Eiv) to the Italian's '*Disputatio adversus astrologos*' [*Argument against the astrologers*]. Volusenus, moreover, was not the only Scottish scholar familiar with Pico's works. John Mair inserted a eulogistic reference to Pico in the preface to the fourth book (1509) of his own *Commentaries* on the *Sententiae* of Peter Lombard (Lubac 1974: 25, 40). These commentaries of Mair were printed by Giovanni Ferrerio in 1541, when the latter for a few years was back in Paris from the abbey of Kinloss: that was in Ferrerio's edition of Pico's *De animae immortalitate* [*On the immortality of the soul*], which itself deals with the third book *De Anima* of Aristotle. Also relevant is that, in his own *Auditum visu praestare* [*Seeing surpassing hearing*] (Paris, 1539: fol. 21), a volume dedicated to Abbot Reid, Ferrerio quotes a passage from Nemesius of Emesa (fourth century), a writer with roots in Hermeticism and who was of real interest to Pico. Giorgio Valla's Latin translation of this early Christian philosopher was printed at Lyon by Gryphius in 1538, and Volusenus, who is known to have acted as corrector for the publisher, may in that capacity have encountered this very edition, and it may be noted that Baker-Smith (1969: 282) detected in one aphorism (§158) of the *Commentatio* an influence from Nemesius. Given the general contemporary context of humanism, and in particular the aphoristic method shared by the *Commentatio* of Volusenus and the *Oratio* of Pico, the hypothesis that the Scot could have chosen to follow the example set by the Italian's famous text seems altogether reasonable. Indeed, early sixteenth-century Scottish interest in Florentine humanism extended beyond only Pico: Hector Boece's personal copy (c.1494) of Ficino's *De triplici vita* is still preserved at Aberdeen, where the very architectural arrangements of King's College have been shown to be indebted to the astrological and medical principles informing this latter work (Stevenson and Davidson 2009: 17–26).

Other features of the *Commentatio* that reflect the influence of humanism include the following: (1) the reliance upon, and continual quotation of, biblical and Classical source-texts; (2) the evident care taken over the Latin prose style; (3) the use of Classical terms for Christian reference (Lucifer §2; Olympus §§12, 56; Amphitrite §70; Tartareus §§71, 76); (4) the visual effect of words printed in Greek letters; (5) the enthusiasm for rare and/or Greek-based vocabulary (*coryphaeus* §31; *epithalamio* §131; *nauarchus* §139; *monogrammon* §140; *hypostaseos* §147; *syngrapha* §197; *metamorphosi* §282).

Although such aspects are exhibited by both the *Commentatio* and the *Oratio*, the two texts also show significant differences of inspiration and function. On the one hand, the *Oratio* was intended to serve as an introduction to the public defence of Pico's 900 philosophical *Conclusiones* (the planned event was ultimately prevented by Innocent VIII). The *Oratio* is manifestly the work of a young and intrepid scholar, keen to demonstrate his learning by parading the host of authorities whose works he has mastered: he looks forward 'non sine magna voluptate' [not without great enthusiasm] to his anticipated encounter with the scholarly establishment of the day, and he even boasts (OHD §266) of being able to divide each one of his theses into at least 600 subsections. On the other hand, the Commentatio, which has been described as 'certainly [Volusenus's] most ambitious piece of Latinity' (Baker-Smith 1969: 50), is more modest. In it, not a single authority, whether ancient or modern, is identified by name, and neither is the title of any religious, philosophical or literary work (biblical allusions are indicated merely by means of quotation marks in the margin). While Pico's references to God arise in the context of the exposition of his philosophical tenets, Volusenus engages with God not through logical argument but through direct speech. The effect of this approach is to create the illusion that the reader has been given privileged access to the private thoughts of Volusenus. Despite this, however, the Scot's real purpose is in reality to provide articulated thoughts that an imagined potential reader can adopt and employ in his own meditations. For Pico, the term 'oratio' connotes formal and public speech; for Volusenus, as the prefatory letter to the Commentatio makes explicit, it has rather the sense of prayer ('quae eadem precatio est'). Whereas the Italian anticipates a great and splendid audience, the Scot aims at the individual reader learned and pious ('erudito et pio'). Nonetheless, to the extent that the work of Volusenus may be described as prayer, it is prayer of a kind in which praise and oblation is more in evidence than imploration, and in which humility before God does not necessarily correlate with simplicity of rhetorical style in the expression of that humility.

Jakob Burckhardt, in his landmark The Civilization of the Renaissance in Italy (1860), viewed Pico's Oratio de hominis dignitate as heralding the concept of 'Renaissance man' (Burckhardt 1995: 128, 231). In more recent times, the over-secularising tendency lurking in this concept has been qualified and diminished (Pico 2012: 52–65). Despite this, the topic of the dignity of man remains highly important for both the Italian and the Scot, even if in the Commentatio such dignity tends to be defined negatively, in terms of what is unworthy of mankind. It is namely that which distinguishes man from things inanimate and from the beasts (§266), and equally it is what distinguishes man from God (§305). The concerns of ordinary human life (§5) are perceived as unworthy (§316) to the extent that they lead the mind away from thoughts of God, and, for Volusenus, they detract from the true dignity of humanity, which, founded on religion, is properly directed towards salvation. Whereas in the Oratio Pico's intention is to make a case for the reconciliation of pagan and ancient philosophy on the one hand and the truths of Christianity on the other, Volusenus focuses on reminding man that, for all his fallible humanity, he yet possesses a gift of rationality that is capable of leading him away from sin and in the direction of God.

The clue to Volusenus's purpose lies in the root-word of his title: *mens* [mind]. Dictionaries offer more than one meaning for the term '*commentatio*' – for example, a serious meditation, or a preparation for something significant. To Cicero, *commentatio* could signify a preparation for death: '*Tota enim philosophorum vita, ut ait idem, commentatio mortis est*' [For the entire life of philosophers, as [Plato] says, is a preparation for death] (*Tusculan Disputations*, I.xxx.74). In very similar words, this is echoed by Volusenus's contemporary – and successor at Carpentras – Claude Baduel, who very boldly opens his *De morte Christi meditanda ac contemplanda oratio* [*Discourse for meditation and contemplation on the death of Christ*] (Lyon, 1543: 7) with the name of Socrates. For Volusenus, philosophical enquiry takes the form of a staged progression from an initial call to the soul, to a consideration of man and his position within the great scheme of creation, and thence on to visions of *post-mortem* blessedness. Such a mental and spiritual journey underlies the series of often lyrical outbursts uttered by the speaker-persona in the *Commentatio*.

In the *De animi tranquillitate*, the equivalent progression is indicated more straightforwardly via the dream-narrative of a progress from the temple of Democritus (pagan philosophical reasoning) to that of St Paul (Christianity). The narrative element herein is reminiscent of that found in much medieval allegorical literature, where the ethical or religious argument proceeds via a significant series of symbolic locations. Among the many vernacular specimens employing this technique – and that may be presumed to have been familiar to Volusenus – are Chaucer's *House of Fame* and *Parliament of Fowls*, and, in Older Scots literature, the *Kingis Quair* attributed to James I, and the *Palice of Honour* of Gavin Douglas (MacDonald 2009b).

In as much as the *Commentatio* partakes of the nature of prayer, most of the aphorisms, naturally, are addressed directly to God: however, some 14 are addressed to the soul, five to Jesus, and four to man in general. In addition, more than 100 do not consist of prayer at all, but have other functions – for example, scene-setting (§§2, 3), accounts of heaven and its inhabitants (§§21, 67), echoes of the Bible (§§33, 62, 129, 323), meditations on felicity (§§331, 337, 345), deplorations of human fallibility, inadequacy or sin (§§47, 81, 198, 213, 268), laudatory and discursive accounts of the nature and properties of God (§§64, 131, 132), praise of creation (§§138, 158, 175), self-reflexive ruminations by the author (§§98, 99, 110), approving comments on the man of virtue (§§123, 278). This variety of rhetoric and topic, already noted as perhaps the most conspicuous property of the *Commentatio*, nonetheless leaves almost no room for petition and injunction, elements typically and fundamentally present in prayer: instead, the emphasis is on declaration, descriptive statement, and rhapsodic comment.

Particularly striking is the fluctuation in pronoun forms between the grammatical first-person singular (one third of the total number of aphorisms) and the plural (one quarter). The work opens (§§1–8) and ends (§§346–50) with an individual speaking voice, and such aphorisms occur throughout. These are most commonly found individually, but there are also places where the singular reference (I/me/my) may continue through concatenations (for example: §§108–11, 171–8, 243–5, 317–23); such self-referencing is characteristic of an ego-document. Yet there are almost as many aphorisms where a more generalising first-person plural subject (we/us/our) is encountered, be that in single aphorisms or in linked groups (for example: §§82–8, 294–307). Though the inconsistency in pronoun use might have been supposed awkward, there is in fact little sense of jarring contradiction, since the voice of the individual speaking persona readily modulates into that of the spiritual leader of, and spokesman for, a wider audience. As a result, the reader of the *Commentatio* is not so much cast into the role of eavesdropper on the author's exclamations and adhortations, but is rather enabled to voice his own thoughts via the words provided by the author. Thereby, as it were, the reader 'becomes' the speaker, and thereby the virtual associate of all other reader-speakers; in this way Volusenus's *theologia rhetorica* works to draw the reader into an identification with an unknown number of voices participating in a collective address to God.

The *Commentatio* exhibits strikingly little affinity with most late-medieval and early modern religious literature in the vernacular. It eschews such tried and trusty literary modes as allegory, narrative, sermonising and moral didacticism; neither can it be said to comprise a spiritual exercise. It makes no use of any available enumerative and/or mnemonic technique, nor does it amount to a course of meditations, which, for example, might have been built up of logically demarcated sections within a hebdomadal framework (as in the *Contemplacioun of Synnaris* (c.1494) of William Touris). The coherence of the *Commentatio* is more subtle and tonal than any resulting from such obvious and/or robustly structured organisational procedures. Although, as a consequence, the overall progress of thought in the work is difficult to track in relation to specific aphorisms, it can be argued that it is this very imprecision that constitutes the distinctive feature (and perhaps the strongest literary attraction) of the *Commentatio*.

At the beginning, middle and end, there occurs the image of heaven and earth as a great temple, in which the speaker-persona is called to be the *Antistes*, or chief priest (§§3, 154, 347), whereby the speaker is summoned to the divine service of God and is given licence to address him directly (cf. 1 Samuel 3:1–10). The connotations of this multivalent temple image extend to the following: the imperfect Church of the day (§299); the protective abode of the Christian (§349); the human mind (§314); the physical temple in Jerusalem (§4); the conception of the universe as one vast edifice (§154); the house of God (§325); the location of felicity (§327). In addition, the associated term '*theatre*' is at two places (§§154, 347) used to express the same idea of a great and perfectly ordered physical structure. This image, moreover, links earth and heaven (cf. Psalm 83/84), since the life of the virtuous man is seen as a period of waiting in the temple forecourt (§349), before finally being admitted into the proximity of God.

When all the foregoing is taken into account, it leads to the perception that the most convincing genre-model for the *Commentatio* is not one derived either from the Classics or from medieval literature, but is rather one provided by the biblical psalms. As a later chapter will show, psalms predominate among the sources (whether biblical, Classical or medieval) upon which Volusenus draws. It is moreover just what one might expect from a scholar whose earliest publications consisted of interpretative *enarrationes* of psalms, following the example of Erasmus and Sadoleto and the many other humanist scholars dedicated to elucidating the meaning of Scripture via the assiduous study of Latin, Greek and Hebrew. It might almost be claimed that in the *Commentatio* Volusenus has composed a psalm-like text suited to his own day.

For the psalm genre within the original, purely Hebrew context the reader may be referred to studies by Alter (1985) and Mowinckel (2004) among others. Characteristic psalm features reflected in the *Commentatio* include the following: changes in the speaking voice (between singular or plural); switches of allocution (as between God, man, the world, the self, the soul); variation of style and mode (praise, worship, prophecy, devotion, confession, objurgation, narrative). Longer psalms may well display combinations of such features (e.g. Ps 61/62, which displays a wide variety of rhetorical method, and Ps 90/91, where it is sometimes not immediately clear just who is speaking to whom), but even shorter ones are not immune (e.g. Ps 22/23, which shows the irruption of second-person address into what otherwise is couched in the third- or first-person form). In addition, the final verse of many a psalm carries the reader back to the respective opening lines (e.g., Pss 60/61, 69/70, 102/103), and the temple image that opens and closes the *Commentatio* may be inspired by this practice.

While the knotty Latin prose of Volusenus is obviously uninfluenced by the pairing of internally balanced verses that is so fundamental in the prosodic structure of Hebrew verse, several of the larger-scale rhetorical habits of the psalmist have nonetheless made a mark upon the *Commentatio*, especially where there is direct address to God in tones full of urgency but devoid of presumption. This is seen in those aphorisms where Volusenus might naively be thought to be reminding God of his greatness, and of what he in the past has done, and will yet do, for the benefit of man. Similar also would be the case where (§§ 255–61) Volusenus superficially appears to offer God a supererogatory explanation of the Incarnation and Passion. At such places, it is clear that the speaking voice is best understood not as that of Volusenus the individual, but rather as that of the envisaged erudite and pious reader, who in his own affirmations will use the words provided in a quasi-credal act of self-instruction. In this way, author-focused subjectivity, which is a typical and prominent feature of much lyrical poetry, gives ground to a de-individualised and generalised style of utterance, suited to the rhetorical consensus with which the reader will voluntarily self-associate. The speaker-persona of the *Commentatio* is therefore not so much like a figure from the Old Testament — who at moments may be variously monitory, minatory, paraenetic, prophetic or didactic — but becomes rather the representative and evangelical voice of a Christian Everyman. The merit of the aphorisms of Volusenus, when viewed within a literary-historical perspective, is that they steer clear of the cramped and technical diction typical of scholasticism as well as of the elaborated structures of late-medieval devotional exercises: instead, they evince a novel style of eloquent, affirmative, at places almost ecstatic, psalm-like, prayerful oblation. For such a work of literature the label *theologia rhetorica* is appropriate, and it is also not entirely surprising that in relation to Volusenus the word 'mystical' has occasionally been used (de Groër 1995: 24–6). As an articulation of Christian faith, the *Commentatio* is indeed remarkable — a new style of rhetoric, peculiarly suited to a new age of contested doctrine and cultural change.

II. Volusenus and Latinity

A. FIRST IMPRESSIONS

This chapter discusses the characteristics of Volusenus's use of Latin and considers his success therein; in passing, a brief sketch is given of the development of the literary language from Classical times to the Renaissance, since such a perspective is essential in any appraisal of the author as a Latin stylist.

Volusenus was a Latin tutor and schoolmaster for most of his life and, as such, has a complete mastery of Classical Latin syntax, idiom and vocabulary, which he delights to deploy for his contemporaries' and our admiration. No problems for him with the intricacies of the modal force of the subjunctive forms of verbs in main and subordinate clauses (voluntative, potential, deliberative, concessive, subordinating). He can confidently wield the gerundive of attraction and deploy all the case uses of nouns (such, for example, as the predicative dative and the genitive of 'price'). To give some samples: §258, *'retundenda erat nostra arrogantia'* [our arrogance had to be beaten down]; §267, *'sit argumento locupleti'* [let that be [for] a convincing piece of evidence]; §94, *'non esse praestando'* [not to be [able] for performing]; §307, *'quos tanti redemeris'* [whom you have redeemed at such a price]; also that rather esoteric construction employing *'iri'* (impersonal passive infinitive of *ire* [to go]), together with the accusative case of the supine, actually a fourth declension verbal noun (as Volusenus would know), to express future passive concepts in reported speech: §198, *'eam rescitum iri credit'* [believes it will be found out]; also §238.

In fact, he seems so inordinately fond of using the supine in various cases, compared with its frequency on a page of Classical Latin, and of fourth declension nouns in general, that it draws the reader's attention and seems an idiosyncrasy of his personal style. See for a particularly striking example, §30, *'uno eodemque obtutu* [ablative] ... *quicquid angusti temporis fluxus* [nominative] *separatim edit et tamquam in transcursu* [ablative] ... *contuetur'* [in one and the same present view ... whatever the flux of brief time brings forth separately and observes as it passes ...]. All this is the kind of material that can be found in a comprehensive Classical Latin grammar – Volusenus wrote a simple one for students – but expertise in it needs, as ever, to be honed by the reading of Latin texts and, above all, by writing in Latin. Volusenus also casually throws in many an idiomatic phrase which he would have assimilated from consulting the Latin dictionaries being produced at the time, if he needed to. Some examples: §8, *'qua datur'* [as far as possible]; §196, *'quoad eius fieri potest'* [as far as is possible]; §40, *'in causa esse'* [to be responsible for]; §75, *'eousque'* [to such an extent]; §164, *'pili non facere'* [care not a whit]; §51, *'tui copia'* [access to your presence]; §237, *'pene dixerim'* [I might almost say]; §188, *'ut semel dicam'* [to say it once for all]; §117, *'ne multa'* [to say no more, to cut it short]; §63, *'tua solius virtus est'* [virtue is yours alone].

The most obvious and superficial element in a language is the store of words, the vocabulary. The fanatical 'Ciceronian' in Erasmus's 1528 dialogue of that name on 'the ideal Latin style' (see below) boasts that he is very selective in his reading 'in case some alien phrase attach itself from somewhere or other and besmirch the pure sheen of my Ciceronian diction' (Erasmus 1986: 346). Volusenus, by contrast, collects from his reading and relishes the introduction of words of all kinds: Early Latin words, e.g., from the dramatists; 'Silver' Latin words, i.e., from the century after Cicero; Late Latin words, i.e., second century and later (e.g., from Apuleius, the much-admired third-century purveyor of extravagant performance oratory); poetic words; words belonging to specialised contexts; and words Classical but rare. The following list will give some idea of this range, but does not claim to be exhaustive:

§12, *'exsuperantissimus'* [surpassing] (Apuleius, *De mundo* 27.3); §35, *'penitissimus'* [deepest] (Plautus, *Cistellaria* 63; Aulus Gellius, *Noctes Atticae* 9.4.6.2; Apuleius, *De Deo Socratis* 16.26; Varro, *Menippeae* 522.2); §29, *'vilicatio'* [function of farm overseer] (Columella, *De re rustica* 11.1.13.2; Petronius, *Satyrica* 69.3.4); §16, *'ignoscentissime'* [most forgiving] (not cited at all); §292, *'praesentaneo'* [instant] (Silver Latin); §291, *'veternus'* [lethargy] (poetic and Silver Latin); §21, *'helluo'* [glutton] and §341, *'gurgustium'* [hovel] ('vulgar' words from a different and/or inappropriate register); §260, *'vastitas'* [frightening immensity] (Silver Latin); §175, *'tesqua'* [waste land] (a very specialised word belonging to the priestly language of the augurs); §161, *'insensilis'* [non-sentient] (Lucretius only, *De rerum natura* 2.866, 870, 888); also a number of words borrowed from Greek or invented by Cicero for use in a specialised philosophical context, which supply Volusenus with useful vocabulary: §140, *'monogrammon'* [sketched out]; §249, *insipientia* [lack of wisdom]; §149, *'innumerabilitas'* [innumerability, number beyond counting]. There are also a few Greek words in Greek script, e.g., §165.

To add to the mix, we find a sprinkling of archaisms and older forms, both in spelling and word formation: §40, *'tuapte'* (mostly early Latin), emphatic form of *'tua'* [your]; likewise, §§46, 330, *'hisce'*, *'hosce'*, for *'hi'*, *'hos'* [these]; §134, *'ne hilum'* [not a whit] for *'nihil'* [nothing]; §11, *'queis(cum)'*, old ablative plural of *'qui'* [who] (relative pronoun), later *'quibus(cum)'*.

B. THE RISE OF CHRISTIAN LATIN

Volusenus, as a Christian author writing on a Christian topic, is the inheritor of the many adjustments made by Latin in its response to the new religion. The Gospel, of course, was first preached among people who spoke Greek, either as a first or second language, together with Aramaic or Syriac or one of the local languages of Asia Minor. This Koiné (common) Greek was a useful work-a-day language throughout the eastern Roman empire, and it was far from the refinements of the Classical Attic of the fifth to fourth centuries BC. Both the morphology and syntax had been simplified and the linguistic resources reduced, e.g., by the loss of the optative mood and the dual number, by much simplification in the conjugation of verbs, and by the preference for parataxis over subordination in sentence structure.

Any social group linked by special interests will develop its own terminology to express its common concerns where the existing language does not provide this, and these specialised terms may not be understood by those outside the group. Thus the new Christian faith brought a multitude of new and startling ideas, e.g., salvation, redemption, remission of sins, grace, resurrection, eternal life, for ever, faith in Christ, saints (i.e., Christian believers). For most of these, the existing Koiné Greek had no ready means of expression, albeit that the Christian communities could build on the language used in the third century BC Greek translation of the Hebrew scriptures, the Septuagint, especially the Psalms. There they would find, for example, the fundamental words εὐαγγελίον [evangel] and εὐαγγελιζέσθαι [bring good tidings, evangelise], also τό πνεῦμα τό ἅγιον [the Holy Spirit]. The preaching of Christ's followers presupposes an already developed Christian linguistic resource, to which the sermons of St Paul would have contributed; the same goes for the liturgy, with its 'psalms and hymns and spiritual songs' (Col 3:16) and with its own characteristic usages. The Gospels and other writings that were later incorporated into the canon of the New Testament were likewise written in Koiné Greek during the later first century AD, and the second century saw the start of the long series of works giving instruction about Christianity, defending it, or opposing heresy (e.g., Clement of Alexandria, c.150–215 AD).

The extension of Christianity to the western Roman Empire followed similar lines. There too the first Christian converts were speakers of Greek, and, as speakers of Latin were converted, it again became necessary to develop linguistic resources to express Christian ideas and beliefs. One method was simply to borrow the established Greek words and adapt them to Latin morphology, e.g., *ecclesia, apostolus, baptismus/baptismum, evangelium*, or to translate literally, using existing Latin words and adding to them a new layer of meaning: *Spiritus Sanctus* (ἅγιον πνεῦμα) [Holy Spirit]; *sancti* (ἅγιοι) [Christian saints, i.e., believers]; *fidelis* (πιστός) [believer]; *gratia* (χάρις) [grace]; *Servator* (Σωτήρ) [Saviour]; *salus* (σωτηρία) [salvation]; or to invent new words: *repaenitere* (not *paenitere*) (μετανοεῖν) [repent]. These were often formed on the basis of common Latin word types: *salvatio* [salvation], together with *Salvator* [Saviour], partially replacing *Servator*, and new first conjugation verbs, such as *salvare* [to save] and *praedestinare* [to predestinate]. Some new concepts required the development of new grammatical usages: *credere in*, followed by accusative case [to believe in, e.g., God], whereas in the general language *credere* governed the dative case and meant 'believe someone's statements'; *bene dicere* (two words), followed by the dative case, generally meant 'speak kindly to' or 'commend'; now as one word with the accusative case, it meant 'bless', and brought in its train *benedictus* [blessed] and *benedictio* [blessing].

By the late second century there were enough monolingual Latin-speaking Christians to make a translation of the Greek Bible into Latin necessary. The so-called 'Septuagint' version had often been crudely translated word for word, no doubt out of fear of tampering with the holy text, and many Hebrew lexical, syntactic and stylistic features had been imported as neologisms. This Greek version of the Old Testament scriptures was translated into various regional Latin versions, some of which became established and authoritative (e.g., the versions from Italy and the Roman provinces of southern Gaul and Africa). Once again, the base text was translated literally, with Hebrew features being imported into Christian Latin, for example: *caeli* [heavens], plural, a Hebrew cosmological concept (e.g., Ps 8:2, '*posuisti gloriam tuam super caelos*' [Thou has set thy glory above the heavens]); *confiteor* with dative case, meaning both 'confess (sins)' and 'offer praise (to God)', translating a Hebrew word expressing both these concepts (e.g., Ps 105/106:1, '*confitemini Domino quoniam bonus*' [O give thanks to the Lord for he is good]); the preposition *in* with the ablative case to express 'instrument' or 'with', in Classical Latin ablative alone (e.g., Ps 91/92:5, '*laetificasti me ... in opere tuo*' [Thou hast made me glad through thy works]); phrases such as *rex gloriae* [king of glory, glorious king] (Ps 23/24:7), *sapientiae verba* [words of wisdom, wise words] (I Cor 2:4), the genitive case being used to express the Hebrew mechanism for expressing attributive concepts, there being no 'adjective' as such; and a new vocative form '*domine deus meus*' [O Lord, my God], to render the Hebrew form of address to God in the Psalms. (There was no vocative singular form of *deus* in Classical Latin.) Further examples of ultimately Hebrew stylistic features are: the antiphonal structure of the verses of the Psalms; the use of repetition for emphasis, e.g., Ps 39/40:1, '*expectans expectavi*' [I waited and waited] (compare with the Authorised Version, 'I waited patiently'); a simple narrative style with parataxis rather than subordination (e.g., the Vulgate's rendering of I *Sam* 17). Similarly, in the translation of the New Testament, certain linguistic features reproduce those peculiar to the Koiné Greek basic text, such as the frequent use of participles – in practice, this meant the present participle, as Latin does not have the same range of participles as Greek; e.g., Luke 8:25, '*qui timentes mirati sunt dicentes ad invicem*' [and they being afraid, wondered, saying to one another]; or Mark 12:31, '*maius horum*' [greater than these], where the genitive case is used to express comparison, not (as in Latin) ablative.

The first translators of the Bible into Latin were not scholars but unknown individuals in various places who, in the second century, felt competent enough to embark on this project. (cf. Augustine, *De doctrina christiana* 2.11,13; for his part, Jerome complained of the inaccuracy of these multiple versions:

'*Praefatio in libro Iosue* ...'). Spoken Latin, like Greek, had by this time developed many features in the way of simplification and regularisation, and this made translation by bi-lingual speakers much easier. As ordinary people, the latter naturally translated into artless everyday Latin, adding a layer of 'popular' features to the biblical text. The following are some examples:

> (a) *ille* or *ipse* for the weaker *is* [he], used both as pronoun and as subject of a verb, e.g., Luke 4:14–15, '*fama exit ... de illo et ipse docebat...*' [there went out a fame of him and he taught ...]; (b) *credo quia potest* [I believe that he can], instead of the cumbersome accusative with infinitive construction of Classical Latin, though this is found too; (c) *dixit* followed by the actual words, e.g., Luke 7:43, '*respondens Simon dixit, aestimo quia is ...*' [replying, Simon said, I think that the one ...]; (d) *quoniam* [since], with indicative, instead of *cum* with subjunctive; (e) *ne* with present subjunctive to express negative commands, e.g., Ps 68/69:18, '*ne abscondas faciem tuam*' [Hide not your face], instead of the formal *noli/nolite* with infinitive; (f) *facere* with infinitive, 'make (somebody) do something', e.g., Luke 9:14, '*facite illos discumbere*' [make them sit down]; (g) infinitive used to express purpose, e.g., Matt 10:35, '*veni separare*' [I am come to set at variance].

Again, this is only a sample list. The developing Christian speech played its part and, in turn, the biblical text, as it became more familiar, affected Christian language. The cumulative effect of all this was found distasteful by educated pagans. St Augustine (*Confessiones* 3.9) tells how, in his youth, when he was still aiming at a career as a rhetorician, he had to force himself to read this unsophisticated stuff, so inferior to Cicero. Nonetheless, as time went on, familiarity with it had made it generally acceptable; indeed, it became sanctified, and when Jerome revised the errors in the Latin versions of the Bible in the fourth century, he had to leave much stylistically unchanged, especially in the version of the Psalms.

At the same time as the first Latin translations of the Bible were being made, i.e., late second century, educated Christians began to write in defence and justification of the Christian faith: e.g., Minucius Felix, Tertullian and Cyprian, all incidentally from the Roman province of North Africa. They wrote in contemporary educated Latin style, with which the educated pagan reader could immediately engage, and there was as yet no other style available. This Latin was, of course, not equipped to express the new Christian ideas and, in order to discuss these, it was necessary to incorporate elements of the Christian vocabulary and idiom that had been and were still being developed within the Christian community. Some examples from Minucius Felix's *Octavius*, an elegant justification and defence of the new faith and a demolition of the claims of paganism, are: *resurrectio* [resurrection], *fides* [(Christian) faith], *fratres* [(Christian) brethren], *confiteri* [confess (to being a Christian)], *spei coheredes* [joint heirs of faith], this last using the already existing word *coheres*. The Christian contribution to the written text is in fact at this stage quite small, and even the vehement Tertullian, in his *Apology*, can write at length using mostly unremarkable vocabulary. This early Christian writing shows a basic conformity to contemporary stylistic expectations. It is not popular in style nor obtrusively biblical in idiom, though there are references to biblical content. At the same time, one observes the all-pervasive influence of rhetoric — that ability to put forward a case systematically and persuasively which had long been the aim of Roman education from schooldays onwards.

It was not until about the fourth century that a written Christian Latin developed that was uninhibited by pre-existing stylistic models. The mature St Augustine was by then writing a very individual kind of Latin, especially in the *Confessions*; but even in the less personalised *De civitate Dei* [*The City of God*], he employs a style that allows free use of Christian idiom and constant verbatim quotation of the Bible with all its infelicities of language and simpler sentence structure, very different from the Latin of the Classical Age, now 400 years in the past. It is also a language that freely invents new verbs, especially of the first conjugation type, and new agent nouns in -*tor*. It is not, however, without its own type of rhetoric (Augustine had in early life intended to become a teacher of rhetoric). His contemporary Jerome, e.g., in the *Prefaces* to his translations of the Old Testament scriptures, writes in a Classical style freely incorporating Christian features as required, but it is the kind of Latin exemplified in Augustine that has a future in the Middle Ages.

In an increasingly Christianised empire, especially after Constantine's decree of religious tolerance of 313, the vehicle of school education remained essentially a canon of (pagan) Classical Latin texts, especially Virgil and some of Cicero's philosophical writings. Consequently, this Late Latin retained strong links with the Latin of the past. The traditional way of life and system of education might have continued indefinitely, had it not been for the settlement in wide areas of the western Roman empire during the late fourth to eighth centuries of incoming pagan peoples — Saxons, Franks, Vandals, Visigoths, Ostrogoths — who did not speak Latin. This hastened the disintegration of the western empire, and, in the resultant confusion, the school system survived only patchily, being carried on mainly by the Church in schools attached to churches and in the growing number of monastic institutions. In fact, the expanding Church provided an element of stability through its interconnectedness with Rome, which was increasingly claiming supremacy over the whole Church as the legacy of St Peter. Classical culture survived better in Italy than anywhere else and in the fifth and sixth centuries good (Christian) Latin was being written, still very Classical in style, by upper-class persons like Boethius and Cassiodorus.

C. THE DEVELOPMENT OF MEDIEVAL LATIN

From the third century onwards, missionary activity by monks carried Christianity to areas on the fringe of the western empire where Latin had never been spoken or was not the main language. This evangelisation probably originated from the Celtic-speaking parts of (modern) France, with perhaps some input from the southern part of the province of Britannia. Christianity brought with it both Christianised Latin and the Latin Bible, inextricably combined, and both had to be assimilated, especially by those associated with the organised Church. The missionaries also brought such Classical Latin texts as they valued. Christian writing followed, but writing not now inhibited by the restrictions of Classical style, but following on from the Christian writing of the later Roman empire: e.g., Patrick (fourth century) and Adomnan (sixth century) were active in Celtic-speaking areas, where a distinctive Celtic Church was developing. From Iona, Celtic Christianity was carried to Lindisfarne and, by the seventh to eight centuries, Christian Latin culture had reached a high standard there, personified by the impressively learned Bede, best known for his *Historia ecclesiastica gentis Anglorum* [*Ecclesiastical History of the English People*] but also author of treatises on a wide range of subjects. Another outstanding scholar and prolific writer from the same area, Alcuin (c.704–804), was invited to the court of Charlemagne, where he became a major figure in the so-called Carolingian Renaissance, and a number of Irish scholars were welcomed throughout Europe not only for their general learning but for their famed, but possibly over-estimated, knowledge of Greek.

The significant feature of all this Latin being taught by the Church is that it was correct Latin, being learnt from books; this was true even in the old western provinces of the late Roman Empire, where the majority of the population were now speaking early forms of Romance languages. This learnt Latin never lost its connection with Classical Latin because it continued to be taught in the time-honoured traditional way. The bare bones of the language were learnt from the grammarians, of whom there were many. The most influential was the fourth-century Aelius Donatus, whose two textbooks continued to be hold sway for centuries – alongside other traditional elementary school textbooks (e.g., the *Disticha Catonis* and the *Sententiae* of Publilius Syrus, collections of short sayings of conventional wisdom in simple Latin), together with a selection of Classical texts (Virgil of course, and Cicero's *De officiis* [*On Moral Duties*], and works purveying useful information, such as the Elder Pliny's *Historia Naturalis* [*Natural History*]).

With the passage of time a vast corpus of writing appeared, known collectively as 'Medieval Latin', a title acknowledging that it is Latin, but a Latin unlike Classical Latin in many ways. It is easier to feel this difference than define it, since, apart from some specific changes in grammar and syntax, it seems often to depend on such things as: different patterns of word order; a fondness for pairs of words (often abstract nouns) and pairs of phrases, linked by *et* and separated by the verb (unlike the usage of Classical Latin). This, together with a generally looser sentence structure, results in a different sentence rhythm – it has lost the tautness of Classical Latin, where an extended sentence has an over-arching main unit to which all other elements are grammatically subordinated, and are usually embedded rather than being added in linear fashion. Always there is the pervasive influence of the biblical text and the liturgy and the ambience of Christianity and the Church, which dominated every aspect of life. This Latin was a vehicle for competent and stylish writing in many genres, some of them new (devotional literature; commentaries on biblical texts; expositions of doctrine; hagiography; sermon collections; chronicles and other types of record, and a well-developed genre of history), as also in wholly new types of verse and rhythmical prose, for use in the increasingly innovating liturgy. This vast body of writing, though not uniform, retains a certain homogeneity, and does not diversify into marked regional variations as would a natural language. Several factors may have contributed to this – the writers were reading the same texts, the language was constantly being relearnt as a foreign language from the same sources by new entrants into the church system, and it was in constant use as the language of officialdom – ecclesiastical, civil and diplomatic – over the vast area of Europe.

It is also true that the standard of Latin in non-literary writings depended very much on the ability of the writer. For example, there is the arid logical Latin developed by the schoolmen, which was in a class of its own. However, the Latin found in matter-of-fact charters and diplomatic correspondence, though formulaic and following set patterns, was written by clerks educated in the church system and was grammatically correct; but as the general language of communication, Latin sometimes had to be employed by people with no more than an adequate knowledge of the language, e.g., town clerks. Medieval Latin comes in various sorts.

D. LATIN IN THE RENAISSANCE

This was the situation until the middle of the fifteenth century, when a number of previously unknown Latin texts was discovered in Italy, most notably many of the *Letters* of Cicero. The copying and distribution of these, first in manuscript and then in print, revealed to ever more people how far the Latin they were used to diverged from the Classical style. The work of Lorenzo Valla, an early pioneer of textual criticism, in his *Elegantiae* [*On Correct Latin*] of 1499, demonstrated how corrupted by centuries of miscopying, and how far from what Cicero and others had originally written, were the texts they were taking as authoritative. As a result, there was a determination to rediscover the true Classical Latin and make it the new norm, together with a revival of interest in Classical culture in all its forms. The aim was to take the best that that world had to offer and make it serve Christian ends: this is where Volusenus comes in.

The intense study of these freshly discovered and emended texts led to an adulation of Latin as written by Cicero, newly acknowledged as the supreme stylist and manipulator of Latin. This judgment had been first promulgated by Quintilian in the first century AD in his *Institutio oratoria* [*The Education of the Orator*], to the neglect of other writers as stylistic models, and Cicero had never lost that pre-eminence in theory, if not in practice. The rediscovery of a complete text of the *Institutio* by Poggio in 1416 further promoted it (Murphy 2016: 107). Those who now endeavoured to write Latin like that of Cicero were called 'Ciceronians', possibly as a mocking term. A whole 'Ciceronian' movement developed, at first confined to Italy but spreading to northern and central Europe, as students of Ciceronian tutors returned to their home countries. Some fanatical Ciceronians took to excess the idea of copying Cicero's Latin, proclaiming that one could employ only linguistic features, including even specified grammatical endings, that actually occurred somewhere in the master's works, and at the same time must exclude anything with no precedent there. This unnatural narrowing of the stylistic canon re-created the problem faced by the first Christian writers in Latin − how to write about things Christian in a language not equipped to express it. In fact, it meant a return to a time over 200 years earlier than the first tentative Christian writings in Latin, with an abandoning of all that Medieval Latin had to offer. Sensible Ciceronians, including the two most distinguished members of the movement, the eminent churchmen Pietro Bembo and Jacopo Sadoleto, advocated a thoroughly Ciceronian style of Latin, albeit not one so subservient to cramping rules that it inhibited the natural expression of anything Christian. In his dialogue of 1528, *Ciceronianus* [*The Ciceronian*], subtitled '*On the ideal Latin Style*', Erasmus comments that Sadoleto 'is not so keen on being thought a Ciceronian as to forget his own position as bishop of Carpentras' (Erasmus 1986: 436).

The whole topic was passionately debated, together with the related topic of imitation or copying of stylistic models. In his dialogue, Erasmus made a belated contribution to it, mocking the Ciceronians mercilessly, as he saw their obsession as ludicrous and time-wasting, cramping and unnatural, and indeed hampering the expression of Christian faith. He advocates instead a kind of baptised Classical Latin, 'the kind of Latin that Cicero would naturally write if he were living today as a Christian among Christians' (Erasmus 1986: 392). This is too vague to mean anything much. However, by it he presumably advocates the kind of Latin he himself was writing, Classical in grammar and syntax and idiom and with Cicero's fluent rich style, but embracing every topic and employing any and every word and image and sentiment where appropriate.

E. VOLUSENUS AS LATIN STYLIST

Volusenus was writing his *Commentatio* in 1539 when this controversy was still live, and when, moreover, he was in daily contact with Sadoleto. So how does he respond to the Classical *versus* Christian question? Throughout the whole text there are some 20-plus references to Classical literature and nearly 200 quotations from the Bible. These are not marked by any acknowledgement or obtrusive references in the text, as this would break the flow of thought: instead, the well-educated Christian humanist should recognise most of them for himself, but he is nonetheless alerted to a biblical source by quotation marks in the margin. Volusenus wants his reader to mark and appreciate especially the contribution of this element to his *Commentatio* – as he makes clear in the dedicatory epistle, concerning the effectiveness of the words of Scripture.

The Classical material is homogenous in nature with the surrounding text and can be seamlessly incorporated with small syntactical adjustments (see Chapter III). The biblical quotations and echoes are more difficult to integrate stylistically because of the peculiarities of biblical idiom (noted above), and Volusenus deals with them in several ways. A good many are quoted *verbatim* regardless, e.g., §§125–7 (all from Job); this is what Augustine does in the *Confessions*. Volusenus, however, not seldom makes little verbal changes to the biblical text, the effect of which is to give immediacy and draw the reader in – as, for example:

> §12, Ps 4:3
> Vulgate: '*diligitis ... quaeritis*' [you love ... you seek]
> Volusenus: '*diligimus ... quaerimus*' [we love ... we seek]
> or §201, Col. 32:2
> Vulgate: '*quae sursum sunt sapite*' [set your affections on things above]
> Volusenus: '*quae sursum sunt sapiamus*' [let us set our affections on things above ...].

There are constant other little changes in vocabulary and word order, and there are omissions, variations and additions, varying from the quite minor – e.g., §26, Ps 35/6:10, '*quoniam tecum est fons vitae*', which becomes '*apud te unum est vitae fons*') – to places where the changes amount to a paraphrase of the whole quotation, though there is always enough of the original left to make it recognisable, as in §24, 2 Cor. 12:2–4:

> Vulgate: '*Scio hominem in Christo ... raptum eiusmodi usque ad tertium caelum, quoniam raptus est in paradisum et audivit arcana verba quae non licet homini loqui*' [I know a man in Christ...caught up to the third heaven, for he was caught up into paradise, and heard secret words, which it is not granted to man to utter].

Volusenus: '*Ille quem coelestis quidam mentis aestus ab terris ad tertium usque caelum ultra astra abripuerat, quique arcana verba quae proloqui nefas esset audiverat ...*' [That man, whom a sort of celestial mental impetus had carried from the earth as far as the third heaven beyond the stars, and who had heard secret words which it was not permitted to speak aloud ...].

Sometimes Volusenus repeats a whole biblical phrase in different wording as a kind of gloss or explanation – for example, in §77, Ps 129/130:3, '*nam si tu iniquitates observaveris*' [for if you should closely examine our sins] is glossed as '*si nos pro meritis tractaris*' [if you should treat us according to our merits]. Many of these changes do incidentally improve the Latin from the Classical point of view. This might be intentional but, if so, like the Classicising of the vocabulary (see below), it is not carried through with any consistency. It seems more likely that, as Volusenus freely quotes (from memory?) and adapts to his immediate purpose biblical verses that come to mind, his natural style takes over.

Another element in this richly compounded text is contributed by a number of passages reflecting ideas from Plato and from Aristotelian metaphysics: e.g., §136, 147, 163 (see Chapter IV). Add to these a number of aphorisms of general moral import which draw on the language of a popular Stoicism, derived probably from Cicero's *De officiis* (which was much read in the Middle Ages) and *De finibus*, and from the Younger Seneca's *Epistulae Morales* – examples are: §7, the moral obligation of showing gratitude; §§190–5, virtue, which, as the goal of the good life, is its own reward; §327, *honestum*, the honourable as a standard of conduct; §121, *officium*, duty as a moral imperative; §172, *decorum*, appropriate behaviour; §§122, 208, the unshakeable nature of the man of principle. In fact, there is a latent thread of Stoicism running through many of these aphorisms. These apparently alien elements are all turned to fit the devotional context, but one might ask whether they are really appropriate to a Christian meditation. Volusenus himself gives us an answer in §§192–3, where he reminds us that, when we consider the wise words spoken on the subject of virtue by pagan philosophers who did not have the light of the Gospel, we spineless and ineffectual Christians should be ashamed. Such aphorisms are among the many urging constant attention and effort in the spiritual life.

What is Volusenus's practice in writing about things Christian in his own words? His favourite word when speaking about God is *numen*, that Classical word signifying the awesome sense of presence and power; and he also draws on a rich supply of Classical abstract nouns (*maiestas, dignitas, benignitas, divinitas, bonitas*, etc.), many of which are provided in Cicero's philosophical writings. He often has one abstract noun depending on another in periphrases, such as §35, '*magnitudinis tuae opes*' [the riches of your magnitude], and §304, '*bonitatis tuae divitiae*' [the riches of your goodness], which remind one of the language of St Paul in Eph 3:16, '*secundum divitias gloriae suae*' [according to the riches of his glory]. He often employs the Classical *virtus* to express the effective power and might of God, again with precedent in St Paul's Epistles and in the Psalms. These are all Classical words, but turned to express non-Classical concepts. It is as he struggles to express the ineffable majesty of God that Volusenus draws on the imagery of Classical poetry, which brings with it the pagan implications so disapproved of by Erasmus: §12, '*immensi Olympi sempiternus regnator*' [O eternal ruler of this immense Olympus]; §56, '*tu totum nutu tremefacis Olympum*' [with a nod of your head you cause all Olympus to tremble]; (both of these from Virgil); §146, '*tu summus Iupiter*' [you are the supreme Jupiter]. One might also mention in this context: §233 '*horrida Tartara*' [Hell]; and §76 '*Tartareus tyrannus*', and §153 '*vaferrimus hostis*', for Diabolus, Satanas, which is not a Classical concept. This, however, is a very slight element, and Volusenus is perhaps merely demonstrating another possible source that could be drawn on, as was done of necessity by the first Christian Latin poets and was drawn on to excess by some of his contemporary Renaissance Classicisers.

One might also consider to what extent Volusenus uses or avoids long-established Christian vocabulary. In §§270, 271, 273, 290, we find not the usual word *Salvator* [Saviour], but Classical Latin *servator* [preserver], as noted already; the latter term was never totally displaced by *Salvator*. Similarly, *salus* [health, well-being], a good Classical word, was early pressed into service for the new concept 'salvation'. Thus Volusenus uses §257, '*salutis negotium sic transigendum erat*' [the business of our salvation had to be transacted in this way], but he does not employ the related *salvatio* or *salvare*, which seem to have developed in the Late Latin period. Again, in the Lord's Prayer (Luke 11), we have '*dimitte nobis peccata nostra*' [forgive us our sins], and *dimittere* and *peccata* became the established terms; Volusenus, however, also uses *ignosce*, and has a series of words for sin: §238, *delicta;* §235, *scelera;* §304, *nequitia.* At §259, in '*delictorum omnium gratiam fieri*' [all our sins to be forgiven], he employs the Classical phrase '*gratiam facere*' [to forgive]; also, at §243, we have '*facinorosus homo*' (a good Classical usage) as an alternative for *peccator.* He does not employ *saeculum* with the meaning 'this (wicked) world', though he often speaks of it and its burden. For other topics too, Volusenus opts for unusual terms: thus, in §11, instead of the established *Trinitas*, we have *arcana trias*; and for *Spiritus Sanctus* we have §25, *afflatus tuus,* and in §310, *arcana afflatus tui opera;* at §282 and §286, he even has *sacra persuasio* for 'Christian faith'.

In the earlier part of the aphorisms, much that Volusenus has to say as he contemplates the surpassing wonder of the Creator and his creation would be acceptable to any philosophically minded pagan, but in later sections, especially §§219–44, the tone changes; more specifically Christian concepts arise, and the language becomes more emotional. Now we find §224, *evangelium* [Gospel]; §231, *agnus immaculatus* [spotless lamb] and *sacramenta* [sacraments]; §242, *intemeratae virginis proles* [offspring of the immaculate Virgin], *patris verbum*

[Word of the Father]; §307, *redimere* [redeem, but not *redemptio*]. *Fides* (§§239, 284, 299) is now definitively 'faith', *gratia* (§286) is 'grace'. Yet even here we find that the Holy Spirit is *sacer*, not *sanctus* (§§229, 289). Volusenus does not employ the word *resurrectio* [resurrection], but he speaks of *corpus redivivum* [body restored to life], where *redivivus* is a Classical word, meaning mainly 'reused': it was moving in the direction of 'given life again' and Volusenus has boldly claimed that meaning. There is an unusual depiction of the Ascension, avoiding the actual word *ascensio*, at §232 (for which see below). Volusenus seems to go out of his way to avoid using 'angels' and 'archangels' (see §§50, 52, 66, 69, 179), but he does allow 'seraphim' (§49), apparently so that he can indulge in a Hebrew etymology, though it is not gratuitous in the context. For a humorous list of comparable possible alternatives for established Christian words – a list that Volusenus would have known – see *Ciceronianus* (Erasmus 1986: 388–9).

As for biblical expressions, he prefers Classical *caelum* (neuter singular), but is quite prepared to use *caeli* (masculine plural) on occasion: see §19, '*intra ardua caelorum penetralia*' [within the lofty halls of the heavens]. He has many expressions of the *rex gloriae* type: e.g., §294, '*misericordiae gremium*' [the very bosom of mercy]; §345, '*beatitudinis domicilium*' [home of bliss]. In fact, this usage has become so familiar in the language of hymns in English that one hardly notices it. He does not use *sancti,* either for saints on earth or in heaven, preferring *divi*, and rarely (§§11, 186, 220) addresses God as *Deus* (vocative), and not at all as *deus meus*, preferring *parens* (*alme parens, sancte parens, caelestis parens, magne rerum parens*), or, most of all, simple *tu,* as in the Psalms. The other biblical idioms indicated above do not appear generally in his own text, but see §331, '*in voce laudis*' [with a voice of praise], and the very biblical and triumphal §350, '*canticum gloriae, carmen laudum, misericordias domini in aeternum laudabo*' [I shall sing a song of glory, a song of praise, and the mercies of the Lord forever]. These lists do not claim to be complete, but they suffice to create the impression that, while Volusenus does Classicise his Christian Latin to quite a considerable extent, he is at the same time quite relaxed about including all kinds of non-Classical elements. It is in fact a very mixed and inconsistent picture in general, so much so that one may conclude that he is not trying to demonstrate anything or follow any programme, but is happily drawing on his abundant linguistic resources to write just as he chooses at any particular point.

Among the other mannerisms of Volusenus's personal style, a constant feature is the expression of a single concept by a pair of synonyms or near synonyms. He has a huge vocabulary in general, especially of abstract nouns, and translators are challenged to find English synonyms. This is so ubiquitous that it hardly needs exemplifying, but see, for example: §42, '*absque involucro aut integumento*' [without any mantle or covering]; §166, '*tam absurde, tam abiecte*' [so absurdly and so contemptibly]; §140, '*nihil temere ... nihil otiosum*' [nothing is for nothing ... nothing without function]; §81, '*tam amara sors ... tam acerba fata*' [so bitter a destiny ... so harsh a fate]; §215, '*ludificationes et praestigias*' [trickery and illusions]; §40, '*acies caligat ... et hebescit*' [sight becomes darkened ... and cloudy]; or (more extensively) §18, '*hic apparatus loquitur ... haec rerum magnificentia praedicat*' [This fabrication bespeaks ... this wonderful magnificence of creation declares].

He also employs the familiar rhetorical device of having three successive units of much the same meaning, sometimes of increasing length: §128, '*grave nobis cor est, pronum est, in ima tendit*' [Our heart is heavy, it lies prostrate, it heads towards the depths]; §335, '*ne non agnoscas, ne tamquam spurios abdices et exhaeredes*' [that you will not acknowledge, that you will disdain as bastards and disinherit]; §275, '*hos nulla frangunt adversa, nullae emolliunt libidines, nullae liquefaciunt voluptates*' [No misfortunes break, no passionate desires enervate, no pleasures dissolve]; §107, '*mutantur sicut vestis, usu veterascunt, diuturnitate extabescunt*' [subject to change ... like a garment, they grow old through use and wear away over a long period of time]. This device not only gives increasing impact but is actually pleasing to the listener or reader (see Chapter 1). This last example reminds us that, though Volusenus does not employ allegory, there is a fair sprinkling of metaphor throughout – e.g., reaching harbour (§§42, 122, 322); chains and imprisonment (§§47, 102, 337); life as a play (§§214, 285) or training-ground (§344); seeds, plants, fruits (§310). Also, we find occasionally the rhetorical tricks of alliteration: §50, '*etsi totus ille coelitum coetus communiter incredibili quodam amore ... flagrat*' [For, even though the entire company of celestial beings is in concert aflame with an incredible love]; and word-play (§160): '*tu etenim etsi mole vacas omnia tamen et immensam hanc molem sine mole complecteris*' [For, even though you have no mass, you nonetheless, without mass, embrace all this immense massy world]. He also throws in exclamations, rhetorical questions and parentheses, which, like the colloquialisms mentioned at the beginning of this chapter, are designed to create an air of spontaneity and engagement.

Volusenus often chooses to express what he has to say in an unnecessarily complicated and surprising way, such as making the sentence negative instead of positive. Apart from minor and ubiquitous examples, such as §227, '*neque hoc in parvis ducendum est*' [assuredly it is not to be considered a little thing], and §315, '*inter quas non postremas ... tenet*' [among which certainly not in the last place], there are more egregious examples: §239, '*neque temere alia ratione gravius te offendimus quam cum ...*' [there is no easier way we offend you gravely than when ... *rather than* the easiest way ...]; §152, '*nec nos ... .nisi boni species ... permovet*' [we are not swayed unless by a vision of the good *rather than* it is actually a vision of the good]: §153, '*non ... prius ... mali esum ... persuadet ... quam spem aliquam ... ostendat*' [he does not press upon us ... the eating of the apple ... before he has held out some hope *rather than* he persuades us to eat the apple only after he has]; §270, '*neque honestiorem ... rationem ... quisquam excogitaverit*' [no one could think out a more honourable scheme than *rather than* the most honourable scheme anyone could think out]; §232, '*ipsum corpus ... .non prius supra sidera ascendere intermisit quoad perventum esset in eam sedem*' [that very Body ... did not cease to climb above the stars until it arrived right at that seat] (strange terminology for the Ascension).

F. PRAYER AS APHORISM

This 'meditation or prayer' is advertised as being presented in the form of aphorisms, 350 in all. An aphorism is defined as 'any principle or precept expressed shortly and pithily' (see Chapter 1) and, by choosing this format, Volusenus has set himself a challenge. At any point he is obviously full of thoughts and ideas and emotions that he must express, and yet has chosen to condense it all into a concise utterance. Many of the aphorisms are quite simple, especially in the earlier part, but there are also many that are densely compacted, both in thought and in syntax – main clauses, subordinate clauses, ablative absolutes, other participial phrases, adjectival phrases, parentheses, one syntactical element very often having other elements embedded within it, plus all the stylistic features mentioned above. These are all interwoven into one tessellated whole. This needs to be carefully unpicked, so as to give due weight to the constituent parts and so grasp the overall thrust of the complete aphorism, something beyond the nuts and bolts of the mere grammar. The final translation depends on what one senses this to be, and different persons might interpret differently.

Aphorism §312 provides a good illustration of these points: '*Lucis tuae usque affulgentis ope, cum praeter te nihil dulce aut decorum sit, intervenientibus (ut solent) quas vel malus daemon vel caro offundit nubibus ac praestigiis, nihil praeter te dulce aut decorum appareat*'. Of the five (here A–E) main elements present, the main clause (A) is discerned to be '*Lucis tuae usque affulgentis ope ... nihil praeter te dulce aut decorum appareat*' [Through the power of your light, everywhere effulgent ... may nothing other than you be apprehended as sweet and lovely]. The phrase '*lucis ... ope*' is a subordinate unit of the main clause, the whole phrase put first, emphasising 'power' and 'light', with '*affulgentis*' as an affective descriptive word. Everything else is embedded within this main clause. (B) '*cum praeter te nihil dulce aut decorum sit*' [since apart from you there is nothing sweet or lovely] is a causal subordinate clause introduced by '*cum*' [since], containing a reference to the famous '*dulce et decorum*' of the poet Horace. (C) '*intervenientibus ... nubibus ac praestigiis*' is a participial phrase in the ablative case, a (shorter) equivalent to a fully expressed clause, and here probably temporal in force, 'when clouds ... intervene'. For its part, '*nubibus ac praestigiis*' [clouds and deceptions] is a metaphor employing a striking conjunction of words, and seemingly a memory of a phrase in Apuleius; its unusual wording and emphatic position at the end of the phrase seems meant to mark the contrast with the very first word '*lucis*'. (D) '*ut solent*' [as they do] is a parenthesis embedded in C, making the reader recall personal experience ('Yes, that's what happens'). (E) '*quas vel malus daemon vel caro offundit*' [which an evil demon or the flesh puts in the way] is a relative clause referring forwards to '*nubibus*', likewise embedded in C – *daemon* being another word, ultimately Greek, taken from Apuleius. The final triumphal words deliberately repeat the words of the *cum* clause, and the two together make another sub-unit within the whole, bracketing everything in between. In fact, this could be seen as an alternative main focus of the sentence. The entire structure could be schematically represented as follows: A–B–C–D–E–C–A. All this in one aphorism!

This is a very individual Latin style, with its mixture of Classicism and Christianity, concision and elaboration, artifice and emotion. In reality, setting out to write a series of aphorisms seems an odd procedure, as most recorded aphorisms were originally single, off-the-cuff remarks by various individuals in various circumstances. They were written down later because they were thought worth preserving, and often assembled into collections, several of which survive – examples in Latin being the much-read medieval *Disticha Catonis* and the *Sententiae* of Publilius Syrus. There was also Erasmus's recent great collection of sayings, the (over 3,000) *Apophthegmata* of 1531–2 (Erasmus 2014). These were all totally heterogeneous in content, and the *Commentatio*, in spite of its multitude of wide-ranging thoughts, does have an over-riding unity (see Chapters I and IV, for a synopsis of the developing line of thought). At the same time, within the three sections – i.e., in general terms (1) the ineffable majesty and wonder of God and his creation, (2) the dignity of man combined with stupidity, sinful weakness and ingratitude, and (3) the incredible salvation offered in Christ – Volusenus is seeking ever new ways of expressing these deep concepts. Consequently, he plays with each idea as it occurs and the result is, as it were, a series of different and ingenious ways of saying 'God is awesome and at the same time merciful'.

This reminds one of Erasmus's famous demonstration of *variatio* [stylistic variation] in *De copia* (1512), on the rich oratorical style. That work was a best seller, read by everybody with aspirations as a writer of good Latin. Erasmus devises 146 variations on how to say 'Thank you for your letter', and 200 on 'As long as I live, I shall never forget you'. This is a practical demonstration, deploying all the techniques for making one's writing richer and more interesting, listed and illustrated in the preceding pages – namely: employ synonyms, ('collect yourself a vast supply of words', he says); introduce unusual words, poetic words, old words, 'vulgar' words; add a few Greek words; say things in an unexpected way (e.g., passive instead of active, negative instead of positive, question instead of statement); employ metaphor, rhetorical questions, exclamations (Erasmus 2014: 348–65). Volusenus seems to be putting all this into practice, and these are precisely those stylistic features of his Latin here identified and picked out for comment.

G. CONCLUSION

The work is described on the title page as *Commentatio quaedam theologica quae eadem precatio est, de industria tanquam in aphorismos dissecta,* which might possibly be translated as 'A kind of religious meditation which is also a prayer, deliberately divided up as it were into aphorisms'. The word *dissecta,* implying chopping up something whole, may raise the possibility that Volusenus originally wrote it or thought it out as a continuous piece and then divided it up into short units, thinking it would focus the reader's attention and make more impact in that way. This tentative suggestion would square with the fact (see Chapter I) that some aphorisms occur in clusters, linked by theme, and others are actually linked syntactically and form one sentence; also, the aphorisms vary considerably in length. One might compare here the style of the Younger Seneca, who is quite capable of writing at length a continuous series of sentences, every one of which seems designed to make a point.

Erasmus's tour-de-force, his brilliant exemplification of *variatio* in *De copia,* is not entirely cerebral: he is genuinely thinking with affection of his friends Fausto Andrelini and Thomas More as he writes. For his part, Volusenus is writing out of a genuine felt faith. Some readers, however, may feel that the element of religious sincerity in the *Commentatio* has been overlaid by the very richness and cleverness of the presentation, into which Volusenus has thrown all his dazzling resources. One might ponder each aphorism, while sensing that this is hardly the language of natural prayer. In any case, the *Commentatio* is not intended for all and sundry, but it is *'lectori, praesertim erudito et pio, multum sane placitura'* [one that will be greatly appreciated by the reader, especially one who is both learned and pious].

III. Sources and allusions

A. TYPES OF SOURCES AND DIFFICULTIES IN IDENTIFICATION

The *Commentatio* has been described as 'a specimen of *theologica rhetorica*, being a response to Holy Scripture couched in short, lyrical paragraphs containing phrases drawn from the Bible, the liturgy, and the Ancient classics, and all imaginatively recombined in a way designed to appeal to the common ground between both Catholics and Protestants' (MacDonald 2009a: 124). This chapter considers the range of those borrowed phrases, the ends toward which Volusenus directs them, the changes that he, as a Christian and a humanist, frequently works upon them, and the possible effects that such changes achieve.

The printed text of the *Commentatio* purports to identify quoted material by quotation marks in the left-hand margin. This is in keeping with a remark in the prefatory letter: '*Ea de causa nos hic passim sacra admiscuimus, quod libelli margo notis (ut uides) interpunctus indicat*' [Here throughout, for that reason, we have mingled in words of Holy Writ, which (as you will observe) are indicated by punctuation marks on the margin of the booklet]. It should be noted, however, that because of overhanging indentation, the first line of those aphorisms with quotations is never marked. Furthermore, although it seems clear that the first aphorism contains quoted material, the decorated 'E', which extends to all but the last line, renders such notation impossible. There are about 85 quotations or allusions with strong verbal echoes of the original source, located in 75 aphorisms, that are marked in the text. With only one exception, a phrase from §45, which is from an antiphon for the Feast of St Agnes, these sources are always biblical; none of the identified Classical allusions is marked. In four instances where a passage has been marked (§§26, 59, 250, 252), no precise biblical source has been found. In some cases, there might be several quotations, some of which might not be marked.

One difficulty in identifying sources is that the quotation marks, appearing as they do only in the left-hand margin, do not signal the precise beginning or end of a quoted passage. Nor are they always reliably placed. Additional lines not in the identified source might be marked. This raises the question: Do the extra markings indicate an expansion or paraphrase of a biblical quotation, or are they simply the result of a compositor's error? In §287, for example, the quotation, found in both Luke 10:21 and Matt 11:25, technically ends in line 2: '*Abscondis enim haec a sapientibus et prudentibus*' [For you hide these things from the clever and the wise]. However, the next line is marked as being quoted as well, but not the last line. The passage in those two lines – '*qui suo ingenio metiri se posse confidunt arcanas operum tuorum rationes*' [who are confident that by their own lights they can measure the secret reasons behind your works]

– functions as a single unit of thought, whose purpose is obviously to decry the pride of the wise and prudent in this world. Volusenus perhaps alludes to Isa 45:2–3, which contrasts the humbling of the great by the revelation of divine treasures to God's people: '*Ego ante te ibo, et gloriosos terrae humiliabo; portas aereas conteram, et vectes ferreos confringam: et dabo tibi thesauros absconditos, et arcana secretorum*' [I will go before you, and will humble the great ones of the earth: I will break in pieces the gates of brass, and will burst the bars of iron, and I will give you hidden treasures, and the mysteries of secret places]. If any of the passage should be marked, therefore, all of it should be. But this sentence is a far cry from a direct quotation, and it would appear that the extra mark in line 3 is superfluous.

If it is the case that in some passages an extra line or two is marked that should not be, there are other passages where the marking is incomplete. This is true of §33, from Ps 138/139:11, where the last line should be marked, and §145, which is in its entirety a quotation from Ps 138/139:8–10, even though the last two lines are not marked. In one instance, §252 (Phil 2:8), the quoted material is not marked at all, whereas the quotation mark denotes a passage that does not seem to be a quotation. These inconsistencies, superfluous or absent markings, seem to suggest a compositor's errors.

Still, despite these difficulties, some observations about the sources in the *Commentatio* are still possible. As noted in the previous chapter, Volusenus supplements his reflections by numerous biblical references and allusions and with a sprinkling of Classical and liturgical references scattered widely and sometimes densely throughout the text. These number over 200, although some are more allusive than others. Aside from individual references that have been specifically identified, there are sections of multiple aphorisms, particularly those that dwell on the character of God, that appear as if they depend in a more general way on Volusenus's reading (see especially §§135–6, 143–9). Passages from the Psalms are the most often quoted, and comprise nearly a third of the identified quotations or allusions. It must be acknowledged that identical or similar phrasing in various psalms sometimes makes it difficult to determine precisely which psalm is being quoted. And there are instances when Volusenus will expand or rework a passage so as to blur the line between a direct reference and an echo.

Volusenus draws widely from the psalter, from over 40 individual psalms. Most of these are signalled by quotation marks in the text. Ps 41/42 is quoted directly four times (one of these, in §323, is not marked). Ps 138/139 is another favourite with Volusenus, who quotes from it directly in two places (§§33, 145) and seems to echo it in two others (§§24, 35). Ps 89/90 is quoted in two aphorisms, and Ps 103/104 has echoes in another three. Interestingly, Volusenus never quotes from or apparently alludes to the longest of the psalms, 118/119. Nor does he quote from the two psalms that he had previously written commentaries on: 15/16 and 50/51. Other books that Volusenus draws on heavily are Job (11 references) and the Canticle of Canticles (seven). From the New Testament, passages from the epistles to the Philippians, Colossians and the Hebrews seem to be favourites, as do the gospels of John, Matthew and Luke. In the Matthew and Luke passages, however, there is overlap, given the similar or even identical phrasing that is frequent in those Synoptic Gospels. Classical sources and echoes number over 30, with some ten by Cicero, seven by Virgil, three by Horace, two each by Ovid and Silius, and one apiece by Apuleius, Livy, Martial, pseudo-Seneca, Sextus Propertius, Statius and Xenophon (in the prefatory letter). Plato's presence can be detected, with one direct reference and four others that can be surmised. Four of these Classical references and possibly a fifth can also be found in Volusenus's *De animi tranquillitate*. Given the devotional character of the *Commentatio*, it is no wonder that the language in places appears to draw upon the liturgy of the Church, but these references are difficult to pin down with any precision. It is perhaps the case that they arose unconsciously, or, as part of the rhetorical strategy described in the previous chapter, were intended to give that impression. Still, there are several possible texts as sources: a hymn by Prudentius, an antiphon for the Feast of St Agnes from the prose *De virginitate* of Aldhelm of Sherborne, and the *Gloria*, *Te Deum*, and *Paternoster*. In addition, the second of two '*Salue*' aphorisms (§§11, 242) has a series of names for Christ that find parallels in various liturgical hymns and antiphons. Finally, the *Adagia* of Erasmus appears to have supplied phrasing or parallel references in nine aphorisms in the *Commentatio*.

B. TREATMENT OF CLASSICAL SOURCES

Volusenus quotes with some precision all the Classical passages that have been identified with certainty, as in the case of §117, which includes a line from Martial's *Epigram* 10.58.8: '*et in sterili uita labore perit*' [and life perishes in sterile labour]. This is not to say that he might not adapt the word order and the number, tense, or mood of the verb to the grammatical needs of his meditations. We can see two examples of such adaptations in the following quotations from Cicero. The first is from §5, *De oratore* 3.119.5–6:

Volusenus: **teque ad tuum** *munus, pensumque* **reuoca** [Call yourself back to your function and to your task].

Cicero: **meque ad meum** *munus pensumque* **revocabo** [I will call myself back to my function and my task].

The second is from §191, *De re publica* 6.25.8–9:

Volusenus: *natiuis suis illecebris ad uerum decus **trahere debet*** [(Virtue) should draw the mind by her own intrinsic enticements towards true distinction].

Cicero: *suis te **oportet** inlecebris ipsa virtus **trahat** ad verum decus* [Virtue herself, by her own enticements, should lead you towards true distinction].

The Classical sources are usually employed as a means of punctuation. That is to say, a series of phrases, original to Volusenus or biblical in origin, might culminate in a Classical phrase that adds colour or concreteness. For example, the passage from Martial, quoted above, occurs after a list of observations about the fruitless busyness, anxiety and tumult of life, which, in Martial's words is sterile labour and marks the state in which life perishes: '*Huc, illucque discurritur, gestitur, trepidatur, doletur: mille tempestatum conflictationes, mille curarum difficultates oboriuntur, ac ne multa, inanis sane tumultus frustra suscipitur, et **in sterili uita labore perit***' [Hither and thither there is rushing, desiring, anxiety and unhappiness; a thousand colliding tempests, a thousand perplexing cares arise, and, to say no more, vain tumult is taken on to no purpose and **life perishes in sterile labour**] (§117). Shortly afterwards, in §123, a passage from Statius's *Sylvae* (2.2.131–2) performs a similar function: '*Hic turba in imis relicta uallibus, in edita uirtutum iuga euasit, ubi perenni collium uirore, id est, deliciis non perituris, animum exaturat. **Hic alta mentis ab arce despicit errantes, humanaque gaudia ridet***' [He, leaving the disordered throng in the deep valleys, has escaped into the high peaks of virtue, where, with the everlasting verdure of the hills – that is, delights that will not perish – he replenishes his spirit. **Here, from the lofty citadel of the mind, he looks down upon those who wander, and laughs at human joys**]. Turning now to the one who has escaped the tempest of this earthly life (described in the earlier aphorism), Volusenus invokes the Latin poet to provide a fitting conclusion to the new life above, namely, a kind of cosmic laughter, recalling that of Troilus from the seventh sphere at the conclusion of Chaucer's *Troilus and Criseyde* (5.1807–25). Another example occurs in §129: '*Siquidem omnis caro foenum, omnis gloria eius tanquam flos agri: diluculo efflorescit, ante uesperum decidit, et arescit. **Sola perpetuo manent mentis atque animi bona: florem decoris singuli carpunt dies***' [Indeed all flesh is grass, and all its glory is as the flower of the field; it blossoms with the dawn, and before evening falls and withers. **Only the good things of the mind and the spirit remain forever; one by one the days pluck the flower of beauty**]. After stitching together a series of biblical comments about the transience of human life, Volusenus once again turns to a Classical author, in this case pseudo-Seneca (from his play *Octavia* 548–50), to summarise his observations. Another such example of summarising occurs in §208: '*si fractus illabatur orbis, impauidum ferient ruinae*' [If the world should break up and collapse, the ruins will strike this man still fearless]. Here, Volusenus employs Horace's *Carmina* 3.3.7–8 to add poignancy to his observation that the person of unconquerable mind (*'inuictum mentis'*) will not be thrown off step – even if the whole world were to lie in ruins. In §278 the pitiable condition of Achemenides, the Greek trapped on the island of the Cyclopes, is woven seamlessly into a series of aphorisms (§§272–80), largely biblical, describing those who follow Christ without thought of personal comfort: *'ubi uictum non iam infelicem bacchas, lapidosaque corna dant rami, et uulsis pascunt radicibus herbae'* [where branches yield berries and stony cornel-cherries, by way of sustenance, miserable no more, and where they support themselves on plants they root up] (see *Aen* 3.649–50).

A series of aphorisms (§§141–5) praising God for his care of Creation culminates in this doxology (§146): *'Tu unus ille hominumque deumque pater, summus Iupiter, cuius numine omnia sunt plena. Tu spiritus, qui coelum, terram, camposque liquentes intus alit. Tu mens illa, quae per magni huius corporis artus infusa totam molem agitat'* [You are the sole Father of men and of gods, the supreme Jupiter, with whose Godhead all things are filled. You are the Spirit which from within nourishes the heaven, the earth, and the watery plains. You are the mind which, poured in among the joints of this huge body, moves the entire massy world]. Volusenus is, in fact, importing, almost wholesale, the apostrophe of Anchises in *Aen* 6.724–7, thus underscoring the universal truth of God's creating and sustaining power:

> *Principio caelum ac terras camposque liquentis*
> *lucentemque globum lunae Titaniaque astra*
> *spiritus intus alit, totamque infusa per artus*
> *mens agitat molem et magno se corpore miscet.*

It should be noted, however, that transmission of the passage could have been mediated through Maurus Servius Honoratus's *In Vergilii Bucolicon librum* 3.60.1–2, 5–6, which names Jupiter/Jove specifically:

> **ab iove principivm mvsae** *vel musae meae ab Iove est*
> *principium: vel o musae, sumamus ab Iove principium.*
> *   … spiritus*
> *intus alit, totamque infusa per artus mens agitat molem.*

In any case, this aphorism adds a Classical voice to the praise of God's greatness and illustrates the ease with which Volusenus's Classical and Christian learning and expression abide with one another. This can also be seen in §187. Sextus Propertius, in his *Elegiae* 4.7.60, lends to the aphorism its final phrase: *'Ad summum istuc aethera nos inuitas, ubi perpetuus spirat ueris honos,* **mulcet et elysias aura beata rosas'** [You invite us thither to that highest heaven, where breathes the perpetual beauty of spring and **where a blessed zephyr soothes the heavenly roses**]. The Christian and Classical blend harmoniously through the surrounding series to create a vision of pastoral tranquillity to which God invites the aspiring soul.

With respect to his Classical sources, Volusenus's practice in §191 (mentioned above) differs slightly. The aphorism reads: '**Siquidem ipsa uirtus sibimet pulcherrima merces est**: ipsa una, quamuis uniuersus fieret interitus, et a funere nihil superesset, **natiuis suis illecebris ad uerum decus trahere debet**' [**For indeed, virtue herself is her own most beautiful reward.** She alone, though there should be universal extinction, with nothing surviving that death, **should draw the mind by her own intrinsic enticements towards true distinction**]. In this case, most of the aphorism (and perhaps all) comprises quotations from Classical sources. The first emphasised passage is from Silius Italicus's *Punica* 13.663; the second, as seen above, a slight variation of Cicero's *De republica* 6.25.8–9. It is possible that even the middle phrase is a Classical borrowing as well. It calls to mind the passage from Cicero's *Tusculanae Disputationes* 1.90.7–10: '*animo et corpore consumpto totoque animante deleto et facto interitu universo illud animal, quod fuerit, factum esse nihil*' [When both soul and body are consumed, and that which gives life is totally erased and **utterly destroyed**, then **that which was an animal becomes nothing**]. Whatever the case, the whole aphorism comes as a conclusion to yet another series (§§187–90), this time on the high calling of virtue and its concomitant glories in the lives of those who heed that call. It is no surprise that Volusenus will use these two quotations – from *Punica* and *De republica* – in conjunction with one another for a similar purpose in *DAT*: 163.

C. TREATMENT OF BIBLICAL SOURCES

If Volusenus adheres closely to the wording of his Classical sources, he does allow himself some latitude when dealing with the biblical text, and his treatment of these quotations is of great value in revealing his humanist training and instincts. True, a number of his biblical quotations appear with little or no alteration from the Vulgate. This can be seen in §§75 (Luke 23:30), 125 (Job 29:2–3), 126 (Job 29:4–6), 240 (Job 7:17, although he substitutes *illum* for *eum*), and 285 (Hab 3:18). But he is not a slave to that translation and will deviate from it. This departure can be explained, at least in part, by practical considerations, namely, adapting a quotation to its specific context. Some of these practical alterations are simple, although the effects can be profound. For example, in the passage from Ps 4:3 (§128), Volusenus transposes the second-person plural verb *quaeritis* to *quaerimus* (first-person plural). In so doing, he includes himself among those who seek after deception. It is in such a change that we catch glimpses, noted in the previous chapter, of his humility and intimacy in associating with his readers, qualities that are hallmarks of the *Commentatio*. In §287, *abscondisti* (the perfect form of the second-person singular) from Luke 10:21 (cf. Matt 11:25) now reads *abscondis* (the present tense), suggesting that God's action of hiding divine matters from those confident in their own understanding is an ongoing process. A change in mood occurs in §340, where the *nuntietis* (second-person plural subjunctive) of Cant 5:8 is transformed into a command, *nunciate* (second-person plural imperative): '*Adiuro uos filiae Hierusalem, nunciate quia amore langueo*' [I adjure you, daughters of Jerusalem, **cry out**, that I am weak with love]. In at least one place, §201, the person and mood of the verb are altered. The Apostle Paul's injunction to the Colossians in Col 3:2, *sapite* (the second-person plural imperative), becomes *sapiamus* (the first-person plural subjunctive), a plea to his readers to join him in 'knowing' and, in the next phrase, 'seeking' the higher things.

But Volusenus moves well beyond such tinkering with verb forms and makes significant lexical choices through options open to him now that he has at his disposal not only the Vulgate, but also the Greek Septuagint and the Hebrew text. And although his purpose in the *Commentatio* is not primarily to provide an accurate and thorough translation of the Bible, it seems clear that he is making conscious decisions that are not only stylistic, but substantive as well. One might turn to one of his own biblical commentaries, *Ps XV*, to gain a sense of his careful reading. A prime example is his investigation of the second verse of that psalm (Aiv^v). He begins by quoting the Vulgate: '*Dixi domino, deus meus es tu: quoniam bonorum meorum non eges*' [I said to the Lord: you are my God; therefore you have no need of my goods]. Then he quotes both the Hebrew and the Septuagint:

> *Hebræus hic habet,* דְּילֵע לב יתבוט, *quod Septuaginta verterunt,* ὅτι τῶν ἀγαθῶν μοῦ οὐ χρείαν ἔχεις. *id est, Quoniam bonitas mea non est tibi conferens, aut vsui. ex hebraeo vertunt alij sic, Bonum meum non est nisi a te. Ad verbum si interpreteris, sonat: Bonitas mea non est super, vel, ad te.* [The Septuagint has rendered the Hebrew: 'Because my goodness contributes nothing to yours or is of no use (to you)'. From the Hebrew, others have translated it thus, 'My good is nothing except from you'. If you interpret the expression literally, it denotes: 'My goodness is not over or near you'.] [Note: This last translation appears to imply that our own goodness is not even in the same league as God's.]

The interpretation continues at some length, with additional meanings proffered. One can see Volusenus attending to the nuances of the Hebrew text and its translations. On Bi^v he also points to the difficulty of translation when he discusses the verb root of the Hebrew Divine Name, or Tetragrammaton (יהוה), which has been translated in the Greek as ὄν and in the Latin as *ens* or *existens*. There is the danger, he adds, of great confusion in the use of *ens* because of a variety of significations. In effect, the Hebrew is much more precise in denoting the highest perfection. It is not surprising that in the *Commentatio*, when describing God as being itself (§136), he resorts to the

Greek ὄν. Thus, it does not seem to be stretching a point to argue that the difference between his version of a Scriptural passage in the *Commentatio* and the Vulgate is the result of careful reflection.

Such differences manifest themselves in a variety of ways. Sometimes he will combine related passages, as in the case of §129, which contains phrasing from 1 Pet 1:24 and Ps 102/103:15, passages that are thematically related. As can be seen, there are also verbal changes, which will be discussed later. More significant are his frequent elaborations on a biblical passage. Into the line from Col 3:2 ('*quae sursum sunt sapite, non quae super terram*') he inserts the phrase '*quae sursum sunt, quaeramus*', with this result: '*Quae sursum sunt, sapiamus: quae sursum sunt, quaeramus: non quae super terram*' [Let us set our affections on those things which are above; let us seek out those things which are above, not those which are on the earth] (§201). The repetition of structure, followed by the verb *quaeramus* [let us seek] lends a certain urgency to the task set before the reader, not only to be mindful of the things that are above, but also to seek them. In §247, when quoting from Rom 11:34, the Apostle Paul's question, '*quis consiliarius ejus fuit?*', is expanded to read, '*quis arcanas consiliorum tuorum rationes scrutetur?*'. The result is much more personal and emphatic. For one thing, the address is now to God directly (from *ejus* to *tuorum*) and, for another, the judgements of his counsels (*consiliorum ... rationes*) are described as being hidden (*arcanas*) to human scrutiny. The verb *scrutetur* intensifies the character of the search into the divine mysteries and only highlights the failure of human reason to pierce the hidden counsels of God. Volusenus thus expresses the tension within the Christian humanist's mind as to limitations of unaided human knowledge.

Canticles 3:3–4 (§325) is a particularly good example of how Volusenus elaborates upon a biblical passage. At the same time it draws attention to the difficulties the reader encounters when trying to designate quoted material. The two versions follow, with the added material in the *Commentatio* in bold type.

Vulgate: *Invenerunt me vigiles qui custodiunt civitatem: Num quem diligit anima mea vidistis? ... inveni quem diligit anima mea: tenui eum, nec dimittam, donec introducam illum in domum matris meae* [The watchmen who keep the city, found me: Have you seen him, whom my soul loves? ... I found him whom my soul loves: I held him: and I will not let him go, until I bring him into my mother's house].

Commentatio: Percontabor de ipsis uigilibus, atque excubitoribus, qui hanc ciuitatem custodiunt, **a quibus naturae perfectio ociosam uacationem remouit:** *de* **hisce, quod propius te referant, solicitius quaeram,** *an uiderint, quem diligit anima mea: neque operam intermittam, quoad aedes tuas subeam, donec te inueniam* [I shall ask from these watchmen and sentries who guard this city, **from whom their perfection of nature has withdrawn idle freedom from**

**service. From these, because they reflect you more closely, shall
I enquire with anxious care**, whether they have seen him whom my
soul loves. Neither shall I cease my efforts until the time that I enter your
dwelling, until I find you].

He substitutes *'percontabor de ipsis uigilibus'* for *'invenerunt me vigiles'*, thus
changing the person, number and tense of the subject, so that now it is the
speaker who seeks out the watchmen of the city, not the watchmen, who, in
the original, find the speaker. He also yokes the rather rare word *excubitoribus*
with *uigilibus* as a rhetorical doubling; inserts material (in bold face), which is
not set off by quotation marks in the text, then picks up the quotation again,
but adjusts it to his own needs (employing the plural accusative *aedes tuas*
instead of *domum matris meae*, to signify God's 'temple' or 'sanctuary' rather
than 'the home of my mother'), and includes phrasing (*operam intermittam*) that
is not part of the quotation. The last line of the text, which includes quoted
material, is unmarked. The passage retains enough of its original phrasing to
identify it, but has been significantly altered and enlarged to reflect generations
of Christian exegesis of the passage. The markings in the left-hand margin
roughly indicate what is quoted and what is Volusenus's brief digression on
the nature of the guardians of the city, but show the compositor's dilemma in
sorting the wording of the original text from the paraphrase or commentary.
Likewise, in §4 the phrase *'et tanquam in die inclyti sacrarii tui'*, for which no
source has been found, is inserted in the middle of a marked quotation from
Isa 52:1–2: *'Consurge itaque Hierusalem, consurge: Excutere de puluere, et* **tanquam**
in die inclyti sacrarii tui, *induere uestimentis gloriae tuae'* [Rise up, therefore,
Jerusalem, rise up; shake off the dust, and, **as in the day of your glorious**
temple, be clad with the vestments of your glory]. The addition underscores
an historical continuity between the past glories of Solomon's temple and
the present-day Christian experience.

The departure from the language of the Vulgate in two passages from Ps
138/139 gives us a clear idea of Volusenus's humanist sensibilities, particularly
in the ways his mind and ear are attuned to language in this exploration of
matters of the heart. The first occurs in §33 with a rendering of v. 11. The
Vulgate reads *'tenebrae conculcabunt me'* [the darkness will trample down, or
fall upon me]. This matches the sense of both the Hebrew (יְשׁוּפֵנִי) and the
Septuagint (καταπατήσει). Volusenus, however, employs *occultabunt* [will hide]
to signal the difference in tone of his speaker, one who foolishly believes that
he can remain hidden from God, in contrast to the Psalmist, who knows that
even if darkness falls on him, he cannot escape God's presence. The second
passage (from §145) quotes vv. 8–10:

Si ascendero in coelum, tu illic es: si ad inferos demigrem, ades. si sumptis diluculo
pennis ad extremum usque mare deferar, manus tua est, quae et ducit, et detinet [If

I ascend to heaven, you are there; if I travel down to hell, you are present. If I were to put on wings at dawn and be carried to the uttermost parts of the sea, it is your hand which both guides and holds me].

The original reads:

> *Si ascendero in caelum, tu illic es; si descendero in infernum, ades. Si sumpsero pennas meas diluculo, et habitavero in extremis maris, etenim illuc manus tua deducet me, et tenebit me dextera tua* [If I ascend into heaven, you are there: if I descend into hell, you are present. If I take my wings early in the morning, and dwell in the uttermost parts of the sea: even there shall your hand lead me, and your right hand shall hold me].

The deviations in the *Commentatio* from the original are small, but, it would appear, carefully nuanced. The phrase *ad inferos demigrem* is substituted for *descendero in infernum*; *deferar* for *habitavero*; *ducit* for *deducet*; and *detinet* for *tenebit*. These substitutions create the sense of one who is travelling, both actively (*demigrem*) and passively (*deferar*), one whom God is not only leading (*ducit*), but also holding back (*detinet*).

In §142, which is drawn from Ps 144/145:16, Volusenus substitutes the more specific *ex[s]aturas* [you satisfy] for the more general *imples* [you fill up], which, admittedly, can also imply 'satisfying'. The Greek ἐμπιπλᾷς (Strong's Greek: 1705) from the Septuagint can mean both. The Hebrew עיבשׁומ (Strong's Hebrew: 7646), however, more specifically denotes 'to satisfy', and it seems likely that Volusenus is seeking the precision of the latter. The same appears to be true of his use of *aspiret* instead of *desyderat* when quoting from Ps 41/42:2 in §322. Again, his goal seems to be precision, coupled with an emotional intensity, a precision that can be found in both the Greek ἐπιποθέω ['to long for ..., (greatly) long (after), lust'] and the Hebrew גרעת ['cry, pant', as well as 'long for'] (see Strong's Greek: 1971; Hebrew: 6165). *Aspiret*, with its root meaning 'breath', captures more fully the 'panting' of the soul after God. Stylistically, he also avoids the Vulgate's repetition of *desiderat*. In §339, he fuses two verses from the Vulgate translation of Ps 76/77:3, 6.

> *Commentatio: Renuat aliunde, quam ex te, consolationem admittere anima mea: dies illi antiqui, aeternique anni animum habeant* [May my soul refuse to admit consolation from anywhere but from you; may those days of old fill my mind and the years of ancient times].

> Vulgate: *Renuit consolari anima mea ... Cogitavi dies antiquos, et annos aeternos in mente habui* [My soul refused to be comforted ... I thought upon the days of old: and I had in my mind the eternal years].

In doing so, he substitutes *consolationem admittere* for *consolari; animum* for *mente*. Although *animum* and *mente* might be considered synonymous, the phrase *consolationem admittere*, which echoes the *consolari* of the previous phrase from the original, suggests more than a cognitive consideration of one's years in the search for consolation. In §331 Ps 41/42:5 is reworked in this fashion:

> *Commentatio*: *In uoce laudis, et exultationis ingrediatur in locum tabernaculi admirabilis* [With a voice of praise and exultation may (the soul) enter into the place of the wonderful tabernacle].

> Vulgate: *Quoniam transibo in locum tabernaculi admirabilis ... in voce exsultationis et confessionis* [For I shall pass over into the place of the wonderful tabernacle ... with a voice of exultation and confession, or acknowledgement].

Besides reordering the phrasing, Volusenus substitutes *ingrediatur* for *transibo* and changes both person and mood (from the first-person singular future indicative to the third-person singular present subjunctive) to match the context. In keeping with practice elsewhere, however, the more precise *ingrediatur* ('enter' as opposed to 'pass over') suggests that the soul more fully enters into, as it were, the experience of processing into the tabernacle. And although *confessio* in the original has as one of its meanings 'praise', along with 'acknowledgement', *laudo* leaves no doubt as to the precise character of the utterance. One might compare the word הדות [a ringing cry] in the Hebrew text (v. 4, Strong's Hebrew: 7440) with ἐξομολογήσεως [confession] from the Septuagint (v. 5, Strong's Greek: 1843).

Volusenus's choices of biblical passages woven throughout the meditations in the *Commentatio* run the gamut in emotional tone: adoration of God the Father and wonder at the greatness of his creation, intense longing for the higher good offered to humankind as the crown of that creation, repentance for one's failure to remain fixed in that desire, recognition of the justice of God's judgement, but humble reception of God's mercy and love through the Son. On occasion, a cluster of related passages from the same biblical source can be found in close proximity to achieve a certain effect. Job, not surprisingly, is invoked in two series of aphorisms (§§125–7, and 305–9) to describe one's absolute dependence on God's mercy (for the first series see Job 29:2–6, 30:15–16, 27; for the second, 14:4, 9:20, 15:15). And as Volusenus draws to the end of the *Commentatio*, he frequently cites the Canticle of Canticles to express the soul's love-longing for God and the desire for a restored intimacy between the two (§§320–5; see also §340). These shifts in emotional register corroborate what has been termed the 'affective' character of Renaissance humanist thought, 'wherein its proponents encouraged an increased role for the emotions in rhetoric, theology, and philosophy in comparison with their scholastic counterparts, who had long dominated intellectual, and especially theological, disciplines' (Essary 2017: 329–30).

Volusenus's lexical choices have the same affective quality. One last and especially moving example might be offered to illustrate this point. In his rendering Ps 146/147:9 (§141), he writes: '*Das enim tu escam et pullis coruorum, qui et ipsi opem tuam, suo more crocitando, implorant*' [You give food even to the young of ravens, which themselves beseech your bounty in their natural way, with their croaking]. (The original reads: '*qui dat jumentis* [beasts of burden] *escam ipsorum, et pullis corvorum invocantibus eum*'.) The gracious care with which God nurtures his creation, a care that extends to feeding even the young ravens, is rendered all the more poignant by the change from *invocantibus*, which follows the Septuagint's ἐπικαλουμένοις [calling upon] (Strong's Greek: 1941), to *implorant*, which more closely aligns with the Hebrew וארק׳ [to call, to cry for help] (Strong's Hebrew: 7121), and by the insertion of the onomatopoeic phrase '*suo more crocitando*', that only deepens the tenderness of the scene. It is with the young ravens that Volusenus casts his lot in the *Commentatio*.

This affective quality of his sources allows a glimpse into Volusenus's attitudes toward his biblical and Classical sources and the way that they might live together in some harmony. There is no doubt, however, as to where he would place the emphasis. As he writes in *Ps L*, the wisdom of the Stoics, which encourages a freedom from passion (*apathia*), and the eloquence of Cicero can induce the soul to desire something beyond (Dii^v, p. 29). But it is the Christian Scriptures, which have an almost magical quality about them, carrying the soul away to God and to the heavens – '*uelut magicae cuiusdam … uirtutis in rapiendis in caelum et Deum uersus animis*' – that remain the source of the highest wisdom (*DAT*: 390).

IV. The context of ideas and faith

A. SOME DIFFICULTIES IN LOCATING THE *COMMENTATIO* IN A PHILOSOPHICAL TRADITION

As Chapter I in this section has made clear, the *Commentatio* is not given to philosophical abstraction or Scholastic argument: it does not deign to examine, prove and defend certain propositions on the attributes of the Deity. And it refers only generally to philosophers and philosophy (§§28, 43, 54, 251, 252, 253, 283, 302), or, slightly more specifically, to Christian/heavenly philosophy (§§261, 268, 282), but only as such philosophical endeavour furthers or hinders our journey to intimacy with God. Its purpose and mode of expression are far otherwise. Yet it is clear that Volusenus accepts certain attributes as given, and there are many occasions when his manner of addressing God and reflecting on the Creation has a distinctly philosophical cast to it, evoking such concepts as being, substance, infinitude, limitation, causation, virtue, and the like. It seems reasonable, then, that in his struggle to name the un-nameable and to describe the ineffable, he would turn to places that seem to provide a ready-made vocabulary. In this, the *Commentatio* might be likened, though imperfectly, to a credal statement such as the Nicene Creed, whose series of deceptively straightforward assertions disguise the arduous, even bitter debates that forged them.

This fusion of the devotional and philosophical, the heart and the head, might be illustrated in simple ways, as when Volusenus declares that he is a senseless and stupid hunter of the truth (*'oppido profecto excors, et inscitus ueri uenator sum'*), struggling, through exploring the riches of Creation, to get some sense of who God is (§38). Like any good philosopher, he searches for truth, but in an attitude of praise for God (*'tua solius laus haec est'*, §39). This struggle is signalled in philosophical language once again in §47, this time by a different metaphor, where he observes: *'Nos tantisper, dum in caeco hoc carcere positi, perturbationum uinculis constringimur, umbras circunfusas, circumque uolitantes admiramur'* [We ourselves, as long as we are held in this blind dungeon, are bound by the chains of perturbation, and wonder at shadows surrounding us and flitting around]. This passage, along with several others — §§24, 53, 54, 102, 108, 128, where the concept of shadows is alluded to — recalls Plato's Allegory of the Cave (*Republic* 514a–520a). But the metaphor, only sketched here, Volusenus had expounded more fully several years earlier (1534?) in his *Scholia* (Biv^v), and was yet to do so again in *De animi tranquillitate* (*DAT*: 44). Both works point more specifically to Plato's *Phaedo* 66b–e and Virgil's *Aeneid* 6.730–4. The following passage is from *DAT*:

*non immerito Plato perturbationes morbosque animi omnes in corpus, tanquam in
fontem et originem confert: sicut tum primum perturbari incipiat animus, quum in
tam insolitum et perturbatum immigrat domicilium: et tum demum, et non aliter,
beatus futurus sit, cum relicto corpore, cupiditatum, atque aemulationum erit expers.
Hac ipsa de re insignis est ille apud Virgilium locus, qui ex Platonis officina totus
est depromtus,*

*Igneus est illis (de animis loquitur) uigor et caelestis origo
Seminibus quantum non noxia corpora tardant
Terrenique hebetant artus moribundaque membra.
Hinc metuunt, cupiuntque, dolent, gaudentque, nec auras
Respiciunt, clausae tenebris et carcere caeco.*

[Not undeservedly Plato located the source and origin of all perturba-
tions and diseases of the mind in the body, on the grounds that the mind
first begins to be disturbed when it migrates into such an unfamiliar and
disturbed dwelling-place: and then at last, and only then, will it come to
be blessed, when it will leave the body and be free of desires and strivings.
There is a notable passage about this very thing in Virgil, which is wholly
manufactured in Plato's workshop: 'The strength of those seeds (he is
speaking of souls) is fiery, and their origin celestial, to the degree that they
are not impeded by harmful bodies and their earthly frames and mortal
limbs do not dull them. This is why they fear, desire, grieve and rejoice,
having no care for the light, since they are pent up in shadows and this
dark dungeon' (trans. Sutton, in Wilson 2008)].

Such indications would invite a further consideration of possible philosophical
influences in the *Commentatio*.

This consideration must be undertaken with no little caution; and it is
Volusenus himself who would later, in *DAT*: 343, direct the steps of the
inquirer. There he praises for their eloquence and virtue such Greek and Latin
philosophers as Plato, Plutarch, Xenophon, Cicero, Seneca and Pliny, along
with Aristotle, who discusses nature with art and method: *Naturas rerum arte et
methodo tradit Aristoteles.* Volusenus is, however, no slavish devotee to any one
philosophical school, and none of them receives his unqualified praise. In *DAT*:
82, for example, he lists a number of these schools and names their defects: the
Pythagoreans with their μετεμψύχωσιν, or reincarnation; the Platonists with
their Ideas, their composition of numbers, and '*monstrosas Reipublicae formas*'
[monstrous forms of republic]; the Peripatetics with their '*infinitam seculorum
aeternitatem, et uacillantes de animorum duratione sententias*' [infinite eternity of
ages and their wavering opinions about the duration of souls], the Academics
(σκεπτικοί), who '*in contrarias partes de omni re disputant, ridicule etiam a manifeste
ueris assensione abstinentes*' [take opposing sides regarding everything, absurdly
withholding their assent from manifest truths]. Even the Stoics, that '*sanctum*

sane philosophorum genus' [holy tribe of philosophers], have their *'doctrinae absurditates'* [absurdity of doctrines]. The Epicurean voluptuaries (*'cuius modi fuerunt ex uoluptariis illis philosophis nonnulli'*) are not worthy of consideration or even naming. And although Volusenus warns his interlocutors, Francesco and Demetrio, not to be surprised if Aristotle's name crops up frequently in the conversation, he mildly censures the eminent Greek as 'slippery and obscure, sometimes redundant, and sometimes hard to comprehend': *'Non nego illum interdum lubricum et obscurum, interdum redundantem, interdum uanum denique deprehendi'* (*DAT*: 86). Still, Volusenus's admiration for Aristotle (who, in his opinion, outweighs all other philosophers, Greek or Roman) and the Peripatetics, for the Stoics, and for Plato remains high.

In the *Commentatio* Aristotle's presence, while residing in the shadows, is easiest to posit, but largely because of outside evidence. Volusenus would certainly have been exposed to Aristotle's thought directly and through his interpreters in his studies at Aberdeen and Paris. More specifically, he quotes directly from the *Physics* 3.6.207a in his *Psalmi 15 enarratio* (*Ps XV*): 'οὗ δὲ μηδὲν ἔξω, τοῦτ' ἔστι τέλειον καὶ ὅλον· οὕτω γὰρ ὁριζόμεθα τὸ ὅλον' [On the other hand, what (Being) has nothing outside it is complete and whole]. And the great admiration for the Greek master, as expressed in *DAT*, has just been noted. Admittedly, the latter work, on its own, cannot be used to prove anything definite about an Aristotelian influence in the *Commentatio*. But it has been suggested that Volusenus had been engaged in writing a synopsis of Aristotelian philosophy, a work that either he abandoned or that is now lost (see the Introduction). Thus, even though Aristotle is neither named nor, with the possible exception of a Greek term here and there, quoted directly in the *Commentatio*, it would seem that his spirit is never very far from Volusenus's text.

But the devotional character of these aphorisms urges the reader to go farther afield into a more specifically Christian application of Classical philosophy. Alexander Broadie (1990: 88) argues that, despite strong Ciceronian currents, Aristotelian teaching runs deep in an independent thinker like Volusenus, whose influences include Hector Boece, his teacher at Aberdeen, Erasmus, Melanchthon, and Italian humanists gathered at Lyon in what Broadie terms 'the nearest thing in humanist France to Plato's Academy'. The *Commentatio*, he continues, is a kind of 'litany', that among other things asserts 'the utter otherness' of God and follows in the line of Boethius and later Thomas Aquinas, who declare that God sees all events – past, present and future – in the Eternal Present. In his observations on the *De animi tranquillitate*, Broadie (89) describes Volusenus as being a theologian as much as he was a philosopher, whose Thomistic leanings can also be detected in various places in that work. Though steeped in the humanist thought of his time, Volusenus did, however, remain sympathetic to 'the old order'. Broadie's assessment opens up the possibility for a more thorough examination of the Thomistic tradition in the *Commentatio*.

The case for Thomas's direct influence is still difficult to make. In only a single reference from an earlier work, his *In psalmum 50 enarratio* (*Ps L*), does Volusenus even mention Thomas, and this with respect to the philosopher's discourse on original sin (Ci^v, p. 18). Nor does he quote from the Doctor Angelicus in any conclusive way. As is the case with Aristotle, single words or short phrases do not allow for much precision in identifying particular passages. Too often such terms derive from a common philosophical vocabulary. And, again, Volusenus himself would suggest caution. He argues in *DAT*: 343 that Christian thinkers of an earlier age wrote with spirit and simple erudition, although without much method; but complains that more recent scholars, though methodical, expound on trivial matters, proudly display their learning, and rely almost exclusively on Aristotle, barbarously understood:

> *Recentioribus, qui sunt innumeri, et methodus quaedam est, et acuminis sane plurimum: sed magna est rerum ieiunitas, et saepissime in ludicris, et friuolis ambitiose ostentant ingenium. Siquando illis sacra tractantur, nullae sunt flammae, nullus impetus orationis, quo incendatur ad rerum amorem lector. Ex uno prope Aristotele barbare intellecto, omnis illorum commentatio est composita.*

Unfortunately, he does not name those thinkers, nor does he identify how recently they lived. Presumably, he means the Scholastics. Nor was he alone in this criticism of such scholarship: many of his fellow humanists in the sixteenth century shared this suspicion of Scholasticism (Rice 1962: 135–7). Further, Volusenus bemoans having spent so much of his education learning sophisms, or *captiunculae*, when he might have been learning Greek and Latin more fully. Concluding this excursus, he admits his pleasure at owning St Augustine's *De civitate Dei* (*DAT*: 343–4).

But this disdain for more modern thinkers does not entirely rule out Aquinas's influence, given what appears to be an affinity between some of his conclusions and Volusenus's affirmations. Why the imprecision in identifying the influence? There are at least three possible explanations. The first, of course, is that Volusenus never mentions his other, more obvious sources. The nature of the *Commentatio* would prohibit him from doing so. His is an interior monologue of sorts, addressed alternately to God, to his reader, and to his own soul in language that is biblical, Classical, and philosophical. He is not citing authorities to support a position so much as borrowing their vocabulary. A second reason for the imprecision is likely to have been stylistic. Durkan (1990: 131) remarks the change in the sixteenth century from a Medieval Latin style shaped by local vernacular to a greater emphasis on the elegance of Classical antiquity, and points to the influence of this shift in Scotland. Volusenus, who had a finely tuned ear for style, would not have wanted to perpetuate such Latin 'barbarism' as might be found in Thomas and his fellow Scholastics. Later, in fact, he will criticise even Erasmus, who, he claims, should have been *'paullo accuratior ... in Romani sermonis puritate'* [a little more precise ... in the purity of his Latin style] (*DAT*: 344). This respect for language, as we have seen in the previous chapter ('Sources and allusions'), has given him permission to exercise some freedom even in translating biblical passages. Finally, there is the difference in tone. Whereas Aquinas approaches his topics systematically and discursively, the *Commentatio* appears, on the surface anyway, to have arisen almost spontaneously, one expression spilling over loosely into the other in a kind of stream of consciousness. The reader is swept along imperceptibly from beginning to end, and only upon further reflection realises how careful and thoughtful the organisation and intention are (see Chapter 1).

The purpose of the following, then, is not to prove that at a given point Volusenus refers to any specific passage, as he had done with his biblical and Classical sources, but to suggest his familiarity with a Christian philosophical tradition that was strongly influenced by the work of Aristotle, and whose chief spokesperson was Thomas Aquinas. Along the way it would seem that he offers the occasional nod to Plato, Boethius, Augustine, and perhaps to pseudo-Dionysius.

The opening of the *Commentatio* constitutes a hymn of praise and an acknowledgement of God's being the repository of all wisdom and knowledge (§29), a phrase from Col 2:3, which Volusenus had quoted in *Ps XV* (Ci^v–Cii^r). This passage helps to set the tone for the whole work. What follows is a series of aphorisms that, among other things, consider how we can know God and what we can say of God. This leads naturally into the relationship between the Creator and the Creation. Aristotle and Thomas have much to say about these matters; and, in the language with which Volusenus addresses God, he seems to have imbibed the spirit of both. The means by which we can know God, at least from the standpoint of natural knowledge, is through what God has created (§38), a point that Thomas makes in *ST* I.Q12.A12. As such, our knowledge will always be limited. We might know from this natural reason that God exists, but cannot describe fully such attributes as his power. Volusenus will attempt to assign names appropriate to God, but knows that such attempts are ultimately doomed to be inadequate and imperfect expressions because of the immense gap between us and the Deity (§41). Drawing on what appears to be a reference to Plato's Allegory of the Cave in *Republic* 514a–520a, and on *Phaedrus* 249d–250b in §§52–4, especially §53, he also considers how our view of divine matters is limited by the shadows of forms (*'formarum umbrae'*), which cause us to dabble in trivial concerns (*'in leues quasdam curas'*). His use of the Greek term φιλοκάλῳ (lover of beauty) in §55 would seem to cement the connection with Plato, who employs it in his Allegory of the Chariot (*Phaedrus* 248d) to designate those who, along with the philosopher, musician and lover, embody the highest level of insight in recollecting those things forgotten in the fall from the original divine vision of God. It should be noted, however, that such Platonic language bespeaks an inappropriate attitude toward creation, but in no way diminishes the goodness and beauty of the created order, as will be seen in later reflections (§§135–49). In this, Volusenus would appear to adopt the Augustinian notion that God created each thing good and all things together very good, and that the creation points not to itself, but to its Creator, as worthy of adoration (see, for example, *Confessiones* 7.13–14; in 10.6, Augustine writes: '*Et dixi omnibus, quae circumstant fores carnis meae: dicite mihi de deo meo, quod vos non estis, dicite mihi de illo aliquid. Et exclamaverunt voce magna: ipse fecit nos. Interrogatio mea intentio mea, et responsio eorum species eorum*' [And I said to all things gathered around the doors of my flesh, tell me about my God, you who are not he; tell me something of him. And they exclaimed with a loud voice: he himself made us. My question was my purpose, and their response was their splendour]).

Volusenus will make a similar point about the limitations of our expressions about the divine nature in §90, when he admits that while we might speak of God ('*his uocabulis, nostro modo loquentes te esse facimus*'), we have no notion of the true property of his nature ('*naturae tuae proprietatem*'). Ian Hazlett has suggested that *re* in §91 hints at the familiar contrast between *de re* and *de dictu*, and prompts a thought about *his uocabulis ... loquentes* in §90. Thus, in §90 Volusenus considers a dictum – a statement we might deploy in speaking about a thing. In §91, by contrast, he focuses on the reality of the thing itself – what there is. In the former, he admits that 'the words he has used in §89 – *lux, vita, species*, and so forth – are, in the context, vacuous in the sense of providing us with no notion of the reality at issue'. In the latter, however, the word *ratione* is used 'to indicate that there is an unsurmountable obstacle to our engaging in successful reasoning whose conclusion is about what God is' (Hazlett, personal correspondence). To use Thomas's words, '*Sic igitur praedicta nomina divinam substantiam significant, imperfecte tamen, sicut et creaturae imperfecte eam repraesentant*' [Therefore the aforesaid names signify the divine substance, but in an imperfect manner, even as creatures represent it imperfectly] (*ST* I.Q13.A2). In fact, Volusenus declares, it is easier to talk about what God is not than about what he is, '*potius quid non sis, quam quid sis, ostendunt*' (§41), a point that echoes the words of John of Damascene: '*oportet singulum eorum quae de Deo dicuntur, non quid est secundum substantiam significare, sed quid non est ostendere*' [Everything said of God signifies not his substance, but rather shows forth what he is not] (qtd. by Thomas in *ST* I.Q13.A2). Still, although human knowledge of God suffers under the limitations imposed by the physical body and limited understanding, attempts to speak of the ineffable are justified because, after all, as Volusenus had stated in §18, the magnificence of God's creation bespeaks his excellence and the glory and richness of his kingdom.

A brief digression in §§20–2 serves to introduce a higher kind of knowledge with which the angels are endowed as creatures of pure intellect. Although this knowledge is also limited (no creature can ever comprehend fully its Creator), their minds function like so many eyes (*'quia pene tot mentes toti sunt oculi'*), beholding the divine glory and delighting in its radiance, even if perceived through a kind of lattice-work (*'uelut per transennam'*). In a lengthy examination of the angelic nature (*ST* I.QQ50–64), Thomas will likewise refer to this quality of the intellect (see *ST* I.Q54.A3) and the delight in the contemplation of God it produces (*ST* I.Q60.A5). Further, in his commentary on pseudo-Dionysius's *De Divinis Nominibus* (*DDN* C4.L4), Thomas examines the notion of intelligible light, which is desired more and more (*'magis desideratur, et magis desiderantibus magis immittitur'*) as it cleanses the eyes and expels the darkness. This vision, in Volusenus's words (§23), is *'ipsa felicitas'* [happiness itself]. Later, in §49, he will return to this theme with respect to the Seraphim in particular, the highest order of angels, whose name means *'meros ardores'* [pure burning lights]. Thomas, in his commentary on the *Sententiae* of Peter Lombard (II.D9.Q1.A3), likewise describes these creatures as *'ardens vel incendens'*, but goes further to attribute their special position to their having perfected the will through love and thus having entered most fully into 'the interior things of the beloved' (*'amor facit interiora amati penetrari'*).

Although unable to apprehend God with the pure intellect of the angels, Volusenus will yet address God in the terms available to him, limited though they are, both as to God's character and as to his works. Specific aphorisms are dedicated to some quality of the Divine, whereas others comprise a whole list. The series of apostrophes in §13 is an example of the latter, couched in language that approaches the poetic: *'Tu uita, tu salus, tu communis omnium spes: Tu rerum flos, tu rerum decus: tu rerum delitiae, tu summum, imo unum uniuersi orbis bonum'* [You are the life, the salvation, and common hope of all; you are the flower and beauty of all things; you are the delight of all things, you are the highest, and indeed only, good of the universal world]. And in §89, he adds other names – light, life, beauty, wisdom, power, delight – which are among the list pseudo-Dionysius sets forth in *DDN* cc. 4–10. Some of these names and attributes will be examined in greater detail.

Volusenus, in §96, enlists the apophatic tradition to counterbalance the positive series of attributes:

Nihil in te uarium, nihil concretum, nihil pensile, nihil aduentitium, nihil mole extensum, nihil qualitate affectum, nihil adhaerescens, nihil aliunde mutuatum, nihil alienae opis indigum, nihil duplum, nihil coactum, nihil diuiduum, nihil labefactabile, nihil ulla ex parte mobile [In you is nothing different, nothing coalesced, nothing dependent, nothing extraneous, nothing extending in mass, nothing determined by any quality, nothing attached, nothing borrowed from anywhere else, nothing wanting outside help, nothing double, nothing combined, nothing divided, nothing destructible, nothing moveable in any part].

The language by which he addresses God, whether in positive or negative terms, has strong philosophical overtones, which he will begin to amplify.

B. TERMINOLOGY OF/FOR THE DIVINE

The Divine Essence

Several of the Greek terms scattered throughout the work naturally turn the reader's attention to the Greek philosophers, especially to Aristotle. For example, 'οὐσία' (§§65, 103), or 'essence', names Aristotle's chief category of being, as seen in *Metaphysics* 12, especially c. 7 (1072a21–1073a12), which deals with the divine nature. Volusenus reproduces the term when declaring how the Divine Essence differentiates itself from all its creatures as being incapable of multiplication or division of itself or of suffering any limits to its perfection; as embracing all things; and as allowing no other nature to share in its distinction: '*Multitudinem ac sui partitionem ea natura non admittit, quae nullis perfectionis terminis circumscripta, omniaque complectens, nullam notam, nullum insigne alteri paris naturae relinquit, quod* τῆς οὐσίας *differentiam efficiat*' [emphasis added]. Thomas, commenting not on Aristotle but on pseudo-Dionysius, describes God in similar language, as being without limitation ('*incircumscripte*') and embracing all things ('*in seipso uniformiter esse praeaccipit*'). And he quotes his source: '*Deus non quodammodo est existens, sed simpliciter et incircumscripte totum in seipso uniformiter esse praeaccipit … ipse est esse subsistentibus*' ['God exists not in any single mode, but embraces all being within himself, absolutely, without limitation, uniformly … He is the very existence to subsisting things'] (*ST* I.Q4.A2; the actual quotation comes from Aquinas's commentary on the *Book of Causes*, Proposition 3l; but see *DDN* C5.L1).

Wisdom

God's absolute wisdom, the subject of §39, is the means by which God is known entirely to himself and, as far as possible, is known to his creatures: '*quod ipse tibi plene, et quoad eius fieri potest cognitus sis*'. The ability of the intellect to possess the object of its knowledge is, according to Aristotle, a quality attributable only to the Divine (*Met* 12.7.1072b):

> For that which is capable of receiving the object of thought, i.e. the essence (τῆς οὐσίας), is thought. But it is active when it possesses this object. Therefore the possession rather than the receptivity is the divine element which thought seems to contain, and the act of contemplation is what is most pleasant and best. If, then, God is always in that good state in which we sometimes are, this compels our wonder; and if in a better this compels

it yet more. And God is in a better state. And life also belongs to God; for the actuality of thought is life, and God is that actuality; and God's self-dependent actuality is life most good and eternal. We say therefore that God is a living being, eternal, most good, so that life and duration continuous and eternal belong to God; for this is God. (trans. Ross, in Aristotle 1924)

Likewise, Aquinas, in describing God as having nothing of potential ('*nihil potentialitatis*'), but as being pure act ('*actus purus*'), asserts that God understands himself through himself: '*Deus se per seipsum intelligit*' (*ST* I.Q14.A2).

Goodness

Several times throughout the *Commentatio* (§§16, 135) Volusenus associates the attribute of goodness with God, but in §88 he describes God as goodness itself, '*ipsa est bonitas*'. Augustine, when discussing the character of good and bad angels in *De civitate Dei* (*DCD* 12.1–2), had named God as immutable goodness: '*Dicimus itaque incommutabile bonum non esse nisi unum verum beatum Deum*' (1877: I.512–13). And in an article from the *Summa* quoted above (I.Q13. A2), Thomas subjects the term to some scrutiny as to its adequacy in expressing an attribute of God. He concludes that when we state that God is good, we are in fact declaring, '*id quod bonitatem dicimus in creaturis, praeexistit in Deo, et hoc quidem secundum modum altiorem*' [Whatever good we attribute to creatures, pre-exists in God, and in a more excellent and higher way] (cf. *ST* I.Q6.A1).

The Eternal Present

God exists in an Eternal Present (§30), and it is from this vantage that he sees all times simultaneously: '*Etenim tu, uno eodemque praesente obtutu, ex editissimo isto, stabilique aeternitatis uertice simul prospicis*'. This notion, which Boethius explored in *DCP* 5.Pr6, resembles Thomas's articles from *ST* I.QQ10.A2; 14.A13. In that last article, he writes: '*Unde omnia quae sunt in tempore, sunt Deo ab aeterno praesentia*' [Hence all things which are in time are present to God from eternity]. From this statement in the *Commentatio* about God's Eternal Present and his absolute knowledge and wisdom, there naturally follows a consideration of God's providence and governance (§§31–2). This, according to Volusenus, extends to all things, however small: '*nihil sit in tanta rerum uarietate, et copia tam exile, aut tam minutum, quod iniussu tuo oriatur, aut fiat*' [In the great variety and abundance of things, there is nothing so trivial or slight that it originates or happens without your bidding]. Thomas's *ST* I.Q22.AA2,4 seek to prove that anything that participates in existence must necessarily be subject to divine providence, either by necessity or contingency. While maintaining God's providence, Volusenus also asserts the freedom of the will, adding that the mysterious relationship between the two has not been fully investigated: '*necnon et deliberationis quoque nostrae libertas, arcano quodam, nondumque satis explorato nexu cohaerent*'. Likewise, in *ST* I.Q19.A8; and *SCG* 1.C88; 3.C73, Thomas argues that providence does not exclude free will. But, whereas Thomas allows a role for fortune (*SCG* 3.C74), Volusenus does not: '*fortunam consilia tua excludunt*'. It must be noted, however, that Thomas's understanding of fortune is within the context of divine providence – that is, nothing lies outside the providence of God – and the 'disagreement' between the two positions is likely a matter of semantics. Here, Boethius's *DCP* 5.Pr1 (which draws upon Aristotle's *Physics* 2.3), is a useful bridge.

C. THE CREATOR AND THE CREATION

Volusenus devotes a number of aphorisms (§§135–49) to declaring more fully God's relationship to Creation, a relationship that has been implicit in the statements made thus far. In the first seven, he describes the work of God to create and sustain. In the remaining seven he carefully distinguishes God from his creation.

§§135–42

God's purpose in creation, as laid out in §135, is to manifest that absolute goodness named in §88 (see also §140). This accords with Thomas's statement in *ST* I.Q47.A1, a passage worth quoting at some length because of what it sets forth about the divine simplicity and unity, concepts that Volusenus will invoke in §§91, 103, 148:

> *Produxit enim res in esse propter suam bonitatem communicandam creaturis, et per eas repraesentandam. Et quia per unam creaturam sufficienter repraesentari non potest, produxit multas creaturas et diversas, ut quod deest uni ad repraesentandam divinam bonitatem, suppleatur ex alia, nam bonitas, quae in Deo est simpliciter et uniformiter, in creaturis est multipliciter et divisim. Unde perfectius participat divinam bonitatem, et repraesentat eam, totum universum, quam alia quaecumque creatura*
> [For he brought things into being in order that His goodness might be communicated to creatures, and be represented by them; and because His goodness could not be adequately represented by one creature alone, He produced many and diverse creatures, that what was wanting to one in the representation of the divine goodness might be supplied by another. For goodness, which in God is simple and uniform, in creatures is manifold and divided and hence the whole universe together participates in the divine goodness more perfectly, and represents it better than any single creature whatever].

For Volusenus, the fundamental nature of creatures consists not simply in this or that effect, but in their very being, which God (very Being itself) brought forth out of nothing: '*Tu, qui non hoc aut illud es, sed ipsum* ὄν, *adeoque totum* ὄν *es, totum hoc* ὄν, *nulla eius parte praeuia, nulla quae praecedat subiecta materia, e nihilo producis, atque effingis*' (§136). Thomas describes God's Being similarly: '*est ipsum esse subsistens, omnibus modis indeterminatum*' [He is being itself, subsistent, absolutely undetermined] (*ST* I.Q11.A4; see also Q44.A1). He, too, affirms the ancient notion that God creates all things '*ex nihilo*' (*ST* I.Q45.AA1–2). It is significant that Volusenus three times employs the Greek word ὄν, accompanied by the modifiers *ipsum* and *totum*, rather than *ens*, to name the 'Divine Being'. In *Ps XV* (Bi^r), he had equated the Hebrew word for the Divine Name, הוה ('I AM'), in v. 2 with the Greek ὄν and the Latin *ens*, and suggested that the Latin term had been applied so variously as to cause much confusion unless carefully qualified, which he does. It is at this point he quotes from Aristotle's *Physics* 3.6, as noted above. The phrasing by which he translates the Greek into Latin anticipates in spirit what he declares in the previous aphorism (§135): '*perfectum illud est, et totum, extra quod nihil est, seu cui nihil deest: quod perfectissimum ens dici meretur*' [The Divine Being is perfect and complete, without which nothing exists, or of whom nothing is lacking: worthy to be called most perfect being]. Volusenus's decision to use the Greek ὄν in this Latin context deepens an already profound sense of God's Being, both biblically and philosophically.

§§142–9

In §143 God is described as the mover of all things, although he himself remains at rest: '*Omnia moues, ipse requietus*'. Here parallels might be seen with *Metaphysics* 11–12 (especially 11.9, 1065b5–1066a34), along with Aquinas's lectures on these two books, in their treatment of the concepts of motion and rest, and of the character of the prime mover. This portion of the aphorism follows as the natural conclusion to §97, where Volusenus has earlier argued that '*Motus enim omnis, accessionis gratia fit: accessio defectum, qui in te non cadit, semper arguit. Quicquid igitur in te est, puritas est, diuinitas est, imo ipsum esse est*' [All motion is for the purpose of acquisition: acquisition (and, by extension, motion), which does not apply to you, always argues a defect. Therefore, whatever is in you is purity, is divinity, is very Being itself]. Perfect in himself and thus needing to acquire nothing beyond himself, God remains at rest. Thomas, in *ST* I.Q2.A3, includes as one of his proofs for the existence of God the concept of the prime mover; and in his reply to objection 2, defends the notion that 'all things that are changeable and capable of defect must be traced back to an immovable and self-necessary first principle': '*oportet autem omnia mobilia et deficere possibilia reduci in aliquod primum principium immobile et per se necessarium*'. Like Volusenus in §97, Thomas invokes the phrase '*est ipsum esse*' to underscore what has become a familiar refrain, that God is very Being itself. (This phrase is a common refrain throughout Thomas's writings; in the *Summa Theologiae* alone it appears 21 times; see, for example, *ST* I.Q4.AA1–3).

Ensuing aphorisms in the *Commentatio* describe God's relationship to his creation, a task to which Thomas devotes much attention; but it must be reiterated that Volusenus writes in an attitude of devotion, not in the manner of philosophical debate. The tone is thus one of wonder and humility, which affirms simultaneously the intimacy and the otherness of God. §§144 and 148 are condensed expressions of this tension, which is examined more fully in parallel passages from Thomas. In the former, Volusenus declares that God fills all things, and is everywhere present, but not visible to anyone except by self-revelation (cf. *ST* I.Q8.AA1–2; Q12.A3). In §148 he addresses God himself in a series of apostrophes, a rhetorical strategy that is familiar throughout the work:

> *Tu rerum omnium principium: tu item omnium finis, utriusque tamen iuxta exors. Tu forma, sed libera, ac ab omni materiae conditione multo alienissima. Tu simplicissima quaedam idaea, sed quam tot, tamque diuersae res pro rata quaeque portione imitantur*
> [You are the first principle of all things; you likewise are the end of all, yet having no share in either. You are form, but without restriction, and utterly alien from any condition of matter. You are a kind of purest idea, but one which so many and so diverse things imitate, each in its own degree].

Each of these attributes of God can be found in Aquinas: as the first principle of all things (cf. *ST* I.Q2.A3); as the end of all things: *'ultimus finis omnium rerum'* (cf. *ST* I.Q6.AA2–3); as having no share in any created thing and differing from the condition of everything material (cf. *ST* I.Q3.A8); as form, but without restriction (cf. *ST* I.Q3.A2: *'Est igitur per essentiam suam forma'*); as a kind of purest idea, imitated by so many and so diverse things, each in its own degree (cf. *ST* I.Q3.A7: *'quod ea quae sunt a Deo, imitantur Deum sicut causata primam causam'*). This last point resonates with other passages from Thomas, who attributes to God absolute being (*'Deum omnino esse simplicem'*, *ST* I.Q3.A7), and who asserts that since God is 'the similitude of all things according to His essence, … an idea in God is identical with His essence': *'Deus secundum essentiam suam est similitudo omnium rerum. Unde idea in Deo nihil est aliud quam Dei essentia'* (*ST* I.Q15.A1).

Volusenus concludes this section by maintaining that all creatures, whatever their place in creation, however small, or, for that matter, however evil, preserve the footprints (*uestigia*) of God's greatness and goodness: *'Nihil enim est in hac rerum innumerabilitate tam paruum, quod non magnitudinis: nihil tam malum, quod non bonitatis tuae, tanquam uestigia quaedam, seruet impressa'* [For there is within this innumerability of things nothing so tiny but that it preserves certain traces, like footprints, of your greatness, nothing so bad but that it has traces of your goodness] (§149). For Thomas, as well, traces or 'vestiges' of the Divine are a quality of creation: '*Sed in creaturis omnibus invenitur repraesentatio Trinitatis per modum vestigii, inquantum in qualibet creatura inveniuntur aliqua quae necesse est reducere in divinas personas sicut in causam*' [But in all creatures there is found the trace of the Trinity, inasmuch as in every creature are found some things which are necessarily reduced to the divine Persons as to their cause] (*ST* I.Q45.A7). But for both Volusenus and Thomas some creatures can approach more nearly to God and participate to some degree in divine perfection:

Commentatio (§150): *quo quodque tibi uicinius est, tuique similius, hoc absolutius est, et perfectius* [For the closer something is to you, the more it is similar to you, so it is the more absolute and the more perfect].

ST I.Q44.A.1: *Necesse est igitur omnia quae diversificantur secundum diversam participationem essendi, ut sint perfectius vel minus perfecte, causari ab uno primo ente, quod perfectissime est* [Therefore it must be that all things which are diversified by the diverse participation of being, so as to be more or less perfect, are caused by one First Being, Who possesses being most perfectly].

It is true that in *ST* I.Q12.A6 Thomas does aver that a more perfect knowledge of God's essence derives from intellect rather than similitude with God; but here he is arguing with respect to knowledge of God, not to placement within the hierarchy of creation.

In §147 of the *Commentatio*, Volusenus proposes that it is the creature's *hypostasis* (prime substance) that allows for the relative proximity to the Divine Being, whatever distance might be determined by the body: '*quo longius naturae dignitate a corporibus abscedis, hoc uirtutis, adeoque et hypostaseos propinquitate rerum, quas moderaris, ingenio ita exigente, iisdem praesentius ades*' [The more distinct you are from corporeal things by the dignity of your nature, the more present you are with them by the proximity of your power as the essential underlying substance, the inherent quality of the things which you govern requiring this to be so]. This would seem to accord with Thomas's explanation (*ST* I.Q78. A4) that the eminence of the powers of human thought and memory arises not from the senses ('*non per id quod est proprium sensitivae partis*') but from their affinity and closeness to universal reason ('*per aliquam affinitatem et propinquitatem ad rationem universalem*'), which powers, then, are distinguished as more perfect than those found in the other animals ('*perfectiores quam sint in aliis animalibus*'). The appearance of the word *hypostasis* calls to mind Thomas's discussion in *ST* I.Q29.A2, where the term is used to translate Aristotle's οὐσία (*usia*), meaning 'substance' or 'essence' (οὐσία occurs in this sense in §§65, 103 of the *Commentatio*.) Thomas states: '*Uno modo dicitur substantia quidditas rei, quam significat definitio, secundum quod dicimus quod definitio significat substantiam rei, quam quidem substantiam Graeci "usiam" vocant, quod nos "essentiam" dicere possumus'* [In one sense it means the quiddity of a thing, signified by its definition, and thus we say that the definition means the substance of a thing; in which sense 'substance' is called by the Greeks 'ousia', what we may call 'essence']. This passage Thomas follows with the comment in his reply to Objection 1: *'apud Graecos, ex propria significatione nominis habet quod significet quodcumque individuum substantiae, sed ex usu loquendi habet quod sumatur pro individuo rationalis naturae, ratione suae excellentiae'* [Among the Greeks the term *hypostasis*, taken in the strict interpretation of the word, signifies any individual of the genus substance; but in the usual way of speaking, it means the individual of the rational nature, by reason of the excellence of that nature]. (See also Thomas's lectures 10 on *Met* 5.8.1017b10–26; and 3 on *Met* 10.2.1053b9–1054a19.)

D. HUMANITY WITHIN CREATION

Up until this point Volusenus has considered Creation in general and, in a brief transition (§§150–3), observes: *'Itaque ut ex te omnia manant, sic ad te omnia moliuntur, tanquam in portum recursum, omnia te usque referre student'* [And so, just as all things proceed from you, so do all things work towards a return to you, as if back to harbour, and strive always to reflect you] (§150). But the return is complicated by the work of the serpent, who promised Eve and Adam that they would be as gods: *'Eritis sicut Dii'* (§153, quoting Gen 3:5). Despite this promise Adam and Eve's disobedience sets into motion what results in a separation from God, not a greater kinship with him. The transition introduces a lengthy portion of the *Commentatio*, which is now devoted to the place of human beings in Creation (§§154–218). This section might itself be roughly divided into several parts:

- God's exaltation of us, with our affinity to the divine, as the crown of Creation (§§154–74)
- the benefits of Creation to us (§§175–84)
- God's promise of even greater rewards to us (§§185–91)
- our failure to live into our role (§§192–200)
- Volusenus's determination to live a godly, virtuous life (§§201–8)
- obstacles to the virtuous life: sensuality, Fortune (§§209–18)

The first of these sections might be considered Volusenus's own 'humanist manifesto', celebrating as it does the unique place of humankind as the crown of visible Creation: *'Supremus enim ipse fui in illa nascentis mundi origine tuus labor, et tanquam coronis, imo uero finis'* [For I myself was your supreme work in the creation of the new-born world, and, a kind of finishing touch, the end in fact] (§174). We are appointed by God to be the priests of this great temple: *'Igitur ne templo huic tam augusto deesset Antistes, uel theatro tam magnifico spectator, homo a te conditus est, atque in totius operis meditullio collocatus'* [Therefore, that there should lack no chief priest for so august a temple or spectator for so magnificent a theatre, man was created by you and placed right in the middle of the whole creation] (§154). He echoes a notion espoused by Cicero in the *Dream of Scipio* (*De re publica* 6.15.5–13, especially 8–10), who argues that human beings have been tasked by God to guard that temple: '*Homines enim sunt hac lege generati, qui tuerentur illum globum, quem in hoc templo medium vides, quae terra dicitur'* [For men were created by this law, to guard that globe, which you see in the centre of this temple, which is called the Earth]. The language of Volusenus's commentary on this passage in his *Scholia* (Ci^r) anticipates that found in §154: '*Sumus sane homines antistites huius magni templi quod diuino numine plenum est'* [We human beings are indeed priests of this great temple, which is filled by the divine presence]. This and the following aphorisms also echo similar sentiments from Cicero's *De legibus*, especially 1.22–7, which underscore the exalted position we occupy with regard to our Creator by virtue of reason, virtue and law. In §158, a passage reminiscent in its power and beauty of Hamlet's own praise of this 'quintessence of dust', Volusenus describes humankind as an image of the whole world, or microcosm: '*ut inde absoluta quaedam totius orbis imago consurgat'* (cf. Plato's *Timaeus* 29d–47e). He will return to this concept in *DAT*: 33 with the phrase '*minor quidam mundus'*. As has already been noted in Chapter 1 on Volusenus's rhetoric, Baker-Smith (1969: 282) suggests that this aphorism has patristic roots in Nemesius of Emesa's *De natura hominis* 1.13 (*PG* 40.511B), a work that had appeared in a Latin translation just a year before the publication of the *Commentatio*. The passage in question appears in the Latin version on pp. 25–6:

> *Quis igitur dignis huius nobilitatem animalis laudibus prosequi potuerit? quod intra se mortalia immortaliaque complectitur, quod irrationalia rationalibus coniungit, quod omnifariae creationis in sua natura claudit, fertque simulachrum. quamobrem et paruus mundus homo nominatur … Rerum naturam exquirit, a deo suscitatur, domus et templum dei gignitur: & haec omnia uirtutibus comparat, atque pietate* [Who therefore can worthily describe the dignity of man: who encompasses within himself the mortal and immortal, who conjoins the rational and irrational; who encloses within his own nature and bears the likeness of the whole diversity of creation, for which reason man is called a little world? … He inquires into the nature of things, from God he is stirred (to curiosity), he becomes the house and the temple of God. And he achieves all this by virtue and piety].

This section of the *Commentatio*, especially §166, highlights the assertion that in the Creation our souls have been ordained to a higher and more divine order ('*diuiniorisque cuiusdam esse ordinis'*), even if this status has been imperfectly explained ('*ad unguem exploratus non es'*). One who would content himself with dwelling purely on the material level does not, therefore, value his own worth: '*si quis animus est, qui tam absurde, tamque abiecte ipse de se sentiat, ut se pari cum belluis aetatis spatio circumscribat, ac metiatur, profecto* τοῦ νοῦ, *id est, suam ipsius dignitatem non satis expendit*' [If there is any rational spirit such as to feel so absurdly and so contemptibly about himself that he limits and measures himself to a lifespan equal to the beasts – assuredly, he does not sufficiently weigh the worth of his mind, his own worth in fact]. The sentiment here echoes much Classical and Christian thinking on the dual nature of human beings – the 'bestial' and the divine – and the injunction to seek the things of the spirit. Volusenus will explore the idea in greater detail in *DAT*: 60, where he also employs the Greek expression 'τὸν νοῦν' [the mind] when addressing Aristotle's own treatment of such ideas: '*licet passim* τὸν νοῦν, *hoc est, mentem, aut intellectum magna ueneratione dignetur*' [Everywhere he honoured νοῦς, that is, the mind or intellect, with great reverence]. But he will add that the Greek philosopher's thinking on the matter was tentative and his explanations confusing: '*implicatae tamen orationis forma, in qua plurimum ille esse solet, lectori non mediocres offundit tenebras*' [However, the tangled form of discourse in which he was often accustomed to be engaged, shrouds the reader in no little darkness]. So great then is our position in the created order that it would appear that all things were made for us. Thus has Nemesius argued. Volusenus's rhetorical strategy of *repetitio* in the series of aphorisms beginning with *Mihi* (§§175–8) drives the point home most forcibly.

These blessings of creation, however, are not to be enjoyed as ends in themselves, but as a means of rendering thanks and service to God (see §§186, 201). In an extended section of the *Summa Theologiae* (I–II.QQ2–4), Thomas lists the possible sources of happiness and concludes that only in God can true happiness reside (Q4.A7; see also *SCG* 3.CC26–37). Boethius, in a more abbreviated discourse (*DCP* 3.Pr10), had drawn the same conclusion, that the highest good for humankind is participation in the Divine.

Up until §212 Volusenus's attention has focused on the character of God the Creator, Ruler, and Father of the universe, with only two trinitarian references (§§11, 83). In effect, for much of this portion of the *Commentatio*, certain strands of Classical philosophy and Christian thought can coexist in some harmony. In fact, Volusenus commends pagan philosophers for their commitment to virtue, while he, as a Christian to whom the hope of eternal reward has been revealed, behaves in a most drowsy fashion (§§192–4). But as the *Commentatio* turns to topics that concern the fall and restoration of humankind, the references to the Son and his redemptive work become much more frequent, and there is less need for the philosophical vocabulary that has marked the earlier aphorisms, although such expressions have not disappeared entirely (see, for example §§215, 251–3, 302). Most of the theological statements are both firmly rooted in the Christian scriptures and thoroughgoing in their orthodoxy, so that their sources would be too numerous to identify.

The tone here is deeply personal: it is as a representative of humankind that Volusenus confesses his own sinful nature and voices his thanksgiving for God's grace. It should be added that he, by his own admission, had no desire to enter into religious controversies (either ancient or modern). In *DAT*: 121 he lists some of these:

> *cuius modi sunt et illae de ineffabili Triade, de aeterna immutabilitate diuinorum consiliorum circa salutem hominum, quam Praedestinationem populariter uocant, de modo, quo humana natura sit in CHRISTO diuinitati coniuncta, qua ratione animi corporum expertes torqueantur ab ignibus* [Those concerning the ineffable Trinity, the eternal immutability of divine counsels concerning human salvation, popularly called predestination, the means by which human nature is conjoined with divinity in Christ, the manner in which souls separated from the body are tormented by hellfire].

Instead, he encourages his friends Francesco and Demetrio, if they wish, to read the immediate sources in these debates – the theologians themselves. He, for his part, will gladly (*'libenter'*) join St Paul in confessing his ignorance and exclaim, *'O altitudinem diuitiarum sapientiae et scientiae Dei, quam incompraehensibilia sunt iudicia eius, et uiae nulli peruestigabiles!'* [O the depth of the riches of the wisdom and knowledge of God; how incomprehensible are his judgments, and his ways untraceable!] (Rom 11:33).

E. CONCLUSION

As seen in this and the previous chapter, the influences on the *Commentatio* are wide-ranging. Of the identification of biblical and Classical sources there can be little debate. And even if one must concede that the precise identification of scholastic influences must remain largely conjectural, it is to be hoped that the parallels that have been drawn between the work of Thomas Aquinas and Volusenus's own statements are sufficient to locate the Scotsman's vision of God and the Creation firmly within the Thomistic tradition, however that might have been mediated to him. But to return to the opening chapter of this section, it is not the demonstration of this or that influence that is of primary concern. Rather, it is his subordination of all the resources at hand – the eloquent Classical phrase, the weighty philosophical dictum, the plaintive cry of the Psalmist's heart – to guiding his readers, while walking with them, into a profound devotion.

.

v. Notes on the text

★ passages marked by quotation marks
(★) initial lines, though not marked because of overhanging indentation, which are obvious quotations

Prefatory Letter
The bishop of Winchester is Stephen Gardiner (1483–1555).
The reference to Xenophon is from *Memorabilia*, I.ii.21.

1   (★)*Exurge gloria mea, exurge: Exurge psalterium et cithara, exurge diluculo* … Pss 56/57:9; 107/108:3.

2   *Ales, uicinae lucis nuntia, officii iandudum me admonet* … Echoes from the first stanza of the breviary hymn by Prudentius, sung on Tuesday at Laudes: *Ales diei nuntius/ Lucem propinquam praecinit.*

4   ★*Consurge itaque Hierusalem, consurge: Excutere de puluere, et tanquam in die inclyti sacrarii tui, induere uestimentis gloriae tuae* … Isa 52:1–2. The phrase '*et tanquam in die inclyti sacrarii tui*', for which no source has been found, is inserted. It appears to refer to the Day of the Lord, or Day of Judgement, a common refrain throughout the Bible. *Sermones* 9.1: '*De Resurrectione Domini, II*', attributed to Pope Leo the Great, begins thus:

   In ista die sancta, fratres charissimi, in ista die inclyta atque egregia [On this holy day, most beloved brothers, on this day glorious and celebrated] (*PL* 54.0497B).

5   *teque ad tuum munus, pensumque reuoca* … Cicero, *De oratore* 3.119.6. See Erasmus, *Adagia* I.iii.61 (Saladin 2010: I.304; cf. Erasmus 1982: 285).

   et coelestium rerum commentationem te conuerte … See Cicero, *De finibus* 4.11.4–5.

6   ★*Nonne deo subiecta es anima mea? Nonne ab ipso salus tua?* … Ps 61/62:2; see also Pss 34/35:3; 68/69:30.

   ★*Nunquid non ipse est pater tuus, qui possedit, fecit, et creauit te?* … Deut 32:6.

8   *Lauda anima mea dominum* … Ps 145/146:2.

11   *Salue arcana trias* … The word *arcana* to describe the Trinity is relatively common among the Church Fathers. See, for example, Bernard of Clairvaux, *Epist* 189 (*PL* 182.0355A) '*de arcano sanctae Trinitatis*'. Maximus of Touris, in *Homilia* 23, *Admonitio* (*PL* 57.0273B), writes: '*qui ineffabilis Trinitatis arcanum uno Dei sub nomine confitemur*' [which we acknowledge, under the one name of God, the ineffable mystery of the Trinity].

14 *tibi regi seculorum immortali, inuisibili, soli deo, omnis sit honos, omnis sit gloria ... 1 Tim 1:17.

17 Parts of this aphorism and the next seem to recall, in spirit, the sentiment of Ps 18/19:2, which states: 'Caeli enarrant gloriam Dei, et opera manuum ejus annuntiat firmamentum' [The heavens show forth the glory of God, and the firmament declares the work of his hands].

18 regni tui gloriam ... Ps 144/145:11.

admirabilis haec rerum magnificentia ... Ecclus 43:32.

19 *lucem habitans inaccessam ... 1 Tim 6:16; the last line is not marked.

22 et uelut per transennam intermicas ... See Erasmus, Adagia III.i.49 (Saladin 2010: III.1508).

24 tenebrae non opacent ... This phrase seems to echo Ps 138/139:11–12.

26 *Apud te unum est uitae fons ... ... Ps 35/36:10. The source for lines two and three (which are marked) have not been identified; but the phrases, by their construction, appear to be an expansion of the initial phrase and the markings are therefore likely to be a compositor's error.

29 *sapientiae et scientiae thesauri sunt repositi ... Col 2:3; also qtd. in Ps XV, Ci^v–Cii^r.

*Tu scrutaris profunda fluuiorum: tu in lucem abdita pandis ... Job 28:11.

*tu sedes super cherubim, et intueris in abyssum ... Dan 3:55.

*tu maris dinumeras arenam ... Ecclus 1:2.

tu coeli stellis nomina imponis ... An echo of Ps 146/147:4. Not marked in the last line of the aphorism.

33 *Non uidebit dominus: non intelligent Deus Iacob ... Ps 93/94:7.

*Tenebrae occultabunt me: nox illuminatio mea in deliciis meis ... A rendering of Ps 138/139:11.

34 *Num tu, qui plantas aurem, non audias? Num qui fingis oculum, non consideres? Num tu rei alicuius nescius esse queas, qui doces hominem scientiam? ... Ps 93/94:9–10. The last line is not marked; the phrase 'Num tu rei alicuius nescius esse queas' seems to be Volusenus's own addition.

35 This aphorism has echoes of Ps 138/139:2–5, 11–12.

36 non temere proponit ante oculos rem iniustam ... Ps 100/101:3 (not marked).

*perambulat in innocentia cordis sui, in medio domus suae ... Ps 100/101:2.

40 nam ita natura passim comparatum est ... Livy, Ab Urbe Condita 3.68.10.1; the phrase is quoted, without attribution, in Adagia I.ix.77 (Saladin 2010: I.754).

45 *pulchritudinem tuam sol et luna admirantur ... According to Aldhelm of Sherborne, De virginitate, Prosa 45, the words of St Agnes, in praise of

the Blessed Virgin Mary (Aldhelm 1844: 60). It forms the basis for an antiphon sung on the feast of the saint (21 January). One of the few instances where the marked quotation is not biblical. See also Pss 95/96:6, 11, and 148:3–4, which echo the sense and, in cases, the language of the whole aphorism.

47 *Nos tantisper, dum in caeco hoc carcere positi* ... The whole aphorism resembles a passage in both *Scholia* (Biv^v) and *DAT*: 44, drawing on both Plato (*Phaedo* 66b–e), and Virgil (*Aen* 6.730–4). See the discussion on these passages in 'The context of ideas and faith'.

52–4 These reflections on the shadows of forms (*formarum umbrae*) and the restrictions such shadows place on our ability to perceive the higher things is a common theme in Plato's dialogues. See particularly *Phaedrus* 249d–250b, and the Allegory of the Cave in *Republic* 7.514a–520a.

55 The Greek term φιλοκάλῳ ('lover of beauty') appears in Plato's *Phaedrus* 248d in the 'Allegory of the Chariot'. For a discussion of this idea, see Chapter III above.

56 *Tu totum nutu tremefacis olympum* ... Virgil, *Aen* 9.106; 10.115, which Erasmus quotes in *Adagia* III.vi.77 (Saladin 2010: III.1793; cf. Erasmus 2005: 178). There is perhaps an oblique reference to this passage in *DAT*: 389, referring to the judgement of Christ: '*Num quicquam est in hoc regno, quod ad illius, uel nutum non contremiscat?*' [Surely there is nothing in this kingdom which does not tremble at his very nod?]

Tu fera terribili iacularis fulmina dextra ... Ovid, *Metamorphoses* 2.61.

57 ★*Tu coelos digitulo appendis: tu palmo concludis orbem: tu montes in statera ponderas* ... See Isa 40:12. The quotation continues into the third line (not marked).

58 *Ante te incuruantur qui portant orbem* ... Job 9:13.

59 (★)*Tu montes et colles humilias* ... Isa 42:15. The word *humilias* is substituted for *faciam desertos*. In lines 2 and 3, which are marked, there is perhaps a distant echo of Jer 49.16.

Deturbas de sedibus potentes, et a puluere usque ad gloriae principatum humiles subuehis ... See Luke 1:52, from the Magnificat.

60 ★*Si populorum insurgant milia* ... Perhaps an allusion to Ps 3:7.

sub alarum tuarum umbra ... Ps 16/17:8. This phrase is not marked.

61 *Altissimum enim posuisti refugium tuum: illo usque malum non pertinet, et flagellam non appropinquat ad tabernaculum tuum* ... Ps 90/91:9–10. The whole aphorism is a quotation, but line 4 is unmarked.

62 ★*Beatus cuius deus Iacob adiutor eius, spes eius in domino deo ipsius* ... Ps 145/146:5.

63 *Tu pensilem hanc molem, et quicquid eius ambitur finibus, assidue fulcis* ... This
echoes a passage from *Ps XV*, v. 2 (Bii^r), where Volusenus describes the
divine essence to be '*solus*' [alone], a term Aquinas employs on numerous
occasions (cf. *ST* I.Q31.A3). That essence is immovable and supports
the dependent life of everything else ('*pensilemque ... aliorum omnium
subsistentiam fulciens*').

te penes est unum uasti custodia mundi ... Ovid, *Fasti* 1.119.

64 For a discussion of God's self-containment, see *Ps XV*, v. 2 (Bi^v–Bii^v).

65 This aphorism echoes Volusenus's comments in *Ps XV*, v. 2, whereby he
distinguishes between the incomplete essence ('*ens inabsolutus*'), which is
marked by potentiality, or a capacity to grow; and the divine essence,
which, as fully realised actuality (Aristotle's 'entelechy'), lacking in
nothing and needing nothing, is necessarily infinite and circumscribed
by no limits to its perfection: '*necesse est sit infinitum, nullisque penitus
perfectionis limitibus circumscriptum*' (Bi^v–Bii^r).

66 *principatus, dominationes, uirtutes, praefecti, procuratores, dioecete, nuntii* ... Cf.
Col 1:16, which identifies the members of the angelic hierarchy as '*throni,
sive dominationes, sive principatus, sive potestates*'. Volusenus's designations
differ from those normally used. See, for example, Bernard of Clairvaux,
De consideratione 5.4: '*Angeli, Archangeli, Virtutes, Potestates, Principatus,
Dominationes, Throni, Cherubin, et Seraphin, haec nomina*' (*PL* 182.0792A).
The less usual in Volusenus's list seem to come from Classical political
and judicial offices; see, for example, Justinian's *Digesta* 4.6.32.4–5,
which names *procuratores* and *praefecti*.

68 This aphorism calls to mind Ps 103/104:27–9.

69 This aphorism calls to mind Ps 103/104:10–15.

71 *Ad minimam nominis tui mentionem, profunda contremiscunt Tartara* ... Likely
an echo of Virgil's *Aen* 7.514–15.

72 ★The whole of the aphorism is from Deut 32:40–1, but the last line is
not marked. In addition to changes in tense, *extendis* is substituted for
levabo.

73 ★The whole aphorism, not just the passage marked, is from Deut 32:22.
incendis is substituted for *succensus*; *desaeuiat*, for *ardebat*; and *exurit*, for
comburet.

75 *montibus dicturi sint, Cadite super nos: collibus, operite nos* ... Luke 23:30.
The quotation begins on line 4 (not marked).

76 (★)*Quis nouit potestatem irae tuae?* ... Ps 89/90:11.

quam impatibilis sit furor tuus ... A rendering of Num 25:4.

77 ★*Ne, amabo, filios in furore arguas* ... Pss 6:2; 37/38:2.

Nam si tu iniquitates obseruaueris, si nos pro meritis tractaris, hei mihi, quis perferat? quis sustineat? ... An amplification of Ps 129/130:3. Lines 4 and 8 are unmarked.

78   *Ignosce nobis parens, ignosce. Nescimus proculdubio, nescimus, quid facimus ...* An echo of Luke 23:34. Volusenus follows what had become a more common way of expressing the word for 'forgive', *ignosce*. See, for example, Augustine, *DCD* 18.32 (1877: II.300): '*Pater ignosce illis, quia nesciunt quod faciunt*'. There are numerous examples from the Church Fathers.

83   *quae in iram apparasti, uasa coniicias ...* Perhaps an echo of Rom 9:22.

84   *manuumque tuarum opificium ...* An echo, perhaps, of Job 10:3 ('*opus manuum tuarum*'), although used here in a context that differs from Job's. Volusenus admits that although he is the work of God's hands, he deserves punishment. Job questions why God would oppress him, the work of God's hand, while favouring the unjust.

86   *contra folium, quod uento rapitur, ostendes potentiam tuam, et stipulam hanc siccam ad internetionem persequere?* ... Job 13:25. The phrase '*ad internetionem*' is added, but occurs on a number of occasions in the Bible and in medieval chronicles to refer to complete destruction (see, for example, Isa 43:28). This sentence also appears in *DAT*: 161. The last line should be marked.

91   *bonorum omnium pelagus es immensum ...* A phrase resembling one found in *Ps XV*, Bii[r]: '*pelagus quoddam substantiae innui infinitum, immensasque perfectionum diuitias contineri*' [The sea has signified a certain infinitude of substance, containing immense riches of perfection]. This passage itself is a rendering of John Damascene's *De fide orthodoxa* 1: '*habet ipsum esse velut quoddam pelagus substantiae infinitum et indeterminatum*' [It contains existence itself as an infinite and indeterminate sea of substance]. Aquinas quotes from the passage to declare that the Divine Name ('*Qui est*', or 'He Who Is') is most appropriate for God (*ST* I.Q13.A11).

92   *ostendam tibi omne bonum ...* Ex 33:19.

93   *Tibi, inquit, (tanquam proloqui superuacaneum foret) silentium, laus Deus in Syon ...* Ps 64/65:2 (Jerome's translation). Cf. Ps 101/102:22, with perhaps a nod to Hab 2:20.

98   *quando ueniam? quando apparebo ante faciem dei mei?* ... Ps 41/42:3 This quotation is not marked.

     Quis mihi dabit pennas sicut columbae? et uolabo, ut requiescam ... Ps 54/55:7. *ut requiescam in monte sancto tuo ...* Ps 14/15:1.

99   *haec tabernacula Cedar ...* Perhaps an echo of Cant 1:4.

100 The Apostle Paul uses similar language in Rom 7.

104 *neque illae nisi extremis lineamentis, non habitu solido* ... A close rendering of Cicero's *De natura deorum* 1.123.9–10.

107 The whole aphorism, with the addition of '*diuturnitate extabescunt, aut certe uniusmodi perpetuo non consistunt*', is from Ps 101/102:27–8, which itself is qtd. in Heb 1:11–12. Only the passage '*tu uero idem ipse es, et anni tui non deficient*' is marked.

diuturnitate extabescunt ... Cicero, *De natura deorum* 2.5.7.

110 *quod tam serus speciem istam adamarim, quae una ab ipsis aeternitatis primordiis (si tamen hic primordia dicenda sunt) in infinitum aeuum illibata perseruerat* ... This passage is reminiscent, in spirit, of Augustine's *Confessiones* 10.27: '*Sero te amavi, pulchritudo tam antiqua et tam nova, sero te amavi*' [Late have I loved you, O beauty both old and new; late have I loved you].

113 *Quare igitur appendimus argentum, et non in panibus? laborem, et non in saturitate?* ... Isa 55:2.

quae nocuere sequimur: fugimus, quae profore scimus? ... Horace, *Epist* 1.8.11.

116 *Qui bibit ex hac aqua, sitit iterum* ... John 4:13.

117 *et in sterili uita labore perit* ... Martial, *Epigram* 10.58.8.

118 Achieving tranquillity of mind is the subject of *DAT*. Greek terms employed from the Stoic tradition appear in the next aphorism.

119 εὐθύμια/ἀπάθια ... Volusenus, in *DAT*: 30, defines εὐθύμια in this way: '*aequabilis et rationi consentaneus, animi status*' [a state of mind, equable and consistent with reason]. The word ἀπάθια, an indifference to passion, is, as Volusenus states (with, it should be added, no little irony), the position of the Stoics that Cicero should not have held so zealously ('*Non fuit ergo Ciceroni illa Stoicorum* ἀπάθεια, *tam acriter propugnanda*'), given his belief that the poet should write with an inflammation of the spirit and a kind of frenzied inspiration ('*inflammatione animorum, et quodam afflatu quasi furoris*'), *DAT*: 73.

According to Stoic thinking, the Supreme Good is Virtue: compare below §168, where Virtue is *res magna*, the Great Thing. The man who achieves Virtue overcomes emotion.

123 *Hic alta mentis ab arce despicit errantes, humanaque gaudia ridet* ... Statius, *Silvae* 2.2.131–2.

124 The palms from Idumaea, a region south of Judea, were celebrated in Classical literature. See, for example, Virgil's *Georgica* 3.12, and Martial's *Epigrammata* 10.50.1.

125 ★The whole aphorism is from Job 29:2–3.

126 ★The whole aphorism is from Job 29:4–6. The last line should be marked. Butter was well known as an emollient, cf. Dietrich Dorsten (1540: 56ʳ):

'*Conducit etiam ut membra et lumbi eo inungantur, dolorem enim in ijs mitigat*' [It helps also when the limbs and the extremities are anointed by it, for it assuages the pain in them].

127 ★The whole aphorism is from Job 30:15–16, 27.

128 ★*Graue nobis cor est ... diligimus uanitatem, et quaerimus mendacium ...* An expansion of Ps 4:3. The first part of the quotation is not marked.

129 ★*Siquidem omnis caro foenum, omnis gloria eius tanqum flos agri: diluculo efflorescit ...* 1 Pet 1:24; cf. Ps 102/103:15.

ante uesperum decidit, et arescit ... From Ps 89/90:6.

Sola perpetuo manent mentis atque animi bona: florem decoris singuli carpunt dies ... pseudo-Seneca Junior, *Octavia*, 548–50.

131 *Ille speciosus forma prae filiis hominum ...* Ps 44/45:3. This psalm is an epithalamion, or marriage hymn. Although the first part of the aphorism is marked, it is actually the last two lines that form the quotation. This is perhaps a compositor's error.

132 ★*Ille thesaurus in agro reconditus: ille preciosa illa margarita fortunarum omnium ...* Matt 13:44, 46. Volusenus will refer to this passage in his Ode (*DAT*: 397, ll. 81–4):

> *Extra se quid enim uolet*
> *Quidquam, qui pretiosum illud, et omnium*
> *Per dispendia quaerere*
> *Quod solum deceat, margaritum tenet.*

[For what does he crave outside himself, he who possesses that pearl, the only one which it is fitting to seek at the cost of all else.]

133 ★*aut formaretur terra et orbis ...* Ps 89/90:2. Line 4, though not part of the quotation, is marked.

135 The phrasing here resembles that in *Ps XV* (Bi^v): '*perfectum illud est, et totum, extra quod nihil est, seu cui nihil deest: quod perfectissimum ens dici meretur, necesse est intra se complectatur*' [That thing is perfect and whole, beyond which there is nothing, or in which nothing is lacking; what thing deserves to be called most perfect, it is necessary that it be complete within itself].

136 In a discussion of the divine Name (the Tetragrammaton), Volusenus equates the Hebrew with the Greek ὄν and the Latin *ens*, 'Being' (*Ps XV* Bi^v).

140 *nihil monogrammon ...* See Cicero, *De natura deorum* 2.59.9–60.1.

141 ★*Das enim tu escam et pullis coruorum, qui et ipsi opem tuam, suo more crocitando, implorant ...* A rendering of Ps 146/147:9. The last line is unmarked.

142   The whole of the aphorism is a rendering of Ps 103/104:28–9. Individual phrases can also be found in other psalms.

Aperis enim tu manum tuam atque omne animal liberaliter exaturas ... Ps 144/145:16.

Simul uero ac tu faciem auertis ... Pss 12/13:1; 87/88:15.

143   This description of God's relationship with the Creation has parallels, although much abbreviated, with pseudo-Dionysius's *DDN* c. 2, §11; c. 9, §9; c. 13, §§2–3.

144   ★*Si ueneris ad me, non uidebo: si abieris, non intelligam ...* Job 9:11. The last line, although part of the quotation, is unmarked.

145   ★The whole aphorism is a rendering of Ps 138/139:8–10, although only a portion is marked.

146   The aphorism is an expansion of Virgil's *Aen* 6.724–7; but see Maurus Servius Honoratus, *In Vergilii Bucolicon librum* 3.60.1–2, 5–6, which names Jupiter/Jove specifically. For a discussion of the passages, see Chapter III above.

152   In *Confessiones* 2.5 Augustine details the means by which a particular vice imitates its corresponding virtue (for example, sloth:rest; prodigality:generosity).

153   *Eritis sicut Dii ...* This aphorism as a whole draws on Gen 3:5, with the serpent's promise that Eve and Adam will be as the gods.

154   *Igitur ne templo huic tam augusto deesset Antistes ...* Cf. Cicero, *De re publica* 6.15, with Volusenus's commentary on the passage in *Scholia* Ci^r. This and the following aphorisms find similar sentiments on the character of humankind in Cicero's *De legibus*, especially 1.22–7, which, though it names these attributes as gifts of God, does not, however, conclude with an exhortation to love and venerate the Creator.

158   *quicquid maiore illo mundo cohibetur liquido repraesentans ...* Cf. Plato's *Timaeus* 29d–47e, where the correspondences between the Cosmos and humankind (the 'microcosm') are detailed at length. Cf. *DAT*: 33, where Volusenus describes the human being as '*minor quidam mundus*' [a certain lesser world]. Baker-Smith (1969: 282) suggests that this aphorism has patristic roots in Nemesius of Emesa, *De natura hominis* 1.13 (pp. 25–6). For a discussion of the passage, see Chapter III above.

166   The sentiment in this aphorism echoes medieval Christian thought about the dual nature of human beings – the 'bestial' and the divine. Volusenus explores the idea in greater detail in *DAT*. See especially p. 60, where he also employs the Greek expression τὸν νοῦν (*hoc est, mentem aut intellectum*, namely, the mind or intellect), which, he claims,

Aristotle (despite his tangled thinking, '*implicatae tamen orationis forma*')
treats with great veneration ('*magna veneratione dignetur*').

ad unguem ... See Erasmus, *Adagia* I.v.91 (Saladin 2010: I.466; cf. Erasmus
1982: 464), who quotes from Athenaeus's *Deipnosophistae* 3.52.

168   *Vtcunque cadat, certe rei magnae iacturam honesta uita facere non potest* ... The
really Great Thing (*res magna*), according to Stoic teaching, was Virtue,
the achievement of which was the goal of the disciplined life lived
according to the principles of rectitude, duty and right discernment
(see above, Chapter III). See, for example, the Younger Seneca, *Epistulae
Morales* 88.35: *Non dabit se in has angustias virtus; laxum spatium res magna
desiderat*' [Virtue will not give herself over to these restraints of ours;
the really Great Thing needs a roomy place to roam]. Once achieved
in its totality it could not be lost, except temporarily by something
affecting the reason (e.g. drunkenness, illness), but even so the person
so affected could never return to his totally unenlightened state. Again,
see *Epistulae Morales* 50.8: '*semel traditi nobis boni perpetua possessio est; non
dediscitur virtus*' [Once the Good has become ours, the possession of it
is permanent; Virtue cannot be unlearned].

172   ★*Ipse enim fecit nos, et non ipsi nos* ... Ps 99/100:3.

181   ★*Plane omnia pedibus nostris subiecisti* ... A rendering of Pss 8:8; 46/47:4.

       ★*terreni orbis reges nos creasti* ... Perhaps an echo of Sap 10:1–2.

184   ★*Nemo enim uenit ad te, nisi tu illum trahas* ... John 6:44; 14:6. No source
has been found for the third line, which is marked.

187   *mulcet et elysias aura beata rosas* ... Sextus Propertius, *Elegiae* 4.7.60.

190   *totisque ... habenis ferri* ... Silius Italicus, *Punica* 4.339.

191   *Siquidem ipsa uirtus sibimet pulcherrima merces est* ... Silius Italicus, *Punica*
13.663; qtd. in *DAT*: 179, though not attributed to Silius.

       quamuis uniuersus fieret interitus, et a funere nihil superesset ... See Cicero,
Tusculanae Disputationes 1.90.7–10.

       suis illecebris ad uerum decus trahere debet ... Cicero, *De re publica* 6.25.8–9;
Volusenus comments on the passage in his *Scholia*, Eiv^r, and also quotes
it in *DAT*: 179.

192   *unus dies, ex ipsius praescriptis actus, cum ipsa possit immortalitate contendere*
... A rendering of Cicero's *Tusculanae Disputationes* 5.5.16–18.

192–4 These aphorisms on the worth and rewards of virtue echo sentiments
expressed in Volusenus's *Scholia* Eiv^r–v, where he quotes from Cicero's
Pro Marcello 29.8–30.3 and, ironically, from Juvenal's *Saturae* 10.142–5,
the latter of which shows the ill-effects of the greater thirst for fame
than for virtue. Invoking the authority of Augustine in the same

passage – '*ut copiose docet Augustinus*' – he states that if pagan heroes like Cato and Fabricius were committed to virtue for earthly goals, such as the glory of Rome, how much more should Christians pursue virtue for God's sake. See *DCD* 5.18–19.

[196]   The Greek term φιλαῦτοι [lovers of selves] appears in in 2 Tim 3:2 (Strong's Greek: 5367). See below, §227.

[198]   *Oderunt sane peccare boni uirtutis amore* ... Horace, *Epist* 1.16.52. The quotation also appears in *DAT*: 98, though not attributed to Horace.

[201]   **Quae sursum sunt, sapiamus: quae sursum sunt, quaeramus: non quae super terram* ... An expansion of Col 3:2.

ad te unum, unde multa ... Although not marked, this line has parallels in 1 Cor 12:12.

[207]   *sed ad conscientiae iudicium abunde amplum ingenuis mentibus theatrum se componit* ... See Cicero, *Tusculanae Disputationes* 2.64, especially 10–11.

[208]   *si fractus illabatur orbis, impauidum ferient ruinae* ... Horace, *Carmina* 3.3.7–8.

[210]   *uoluptatum Sirenes* ... See Isa 13:22 (*et sirenes in delubris voluptatis*); Cicero, *De finibus* 5.48.12–49.3; and Quintilian, *Institutio oratoria* 5.8.1.6–8. Odysseus' temptation by the Sirens is found in the *Odyssey* 12. In *DAT*: 222, 254, 255, 348, Volusenus refers to the Sirens as temptresses to lust and fame.

[213]   *tellurisque duntaxat pondera* ... See Erasmus, *Adagia* I.vii.31 (Saladin 2010: I.578), who is quoting from Homer's *Iliad* 18.104, and *Odyssey* 20.379.

[215]   This aphorism, on dreaming and waking as related to understanding, has Platonic overtones: *Republic* 5 476c–d; and *Timaeus* 52a–c. See discussion by Tigner 1970: 209.

[216]   *ab ipsis protinus incunabulis inficit* ... See Erasmus, *Adagia* I.vii.53 (Saladin 2010: I.596).

[221]   *sub pedibus nubes, sydera* ... Virgil, *Eclogae* 5.57, which Volusenus quotes more fully in *Scholia*, Cii^r.

[224]   This aphorism is reminiscent, generally, of John 1:5–9 and Rom 1:21–32, which develop the themes much more fully.

[225]   (*)*Plane Deus eras absconditus* ... Isa 45:15.

*notus pene tantum in Iudaea Deus, et non temere alibi, quam in Israel, magnum, et celebre fuit tuum nomen ... An expansion of Ps 75/76:2. The latter part of the aphorism is not, however, marked.

[227]   ἀχαριστίας ... The Greek term for 'ungratefulness', used in 2 Tim 3:2 (Strong's Greek: 884). See above, §196.

[229]   The whole of the aphorism is a rendering and expansion, it would appear, of 1 Pet 2:24. Not marked in the text.

230   *paruulum natum nobis, filium datum nobis* ... Isa 9:6. The quotation begins on an unmarked line.

231   *agnus ... immaculatus* ... 1 Pet 1:19.

232   *quam omnipotens rerum parens ad dexteram filio apparauerat* ... Cf. Matt 26:64; Mark 14:62; 16:19; Luke 22:69; Col 3:1; Heb 1:3, 10:12, 12:2; Apoc 5:1, 7. The phrase '*et sedet ad dexteram patris*' is a common one in the liturgy of the Mass.

236   *⋆ut fugiant a facie arcus* ... Ps 59/60:6.

     nec limina illa uis ultrix aut inimica contingit, quae pretiosus ille agni cruor illeuit ... See 1 Pet 1:19. This passage recalls Ex 12:21–3, when Moses told the Israelites to smear their doorposts with blood so that the Angel of the Lord would pass over their houses when killing the firstborn of Egypt.

237   *in filii tui ... in tutela sumus* ... The repetition of 'in' is unnecessary.

238   *⋆delictorum omnium gratiam fieri, imo ne iudicatum quidem iri eiusmodi* ... The phrase has verbal echoes of Rom 5:9, 16; the whole aphorism follows the general sense of Rom 5. Only line 5 is marked.

240   *⋆Quid est homo, quod sic illum magnificas, et apponis erga illum cor tuum?* ... Job 7:17.

242   Many of these names for Christ have a liturgical ring about them:

     fili dei uiui ... Cf. the trope *AGNUS ... MUNDI Jesu summi fili patris vivi.*

     aeterni patris uerbum ... The opening words of Aquinas from his *Compendium Theologiae* 1.1.

     intemeratae uirginis proles ... Cf. '*Intemerata virgo quae*', an antiphon from week after the Feast of the Assumption.

     salutis autor ... A phrase from Heb 2:10, which forms the basis for the sequence hymn '*Auctor Salutis Unice*'.

     nostri generis decus ... Cf. the hymn '*Christe sanctorum decus angelorum rector humani generis*', sung on the Feast of St Michael.

     immensi orbis dominator ... Cf. a hymn from the Feast of the Epiphany and a trope from the Feast of the Resurrection ('*Dominator orbis*'); and '*Elegiarum et carminum libri tres*' 3.4 ('*Christus totius dominator orbis*') by Georgius Sisgoreus (c.1440–c.1510).

     seruili habitu ... Cf. Phil 2:7.

243   *homuncio* ... Cf. *homunculi* in Cicero, *De natura deorum* 1.123.9.

247   *⋆Quis enim nouit sensum domini? quis arcanas consiliorum tuorum rationes scrutetur?* ... Rom 11:34. Volusenus has expanded the latter part of the passage.

250   *Ille, quem coelestis quidam mentis aestus ab terris ad tertium usque coelum ultra astra abripuerat, quique arcana uerba, quae proloqui nefas esset, audiuerat* ...

A rendering of 2 Cor 12:2–4. The passage is not marked. That part of the aphorism that is marked has not been identified. This is perhaps a compositor's error.

252 Although no precise source for the marked line has been found, the spirit of the aphorism, with some verbal echoes, can be detected in Phil 2:8 and Col 2:8, 18.

256 *stulti stultis stulte placere* ... Perhaps a playful elaboration (adding the adverb *stulte*) of a passage from Erasmus's *Encomium Moriae* (N3ʳ): '*Encomiis sese uicissim laudant, Stulti stultos, indoctos indocti*' [With praises, they compliment one another in turn, fools complimenting fools, the ignorant complimenting the ignorant]. Cf. *Adagia* I.i.98: '*Stultus stulta loquitur*' (Erasmus 1982: 141–2).

uideri, non esse ... An inversion of the well-known tag *esse non videri*, or, more commonly, *esse quam videri*. For the latter, see Cicero, *Lucullus* 44.15–16 and *Laelius de amicitia* 98.5; and Sallust, *Catilinae coniuratio* 54.6.3. The sentiment had been expressed earlier by the Greek playwright Aeschylus in *Seven Against Thebes* 592, which was then quoted by Plato in *Republic* 2.361b.

257 ★*Nam cum mundus per suam sapientiam autorem suum male gratus non agnosceret* ... A rendering of Rom 1:21; lines 2 and 5 should be part of the quotation. Paul also contrasts God's wisdom and that of the world in 1 Cor 1.20–9; 3:19.

262 *homuncionum* ... Cf. *homunculi* in Cicero, *De natura deorum* 1.123.9.

266 *uni homini crudelem se praebuit nouercam* ... The figure of the cruel stepmother, a staple of folk tales, has a long history. See, for example, pseudo-Quintilian, *Declamationes Maiores* 6.10.1–2; and Seneca Senior, *Controversiae* 7.1.8.12 ('*O crudelis et pertinax noverca!*')

269 *manhu* ... See Ex 16, especially v. 15, for the story of God's providing manna for the Children of Israel in the wilderness. Volusenus uses the transliteration of the Hebrew (see Strong's Hebrew: 4478, 1931), which means, 'What is it?' See also Ps 77/78:24; John 6:31, 49, 59. John's verses contrast Christ as manna that brings eternal life with the manna in the wilderness that satisfied only a short time.

270 ★*ut abiecta impietate, et praesentis uitae desideriis, sobrie, iuste, et pie uiuamus: expectantes beatam spem, et aduentum gloriae magni Dei* ... Tit 2:12–13. The last line, though unmarked, is part of the quotation.

271 *Sed et mihi quoque seruator, cum in crucem tuam intueor, sub primum aspectum horror es, ignominia es, et dolorum aceruus* ... Perhaps a reference to Isa 53:2–4, which describes the appearance of the Suffering Servant.

272 *At cum mysterium expendo, et nucleum nuce fracta, ut ualeo, contrecto, decus es, et deliciae* ... The image of cracking the shell of a nut to find the delicious fruit inside was a common way of describing the practice of reading allegorically. Jerome, *Epist* 58 (*ad Paulinum*), writes, '*Qui edere vult nucleum, frangat nucem*' (*PL* 22.0585), quoting Plautus, *Curculio* 55. Peter Lombard, in his *Commentaria in Psalmos* (*Disceptatio de auctoribus Psalmorum*), quotes Jerome (*PL* 191.0038A); and Thomas Aquinas, also referring to Jerome, in his *Catena Aurea* on Mark (C1.L6), renders this version: '*Poenitentiam enim agit qui vult aeterno bono, scilicet regno Dei, adhaerere. Qui enim desiderat nucleum, frangit nucem*'. The application of the maxim applied both to Scripture and literature. For the former, see Thomas the Cistercian, *Commentaria in Cantica Canticorum*, 10:

Siquidem Ecclesia per hortum nucum designatur: propter patientiam sanctorum et fructum patientiae, quae signatur in nuce, quae sub amaro cortice et testa dura, dulcem continet nucleum, sic patientia per amaritudinem passionum et constantiae robur, pervenit ad dulcedinem praemiorum [Accordingly, the Church is designated by the garden of the nut because of the patience of the saints and the fruit of patience, which is signified in the nut, which contains a sweet core within the bitter shell and hard outside; thus patience by the bitterness of suffering and strength of constancy attains the sweetness of rewards] (*PL* 206.0668B).

For the application of the phrase to literature, see Robert Henryson's Prologue to the *Morall Fabillis*:

The nuttis schell thocht it be hard and teuch

Haldis the kirnell sueit and delectabill,

Sa lyis thair ane doctrine wyse aneuch

And full of frute under ane fenyeit fabill. (15–18)

273 ★*Hi exugunt mel de petra, oleumque de saxo durissimo* ... Deut 32:13; Volusenus will draw on this image in his ode at the conclusion of *DAT* (396: 73–6):

Sic (quod non temere solet
  Aut multis dare caelum) mel hic ex petra
Ipsa fugit, et ampliter
  Duro ex saxo oleum, cum lubet, elicit.

[Thus (and this is not something heaven is wont to grant rashly or to many) it drives honey from rock, and, when it chooses, it produces oil from hard stone.]

★*Hi hauriunt aquas in gaudio de fontibus seruatoris* ... Isa 12:3. The word *seruatoris* has been substituted for *salvatoris*.

★*Hi renuunt aliunde, quam ex te, consolationem admittere* ... A rendering of Ps 76/77:3. The last line of the aphorism should be marked.

276 *mori, lucrum* ... See Phil 1:21.

278 *ubi uictum non iam infelicem bacchas, lapidosaque corna dant rami, et uulsis pascunt radicibus herbae* ... Virgil, *Aen* 3.649–50.

★*in montibus et speluncis et cauernis terrae, quibus plane mundus dignus non erat* ... Heb 11:38. The order of the verse has been rearranged. The last line of the aphorism should be marked.

282 *quae coelesti quadam metamorphosi homines uel ante diem, pene dixerim, deos efficit* ... Volusenus here asserts, albeit with due hesitation ('*pene dixerim*' [I might almost say]), that the serpent's promise to Adam and Eve in Gen 3:5 – that they would be as gods – becomes an actuality in Christian philosophy (cf. §153).

283 This aphorism is perhaps an allusion to Chaucer's depiction of Chaunticleer in the *Nun's Priest's Tale*, who vaunts his learning, but clearly has gained no wisdom. In *DAT*: 77–8, Volusenus recounts Plato's story of Socrates' request that a cock be sacrificed to Aesculapius in thanksgiving for his deliverance from the bondage of this life (see Plato's *Phaedo* 118a), but makes no attempt to allegorise the cock. On the other hand, Pico della Mirandola, following Pythagoras, exalts the *gallus*, whom he describes as '*divinam animae nostrae partem*' [the divine part of our soul]. He alludes to Job 38:7, 36. See *De oratio*, §§124–9 (2012: 172–5).

285 ★*In te domino gaudebo, et exultabo in Deo IESV meo* ... Hab 3:18. The last line should be marked.

287 ★*Abscondis enim haec a sapientibus et prudentibus* ... Matt 11:25; Luke 10:21. Line 3 is not a biblical quotation and technically should not be marked, but it perhaps alludes to Isa 45:2–3, which contrasts the humbling of the great with the revelation of divine treasures to God's people: '*Ego ante te ibo, et gloriosos terrae humiliabo; portas aereas conteram, et vectes ferreos confringam: et dabo tibi thesauros absconditos, et arcana secretorum*' [I will go before you and will humble the great ones of the earth. I will break in pieces the gates of brass, and will burst the bars of iron. And I will give you hidden treasures and the concealed riches of secret places].

288 (★)*Reuelas ea paruulis* ... Matt 11:25; Luke 10:21. Line 2 should not be marked.

302 *quod a philosophis de officiis traditum est* ... No doubt a reference to Cicero's *De officiis*.

305 ★*Nam tu solus mundum facere potes, quod ex immundo, et uenenato conceptum est semine* ... An expansion of Job 14:4.

308 *Quid boni fructus ex hac mala arbore enasci ualet?* ... Although not marked, this passage echoes Matt 7:17–18; Luke 6:43.

309   *Non intres in iudicium cum seruo tuo. Nemo in conspectu tuo, si tu summo iure agas, iustus inuenitur* ... Ps 142/143:2.

Si coner me innocentem ostendere, os meum condemnabit me ... Job 9:20. Line 5 should also be marked.

quando ne coeli quidem mundi sunt coram te ... Job 15:15.

312   *cum praeter te nihil dulce, aut decorum sit* ... Perhaps a nod to Horace's famous line from *Carmina* 3.2.13: '*dulce et decorum est pro patria mori*' [It is a sweet and fitting thing to die for one's country].

nubibus, ac praestigiis ... Apuleius *De mundo* 15.1 ('*De nubium praestigiis*').

317   *defecerunt plane in uanitate dies mei, et anni pudendi cum festinatione* ... Ps 77/78:33. The last line should be marked.

320   *tanquam columba in foraminibus petrae* ... Cant 2:14. Line 4 should be marked; the phrase '*perpetuo delitescam*', though marked, appears to be Volusenus's own addition.

321   *qui pascis inter lilia* ... Cant 2:16.

donec aspiret dies felicitatis, et inclinentur umbrae miseriae ... Cant 2:17; 4:6. The last two lines should be marked; the phrase '*cui puritas unice grata*' appears to be Volusenus's own addition.

322   *Quemadmodum desyderat ceruus ad fontes aquarum, sic ad te aspiret anima mea* ... Ps 41/42:2.

323   *Sint interdiu, sint item et noctu mihi lachrymae panes, dum dicitur per singulos dies animae meae, Vbi est Deus tuus?* ... A rendering of Ps 41/42:4.

Quo abiit dilectus tuus, O pulcherrima mulierum? ... Cant 5:17.

324   *Surgam, et circuibo magnam hanc, cui tu praees, ciuitatem per uicos, perque plateas, per omne rerum genus quaeram, quem diligit anima mea* ... An expansion of Cant 3:2. Lines 3, 6–7, though part of the quotation, are not marked.

325   *Percontabor de ipsis uigilibus, atque excubitoribus, qui hanc ciuitatem custodiunt* ... A rendering of Cant 3:3.

quem diligit anima mea: neque operam intermittam, quoad aedes tuas subeam, donec te inueniam ... A paraphrase of Cant 3:3–4. The phrase '*diligit anima meum*' is a refrain in Cant 1:6; 3:1–4. Lines 6 and 9, although part of the paraphrase, are not marked.

326   *The whole aphorism, a rendering of Ps 83/84:11, should perhaps be marked.

329   *Viuam ego iam non ego: quod autem nunc uiuo in carne, in fide tua CHRISTE fili Dei uiui, uiuam: qui dilexisti me: tradidisti temetipsum pro me* ... Gal 2:20. Lines 4–5 should be marked.

tecum uiuere amem: tecum obeam libens ... Although not marked, this seems to be a paraphrase of Phil 1:21.

331   **in uoce laudis, et exultationis ingrediatur in locum tabernaculi admirabilis* ... A rendering of Ps 41/42:5. Lines 3 and 6 should be marked.

333–4   The Utopians, in Sir Thomas More's *Utopia* 2: 'Of the Religions of Utopia' (1999: 190), view dying similarly: it is degenerate souls who fear death and resist it, whereas virtuous spirits embrace it.

336   **[lucis ab autore data est haec]* – not present in 1539. It is presumed that these (intended) words, which are necessary to the sense of the aphorism, were inadvertently omitted by the compositor.

338   *procul este Circea pocula* ... For the story of Circe and her enchanted cup, see Homer's *Odyssey* 10. In *Adagia* I.i.97, Erasmus quotes, in Greek, 10.318–19 (Saladin 2010: I.166; cf. Erasmus 1982: 141); see also *Adagia* II.x.62 (Saladin 2010: II.1448).

339   ** Si oblitus fuero tui Hierusalem, obliuiscatur mei dextera mea* ... Ps 136/137:5. The word '*obliuiscatur*' is substituted for '*obliuioni detur*'.

*renuat aliunde, quam ex te, consolationem admittere anima mea: dies illi antiqui, aeternique anni animum habeant ... A rendering of Ps 76/77:3, 6. The last line of the aphorism is not marked.

340   **Adiuro uos filiae Hierusalem, nunciate quia amore langueo* ... Cant 5:8.

349   Although not marked, this aphorism seems to allude to Ps 83/84:11.

350   **Misericordias domini in aeternum cantabo* ... Ps 88/89:2.

BIBLIOGRAPHY

PRIMARY SOURCES

Augustine of Hippo. 1588. *Confessiones libri tredecim.* Tours.

Augustine of Hippo. 1877. *De civitate Dei.* 2 vols. Ed. B. Dombart. Leipzig.

Aldhelm of Sherborne. 1844. *Operae que extant.* Ed. J.A. Giles. Oxford.

Aldhelm of Sherborne. 1979. *Aldhelm: The Prose Works.* Trans. Michael Lapidge and Michael Herren. Cambridge.

Baduel, Claude. 1543. *De morte Christi meditanda ac contemplanda oratio.* Lyon.

Boethius, Manlius Severinus. 1502. *De consolatione philosophiae.* Deventer.

Buchanan, George. 1725. *Opera Omnia.* 2 vols. Ed. Thomas Ruddiman; rev., ed. Peter Burmann. Leiden.

Calvin, John. 1844–51. *Tracts Relating to the Reformation.* 3 vols. Trans. Henry Beveridge. Edinburgh.

Delitiae poetarum Scotorum. 1637. 2 vols. Amsterdam.

Dempster, Thomas. 1829. *Historia ecclesiastica gentis Scotorum.* 2 vols. Ed. David Irving. Edinburgh.

Dorsten, Dietrich. 1540. *Botanicon, continens herbarum, aliorumque simplicium, quorum usus in medecinis est.* Frankfurt.

Ducher, Gilbert. 2015. *Épigrammes.* Ed., trans. Sylvie Laigneau-Fontaine and Catherine Langlois-Pézeret. Paris.

Erasmus, D. 1515/16. *Encomium Moriae: Stulticiae Laus.* Basel.

Erasmus, D. 1978. *De Copia: Foundations of the Abundant Style.* Trans., annot. Betty I. Knott. In *Collected Works of Erasmus*, Vol. 24. Ed. Craig Thompson. Toronto.

Erasmus, D. 1982. *Adages I.i.1 to I.v.100.* Trans. Margaret Mann Phillips; annot. R.A.B. Mynors. In *Collected Works of Erasmus*, Vol. 31. Toronto.

Erasmus, D. 1986. *The Ciceronian: A Dialogue on the Ideal Latin Style / Dialogus Ciceronianus.* Trans., annot. Betty I. Knott. Intro. A.H.T. Levi. In *Collected Works of Erasmus*, Vol. 28. Toronto.

Erasmus, D. 2005. *Adages: III.iv.1 to IV.ii.100.* Trans., annot. Denis L. Drysdall. In *Collected Works of Erasmus,* Vol. 35. Ed. John N. Grant. Toronto.

Erasmus, D. 2006. *Adages IV.iii.1 to V.ii.51*. Trans., annot. John N. Grant and Betty I. Knott. In *Collected Works of Erasmus*, Vol. 36. Ed. John N. Grant. Toronto.

Erasmus, D. 2014. *Apophthegmata*. Trans., annot. Betty I. Knott and Elaine Fantham. In *Collected Works of Erasmus*, Vols 37–8. Ed. Betty I. Knott. Toronto, Buffalo and London.

Ferrerio, Giovanni. 1539. *Auditum visu praestare*. Paris.

Ferrerio, Giovanni et al., eds. 1541. *Io. Francisci Mirandulae … De Animae immortali*. Paris.

Henryson, Robert. 2010. *The Complete Works*. Ed. David J. Parkinson. TEAMS: Middle English Texts Series. Kalamazoo.

Marguerite de Navarre. 1979. *Le Miroir de l'âme pécheresse*. Ed. Renja Salminen. Helsinki.

More, Thomas. 1510. *Lyfe of Johan Picus erle of Myra[n]dula*. London.

More, Thomas. 1999. *Utopia*. Trans. Ralph Robinson (1556). Ed. David Harris Sacks. The Bedford Series in History and Culture. Boston and New York.

Nemesius of Emesa. 1538. *De natura hominis liber vtilissimus*. Trans. Giorgio Valla. Lyon.

Oxford Latin Dictionary. 2012. 2nd ed. Oxford.

Pico della Mirandola. 1502. *Disputationum adversus astrologos libri duo*. Deventer.

Pico della Mirandola. 2012. *Oration on the Dignity of Man*. Ed. and trans. Francesco Borghesi, Michael Papio and Massimo Riva. Cambridge.

Sadoleto, Iacobo. 1530. *In Psalmum XCIII Interpretatio*. Basel.

Sadoleto, Iacobo. 1538. *De laudibus Philosophiae*. Lyon.

Sadoleto, Iacobo. 1539. *Epistula ad Senatum Populumque Genevensem*. Lyon.

Stuart, John, ed. 1872. *Records of the Monastery of Kinloss*. Edinburgh.

Touris, William. 2022. *The Contemplacioun of Synnaris*. Ed. Alasdair A. MacDonald and J. Craig McDonald. Leiden and Boston.

Traherne, Thomas. 1958. *Centuries, Poems, and Thanksgivings*. 2 vols. Ed. H.M. Margoliouth. Oxford.

Volusenus, Florentius. 1531. *Psalmi quintidecimi enarratio*. Paris.

Volusenus, Florentius. 1532. *In Psalmum 50 enarratio*. Paris. Cambridge University Library, Rare Books.

Volusenus, Florentius. 1534(?). *Scholia seu commentariorum epitome in Scipionis somnium*. London.

Volusenus, Florentius. 1539. *Commentatio quaedam theologica*. Lyon.

Volusenus, Florentius. 1543. *De animi tranquillitate dialogus*. Lyon.

Wilson, Thomas, ed. 1619. *Reverendissimi in Christo patris* [etc.][i.e. Patrick Adamson]. London.

ONLINE

Aquinas, Thomas. *Opera*. Aquinas Institute. Online Text Viewer (Bilingual Editions Online). https://aquinas.cc.

Aquinas, Thomas. *St. Thomas Aquinas's Works in English*. Compiled by Fr Joseph Kenny, OP. https://isidore.co/aquinas.

Aristotle. 1924. *Metaphysics*. Trans. W.D. Ross. Oxford. Internet Archive.

Cantus Index: Online Catalogue for Mass and Office Chants. https://cantusindex.org.

Saladin, Jean-Christophe, ed. 2010. *Les Adages d'Érasme*. 4 vols. Les Belles Lettres et le GRAC (UMR 5037). Paris. https://archive.org/details/ErasmusAdages0-985Tome1BellesLettresEtLeGracJ-cSaladinEditeur; https://archive.org/details/ErasmusAdages1001-2000Tome2BellesLettresEtLeGracJ-cSaladinEditeur; https://archive.org/details/ErasmusAdages2001-3000Tome3BellesLettresEtLeGracJ-cSaladinEditeur; https://archive.org/details/ErasmusAdages3001-4150Tome4BellesLettresEtLeGracJ-cSaladinEditeur.

Strong's Exhaustive Concordance. https://biblehub.com.

Wilson, Florence. 2008 (posted). *De animi tranquillitate* (Lyon, 1543). Ed., trans. Dana F. Sutton. http://www.philological.bham.ac.uk/wilson.

SECONDARY SOURCES

Alter, Robert. 1990. *The Art of Biblical Poetry*. Edinburgh.

Babington, Churchill, ed. 1855. *The Benefit of Christ's Death*. London and Cambridge.

Baker-Smith, Dominic. 1963–6. 'Florence Wilson: Two early works'. *The Bibliotheck* 4, 228–9.

Baker-Smith, Dominic. 1969. 'The Writings of Florens Wilson in Relation to Evangelical Humanism'. Unpublished PhD dissertation. University of Cambridge.

Baker-Smith, Dominic. 1984. 'Florens Wilson and His Circle: Émigrés in Lyons, 1539–1543'. In Castor and Cave, eds. *Neo-Latin and the Vernacular*. 83–97.

Baker-Smith, Dominic. 1991. 'Florens Wilson and the Politics of Irenicism'. In Dalzell et al., eds. *Acta conventus neo-Latini Torontonensis*. 189–98.

Baker-Smith, Dominic. 1996. 'Florens Wilson: A Distant Prospect'. In Hadley Williams, ed. *Stewart Style*. 1–14.

Baker-Smith, Dominic. 2006. 'Antonio Buonvisi and Florens Wilson: A European Friendship'. *Moreana* 43, 82–108; with corrigenda *Moreana* 43, 253–4.

Bath, Michael. 2003. 'Alciato and the Earl of Arran'. *Emblematica* 13, 39–52.

Bawcutt, Priscilla. 1976. *Gavin Douglas: A Critical Study*. Edinburgh.

Biot, Brigitte. 1994. 'Un projet innovant pour un collège humaniste'. *Bibliothèque d'Humanisme et Renaissance* 56, 445–64.

Biot, Brigitte. 1996. *Barthélemy Aneau, Régent de la Renaissance Lyonnaise*. Paris.

Broadie, Alexander. 1983. *George Lokert: Late-Scholastic Logician*. Edinburgh.

Broadie, Alexander. 1990. 'Philosophy in Renaissance Scotland: Loss and Gain'. In MacQueen, ed. *Humanism in Renaissance Scotland*. 75–96.

Brown, P. Hume. 1913. 'A Forgotten Scottish Scholar of the Sixteenth Century'. *SHR* 10, 122–37.

Buisson, Ferdinand. 1892. *Sébastien Castellion: Sa vie et son oeuvre*. 2 vols. Paris.

Burckhardt, Jacob. 1995. *The Civilization of the Renaissance in Italy*. London.

Cadell, P.M. and T.A.F. Cherry, eds. 1983. *The Eye of the Mind: The Scot and his Books*. Edinburgh.

Cameron, Euan. 1991. 'The Late Renaissance and the Unfolding Reformation in Europe'. In Kirk, ed. *Humanism and Reform*. 15–36.

Cameron, Jamie. 1998. *James V: The Personal Rule, 1528–1542*. East Linton.

Campagnac, E.T. and K. Forbes, eds. and trans. 1916. *Sadoleto on Education: A Translation of the* De pueris recte instituendis. London.

Caponetto, Salvatore, ed. 1972. *Il Beneficio di Cristo*. Florence and Chicago.

Caponetto, Salvatore. 1979. *Aonio Paleario (1503–1570) e la riforma protestante in Toscana*. Turin.

Castor, Grahame and Terence Cave, eds. 1984. *Neo-Latin and the Vernacular in Renaissance France*. Oxford.

Christie, R.C. 1907. *Historical Essays*. Ed. T.F. Tout and J. Tait. Manchester. 307–23.

Cowan, Ian B. and David E. Easson. 1976. *Medieval Religious Houses: Scotland*. 2nd edition. London and New York.

Dalzell, Alexander, Charles Fantazzi and Richard J. Schoeck, eds. 1991. *Acta conventus neo-Latini Torontonensis*. Toronto.

Davis, Natalie Zemon. 1983. '*Le monde de l'imprimerie humaniste: Lyon*'. In Martin and Chartier, eds. *Histoire*. I.255–77.

Dawson, Jane. 2015. *John Knox*. New Haven and London.

Dickson, Robert and John Philip Edmond. 1890. *Annals of Scottish Printing*. Cambridge.

Douglas, Richard M. 1959. *Jacopo Sadoleto 1477–1547: Humanist and Reformer*. Cambridge, MA.

Durkan, John. 1952. 'Florens Wilson's Death: A Correction'. *IR* 3/1, 65–6.

Durkan, John. 1953. 'The Beginnings of Humanism in Scotland'. *IR* 4/1, 5–24.

Durkan, John. 1962a. 'Education in the Century of the Reformation'. In McRoberts, ed. *Essays on the Scottish Reformation*. 145–68.

Durkan, John. 1962b. 'The Cultural Background in Sixteenth-Century Scotland'. In McRoberts, ed. *Essays on the Scottish Reformation*. 274–331.

Durkan, John. 1980a. 'Early Humanism and King's College'. *Aberdeen University Review* 163, 159–79.

Durkan, John. 1980b. 'Giovanni Ferrerio, Gesner and French Affairs'. *Bibliothèque d'Humanisme et Renaissance* 42, 349–60.

Durkan, John. 1981. 'Giovanni Ferrerio, Humanist: His Influence in Sixteenth-Century Scotland'. In Robbins, ed. *Religion and Humanism*. 181–94.

Durkan, John. 1982. 'Scottish "Evangelicals" in the Patronage of Thomas Cromwell'. *Records of the Scottish Church History Society* 21, 127–56.

Durkan, John. 1986. 'James, Third Earl of Arran: The Hidden Years'. *SHR* 65, 154–66.

Durkan, John. 1990. 'Education: The Laying of Fresh Foundations'. In MacQueen, ed. *Humanism in Renaissance Scotland*. 123–60.

Durkan, John. 2003. 'Thomas Dempster: A Scottish Baronius'. *IR* 54/1, 69–78.

Durkan, John. 2004. 'Wilson [Volusene], Florence'. *ODNB*.

Durkan, John, ed. 2006. *Scottish Schools and Schoolmasters 1560–1633*. Revised, Jamie Reid-Baxter. SHS 5th Series 19. Edinburgh.

Durkan, John and Anthony Ross, eds. 1961. *Early Scottish Libraries*. Glasgow.

Edington, Carol. 1994. *Court and Culture in Renaissance Scotland: Sir David Lindsay of the Mount*. Amherst, MA.

El Kenz, David. 1997. *Les Bûchers du Roi: La culture protestante des martyres (1523–1572)*. Seyssel.

Essary, Kirk. 2017. 'Enduring Erasmus'. *Church History and Religious Culture* 97/3–4, 322–33.

Fairweather. Eugene R. 1966. 'The Christian Humanism of Thomas Aquinas'. *Canadian Journal of Theology* 12/3, 194–210.

Fenlon, Dermot. 1972. *Heresy and Obedience in Tridentine Italy: Cardinal Pole and the Counter Reformation*. Cambridge.

de Groër, Georgette. 1995. *Réforme et contre-réforme en France. Le collège de la Trinité au xvi siècle à Lyon*. Paris.

Guggisberg, Hans R. 2003. *Sebastian Castellio, 1515–1563*. Trans. Bruce Gordon. Aldershot.

Gwyn, Peter. 1990. *The King's Cardinal*. London.

Hadley Williams, Janet, ed. 1996. *Stewart Style 1513–1542: Essays on the Court of James V*. East Linton.

van Heijnsbergen, Theo. 2004. 'Paradigms Lost: Perceptions of the Cultural History of Sixteenth-Century Scotland'. In MacDonald and Twomey, eds. *Schooling and Society*. 97–211.

Holmes, Stephen Mark. 2008. 'The Meaning of History: A Dedicatory Letter from Giovanni Ferrerio to Abbot Robert Reid in his *Historia abbatum de Kynlos*'. *Reformation and Renaissance Review* 10, 89–115.

Houwen, L.A.J.R., A.A. MacDonald and S.L. Mapstone, eds. 2000. *A Palace in the Wild: Essays on Vernacular Culture and Humanism in Late-Medieval and Renaissance Scotland*. Leuven.

Johnson, A.F. 1922. 'Books Printed at Lyons in the Sixteenth Century'. *The Library*, 4th Series, 3/3. 145–74.

Kaplan, Benjamin J. 2007. *Divided by Faith: Religious Conflict and the Practice of Toleration in Early Modern Europe*. Cambridge, MA, and London.

Kirk, James, ed. 1991. *Humanism and Reform: The Church in Europe, England and Scotland, 1400–1643. Essays in Honour of James K. Cameron*. Studies in Church History Subsidia 8.

Laing, David, ed. 1827. 'Two Letters of Florentius Volusenus'. *The Bannatyne Miscellany*, I.ii. Edinburgh. 325–38.

Linnard, W. 1981. 'Timber Floating: An Early Record on the Tay'. *Scottish Studies* 25, 77–9.

Lubac, Henri de. 1974. *Pic de la Mirandole*. Paris.

MacCulloch, Diarmaid. 2004. *Reformation: Europe's House Divided 1490–1700*. London.

MacDonald, Alasdair A. 2009a. 'Florentius Volusenus and Tranquillity of Mind: Some Applications of an Ancient Ideal'. In MacDonald et al., eds. *Christian Humanism*. 119–38.

MacDonald, Alasdair A. 2009b. 'Allegorical (Dream-) Vision Poetry in Medieval and Early Modern Scotland'. In Suntrup and Veenstra, eds. *Himmel auf Erden / Heaven on Earth*. 167–76.

MacDonald, Alasdair A. and Michael W. Twomey, eds. 2004. *Schooling and Society: The Ordering and Reordering of Knowledge in the Western Middle Ages*. Leuven.

MacDonald, Alasdair A., Zweder R.W.M. von Martels and Jan R. Veenstra, eds. 2009. *Christian Humanism: Essays in Honour of Arjo Vanderjagt*. Leiden and Boston.

Macfarlane, Leslie J. 1985. *William Elphinstone and the Kingdom of Scotland 1431–1514*. Aberdeen.

Macfarlane, Leslie J. 2004. 'John Vaus (c.1484–c.1539)'. *ODNB*.

Macintosh, Herbert B. 1914. *Elgin Past and Present: A Historical Guide*. Elgin.

Macquarrie, Alan and Roger P.H. Green, eds. 2022. *The Poems of Roderick MacLean*. Edinburgh.

MacQueen, John, ed. 1990. *Humanism in Renaissance Scotland*. Edinburgh.

Mapstone, Sally. 2010. 'A Newly Discovered Copy of a Work by John Vaus, and Its Manuscript Context'. In McGinley and Royan, eds. *The Apparelling of Truth*. 30–47.

Margolin, Jean-Claude. 1974. 'Le cercle humaniste lyonnais d'après l'édition des *Epigrammata* (1537) de Jean Visagier'. In *Actes du colloque sur l'humanisme lyonnais au XVIe siècle*. Grenoble. 151–83.

Margolin, Jean-Claude. 1991. 'La notion de dignité humaine selon Erasme de Rotterdam'. In Kirk, ed. *Humanism and Reform*. 37–56.

Martin, Henri-Jean and Roger Chartier, eds. 1983–6. *Histoire de l'édition française*. 4 vols. Paris.

McFarlane, I.D. 1981. *Buchanan*. London.

McGinley, Kevin J. and Nicola Royan, eds. 2010. *The Apparelling of Truth: Literature and Literary Culture in the Reign of James VI*. Newcastle.

McNair, Philip. 1967. *Peter Martyr in Italy: An Anatomy of Apostasy*. Oxford.

McRoberts, David M., ed. 1962. *Essays on the Scottish Reformation 1513–1625*. Glasgow.

Merriman, Magnus. 2000. *The Rough Wooings: Mary Queen of Scots 1542–1551*. East Linton.

Morét, Ulrike. 2000. 'An Early Scottish National Biography: Thomas Dempster's *Historia ecclesiastica gentis Scotorum* (1627)'. In Houwen et al., eds. *A Palace in the Wild*. 249–69.

Morpurgo, Guiseppe. 1912. *Un Umanista Martire: Aonio Paleario e la Riforma Teorica Italiana net Secolo XVI*. Città di Castello.

Mowinckel, Sigmund. 2004. *The Psalms in Israel's Worship*. Grand Rapids, MI.

Murphy, James J. 2016. 'A Quintilian Anniversary and Its Meaning'. *Advances in the History of Rhetoric* 19/2, 107–10.

Nauert, Charles G. 1973. 'The Clash of Humanists and Scholastics: An Approach to Pre-Reformation Controversies'. *Sixteenth Century Journal* 4, 1–18.

Olin, John C., ed. 1966. *A Reformation Debate: John Calvin and Jacopo Sadoleto*. New York.

Péricaud, Antoine. 1850. *Florent Wilson, Guillaume Postel et Louis Castelvetro*. Lyon.

Post, Regnerus R. 1968. *The Modern Devotion: Confrontation with Reformation and Humanism*. Leiden.

Rabil, Albert, Jr., ed. 1988. *Renaissance Humanism: Foundations, Forms, and Legacy*. 2 vols. Philadelphia.

Reid, Steven J., ed. 2024. *Rethinking the Renaissance and Reformation in Scotland: Essays in Honour of Roger A. Mason*. St. Andrews Studies in Scottish History 11. Woodbridge.

Rice, Eugene F., Jr. 1962. 'The Humanist Idea of Christian Antiquity: Lefèvre d'Étaples and his Circle'. *Studies in the Renaissance* 9, 126–60.

Rice, Eugene F., Jr. 1988. 'Humanism in France'. In Rabil, ed. *Renaissance Humanism*. II.109–22.

Robbins, Keith, ed. 1981. *Religion and Humanism*. Oxford.

Ross, Anthony. 1962. 'Some Notes on the Religious Orders in Pre-Reformation Scotland'. In McRoberts, ed. *Essays on the Scottish Reformation*. 185–233.

Royan, Nicola. 2024. 'Sent Abroad to Talk for Their Country: Two Examples of Early Scottish Humanist Diplomacy'. In Reid, ed. *Rethinking the Renaissance*. 98–117.

Sanderson, Margaret H.B. 1986. *Cardinal of Scotland: David Beaton, c. 1494–1546*. Edinburgh.

Simpson, Douglas. 1938. 'Tolquhon Castle and Its Builder'. *PSAS* 72, 248–72.

Slotemaker, John T. and Jeffrey C. Witt, eds. 2015. *A Companion to the Theology of John Mair*. Leiden and Boston.

Somerset, D.W.B. 2018. 'The *Spirituali* Movement in Scotland Before the Reformation of 1560'. *Scottish Reformation Society Historical Journal* 8, 1–43.

Stahl, William Harris, ed., trans. 1952. *Macrobius: Commentary on the Dream of Scipio*. New York.

Steinmann, Martin. 1967. *Johannes Oporinus*. Basel and Stuttgart.

Stevenson, Jane and Peter Davidson. 2009. 'Ficino in Aberdeen: The Continuing Problem of the Scottish Renaissance'. *Journal of the Northern Renaissance* 1. https://jnr2.hcommons.org/2009/591/#back_to_25.

Stuart, John, ed. 1872. *Records of the Monastery of Kinloss*. Edinburgh.

Suntrup, Rudolf and Jan R. Veenstra, eds. 2009. *Himmel auf Erden / Heaven on Earth*. Frankfurt am Main.

Taylor, James. 1861. *A Memoir of Florentius Volusenus*. Elgin.

Tigner, Steven S. 1970. 'Plato's Philosophical Uses of the Dream Metaphor'. *The American Journal of Philology* 91/2, 204–12.

Tracy, James D. 1972. *Erasmus, the Growth of a Mind*. Geneva.

INDEX

GENERAL INDEX

Visigoths   100

Waldensians   xxxi

INDEX OF PERSONS

Adamson, Patrick,
   archbishop   xxxiv
Adomnan, abbot   101
Alciato, Andrea   xxvii, xxxii
Alcuin   101
Aldhelm of Sherborne   115, 144–145
Andrelini, Fausto   111
Aneau, Barthélemy   xxvii, xxxii
Apuleius   96, 109, 110, 115, 157
Aquinas, Thomas   127–138 (passim),
   140, 141, 146, 147, 153, 155
Aristotle   89, 105, 126, 127, 128, 129,
   132, 133, 134, 135, 137, 140, 146, 151
Arran (see Hamilton, James, the
   elder)
Augustine   88, 98, 99, 100, 104, 128,
   129, 130, 133, 147, 148, 150, 151

Baduel, Claude   xxvii, xxx, xxxi,
   91
Bassandyne, Thomas   xvii
Beaton, David, cardinal   xxvi, xxxi,
   xxxii
Bede   101
Bekinshaw, John   xx
Bembo, Pietro, cardinal   103
Berners, Lord (see Bourchier, John)
Bigothier, Claude   xxvii
Blair, Robert   xxxiv
Boece, Hector   vii, xv, xviii, xix,
   xxii, 89, 127
Boethius   100, 127, 129, 133, 134, 140
Bonvisi, Antonio   xx, xxiii, xxvii,
   xxviii, xxix, 2, 3
Borthwick, John, Sir   xxv, xxvi,
   2, 3
Bourchier, John, Lord Berners   xxi

Bracciolini, Poggio   103
Bryan, Francis, Sir   xxi
Bucer, Martin   xxxi
Buchanan, George   vii, viii, xxi,
   xxxiv

Calvin, John   xviii, xxii, xxiv,
   xxvii, xxviii, xxxiii, xxxiv
Caravalla, Demetrio   xxviii, 127, 141
Cassiodorus   100
Castellio, Sebastian   xxvii, xxxiii,
   xxxiv
Charlemagne   101
Charles V, Holy Roman
   Emperor   xxv
Châtelherault (see Hamilton, James,
   the elder)
Chaucer, Geoffrey   xv, 91, 116, 156
Cicero   xxii, xxviii, 91, 96, 99–103
   (passim), 105, 107, 115, 116, 118, 124,
   126, 127, 139, 143, 148–154 (passim),
   156
Ciono, Bernardino   xxix, 2, 3
Clement of Alexandria   97
Colet, John   xxiii
Columella   96
Constantine   100
Contarini, Gasparo   xxiv, xxxiii,
   xxxv
Cop, Nicholas   xxii
Cromwell, Gregory   xxii, xxx
Cromwell, Thomas   vii, xx, xxi,
   xxii, xxvi
Crystall, Thomas, abbot   xviii, xix
Curio, Hieronymus   xxviii, xl
Curione, Celio Secondo   xxviii
Cyprian   99

d'Hocédy, Toussaint (see Hocedius)
Dauphin, the   xxxii
de Guise, Jean, cardinal   xxi
de Sainte-Marthe, Charles   xxvii
Democritus   xxix, 91
Dempster, Thomas   xxii, xxxiv

INDEX OF TITLES